# RIDING THE SPIRIT BUS

"Ahad's metaphoric journey vividly evokes the spiritual awakening that exploded in the '60s. He writes with humor, insight, and a compass needle aimed at Truth. His love is magnanimous, his recollections are luminous, and his prose is visionary. He has a gift for transmitting gems of wisdom embedded in personal parables."

RAMESHWAR DAS, COAUTHOR WITH
RAM DASS OF *BE LOVE NOW, POLISHING THE
MIRROR,* AND *BEING RAM DASS*

"A wonderful telling of an awakening life dedicated to manifesting loving kindness and compassion throughout life's changing conditions. Through Ahad's journey we meet many great teachers and experience firsthand living in spiritual community."

PIR SHABDA KAHN, SPIRITUAL DIRECTOR OF
THE SUFI RUHANIAT INTERNATIONAL AND
COAUTHOR OF *PHYSICIANS OF THE HEART*

ALSO BY AHAD COBB

*Image Nation*

*Every Form You Come In*

*Early Lama Foundation*

*Superconscious, Releasing Past-Life Recordings*

# RIDING THE SPIRIT BUS

### My Journey from Satsang with Ram Dass to Lama Foundation and Dances of Universal Peace

**A Sacred Planet Book**

## AHAD COBB

Inner Traditions
Rochester, Vermont

Inner Traditions
One Park Street
Rochester, Vermont 05767
www.InnerTraditions.com

Text stock is SFI certified

**Sacred Planet Books** are curated by Richard Grossinger, Inner Traditions editorial board member and cofounder and former publisher of North Atlantic Books. The Sacred Planet collection, published under the umbrella of the Inner Traditions family of imprints, includes works on the themes of consciousness, cosmology, alternative medicine, dreams, climate, permaculture, alchemy, shamanic studies, oracles, astrology, crystals, hyperobjects, locutions, and subtle bodies.

Cataloging-in-Publication Data for this title is available from the Library of Congress

ISBN 978-1-64411-535-0 (print)
ISBN 978-1-64411-536-7 (ebook)

Printed and bound in the United States by Lake Book Manufacturing, LLC. The text stock is SFI certified. The Sustainable Forestry Initiative® program promotes sustainable forest management.

10  9  8  7  6  5  4  3  2  1

Text design by Virginia Scott Bowman and layout by Kenleigh Manseau. This book was typeset in Garamond Premier Pro with Abraham, Gill Sans MT Pro and ITC Legacy Sans Std as display typefaces. Artwork by the author unless otherwise indicated.

To send correspondence to the author of this book, mail a first-class letter to the author c/o Inner Traditions • Bear & Company, One Park Street, Rochester, VT 05767, and we will forward the communication, or contact the author directly via **www.ahadcobb.com**.

*To Widad, my wife, love of my life,*
*who inspired me to write this book*
*and who is with me every step of the way.*

*There are some things which cannot be learned quickly, and time, which is all we have, must be paid heavily for their acquiring. They are the very simplest things and because it takes a man's life to know them the little that each man gets from life is very costly and the only heritage he has to leave.*

ERNEST HEMINGWAY

# CONTENTS

Frank Cobb at home, summer 1969, Towson, Maryland.

# 1 SATSANG, SUMMER 1969

Jim pulled over to the side of the road to pick some flowers for his friend. All I knew was that this friend was a guy. When Jim came back to the car with an enormous gathering of goldenrod in his arms, I began to wonder what I was getting into. Giving flowers to guys was unheard of where I came from. This was the first inkling I had that my reality was about to change.

It was the summer of 1969. I was beyond dazed and confused. I had just graduated college, Phi Beta Kappa, magna cum laude, in drug psychosis—and I had no idea where I was going or what I was going to do other than physically remove myself from marijuana. I was lost and bewildered.

I had the good fortune to end up staying with my friend Jim Lytton in the summer house at his grandparents' estate on the end of Long Island. Jim was an artist in the phase of emulating Jackson Pollock with a psychedelic twist. He would climb up on a ladder and dribble vivid luminous paints onto black-painted screens, creating abstract tangles that would glow in the dark under black light.

I was trying to figure out what to do with the rest of my life. I was agitated, restless, anxious, and depressed. My mind never stopped talking. My emotional body, hidden under the nonstop mental chatter, was traumatized, numb, and repressed with occasional outbursts of ecstasy. Inspiration came and went in fitful bursts.

Jim had studied with some guy who had come back from India. Jim practiced yoga. He had this habit of disappearing into his room every afternoon, only to emerge several hours later with a calm glow and far-away eyes. I asked him what he was doing.

"Meditating," he said.

"What's it like?"

"It's more powerful than LSD."

This definitely caught my interest.

I asked him if he would show me how to meditate. He instructed me to sit on the floor in a firm cross-legged posture, close my eyes, concentrate on the breath flowing in and out of my body, put my attention on the tip of my nose, and be aware of breathing in and breathing out.

I sat down, closed my eyes, and tried my hardest to concentrate, but my body would not sit still. I tried this dutifully many times, but my body would spasm, jerk, jump, and twitch in time with my hyperactive mind. No matter how hard I tried, I could not sit still! Meditation did not come easily at first.

I was in need of getting out and doing something, but I had no car to go anywhere. I asked Jim if he wanted to go up to New Hampshire and climb some mountains.

"Let's do it," he said. "Oh, by the way, do you mind if we stop and visit someone on the way? My friend, Ram Dass, is living on his father's estate in Franklin, New Hampshire."

"Sure," I told him, "Why not?"

Early one morning in June we took off and drove in peaceful silence up through New England.

It was when we were approaching Franklin that Jim pulled off to the side of the road, got out of the car, picked that enormous armload of goldenrod to give to his friend, and I found myself wondering about his gathering a bunch of flowers to bring to a guy. Hello?

We drove around the shores of Lake Franklin and then pulled up the long drive to a big white house sitting on top of a wooded hill. We were told that Ram Dass was in retreat in a little cabin behind the big house and was just finishing up an interview with a local radio station. Would we mind waiting?

After a while we were told that the interview was finished and Ram Dass would see us. We walked to a little cabin set apart from the main house. Jim carried the flowers in his arms. The door was open and we walked in. Sitting on the floor in the corner was a large man in a long white robe with a long graying beard and long frizzy hair falling down from a balding head—and the brightest eyes and the biggest smile I had ever seen.

Ram Dass instantly gave us a big smile of delight. The whole room lit up as if a very bright light had snapped on, filling it with white light. I had never seen anything like this. He was positively beaming at us! I didn't have a concept for it at the time, but I knew that here was a being who was brighter than electricity, as bright as sunlight. He literally lit up the whole room!

His first words were, "Are you two coming to my yoga camp this summer?"

Of course, we said yes.

I disremember everything that was said that day, but I did notice that by his side were two stacks of books: a stack of holy books and a stack of Dr. Strange comic books. It was the Dr. Strange comic books that persuaded me that I could trust him.

That was my first meeting with Ram Dass, Baba Ram Dass at the time, formerly Richard Alpert, Ph.D., Harvard professor of psychology and psychedelic pioneer who, together with Timothy Leary, had gotten kicked out of Harvard for giving LSD to some students, who had gone to India and found God in the form of his guru, Neem Karoli Baba, also called Maharaj-ji, and was now back in the States, living in a little cabin on his father's estate.

The yoga camp started in a few weeks. How I got back there without a car I don't recall. But that's what friends are for.

I grew up in a godless family, a family in which God was not a living reality. We did not talk about God, remember God, thank God, or pray to God. We were a very smart family. We prized our intelligence highly. But we didn't even think about God.

We did go to church on Sunday. We did say grace over food sometimes. But even that fell away in time.

When I was a kid I always wanted to know about God. God seemed so important that nobody ever talked about God, not even "God damn" or "God bless" except for once a week on Sunday. I went to Sunday school and was entertained and mystified by stories about Abraham and Moses and Jesus and a whole cast of colorful cartoon characters interacting with an invisible, omnipotent, omnipresent guy named God. I did love the songs about Jesus, but the gestalt of Sunday school on Sunday mornings remained an alternate reality that was never mentioned during the rest of the week.

God seemed like the Wizard of Oz, a big voice behind a curtain of clouds, booming out commandments, raining down blessings, and hailing down punishments. The people prosper—praise be to God! The people are destroyed—God is punishing the people! One thing was clear: obey the commandments God gives the people—or else! Don't question authority.

Who is this God guy anyway? As a child it seemed to me that God was a concept to explain away everything that could not be explained otherwise—God did it!

As I grew older, Sunday school became Bible study and theological discussion. I came to the conclusion that God was a tautology—an inexplicable, unassailable concept that was used to explain everything that could not be explained in any other way. God created the universe—end of discussion. God did it, God willed it, God brought it forth—end of discussion.

I just could not comprehend who this God guy was.

I also came to the arrogant conclusion that I was smarter than all my Bible teachers, which proved that none of them knew what was going on.

The real disappointment in my religious upbringing was my First Communion, which was withheld until I had come of age (thirteen) and had undergone a lengthy communicants' class in which I was asked to memorize and confess to believe in all sorts of incomprehensible assertions fossilized in the Nicene Creed. Not even in my youth could I believe "six impossible things before breakfast." The reward for submitting to all this indoctrination was supposed to be Holy Communion, ingesting the Blood and Body of Christ, albeit symbolically. I was led to believe that this would be a significant, life-changing experience, a participation mystique. It was not. Nothing happened—nothing but a tiny plastic thimble half-full of tasteless grape juice, a stale cube of Wonder Bread. What is this shit anyway? Coca-Cola has more fizz than this!

I had great expectations but, I'm sorry, Jesus, I didn't find you in church.

I went to Mr. Galloway, our minister, and said that I was very interested in finding out about God and pursuing spiritual wisdom, but I was not finding the answers I was looking for in Sunday school or church. I asked him to excuse me from going to his church. He gave me a robust blessing on my spiritual path and told me I did not have to go to church anymore. In response my father resigned as a deacon and stopped taking our family to church.

*Recurring dream . . .*

*I find myself on a long front staircase with a carved mahogany banister in a beautiful old house. I glide down the staircase without touching my feet to the steps, my hand hovering over but not touching the banister. It is as if my body is transmitted in a steady wave through the ether. At the bottom, the front door opens on a resplendent light, and I glide out into the eternal and infinite garden, the hidden garden . . .*

Ram Dass had just returned from a year in India with his guru Maharaj-ji, Neem Karoli Baba. His atmosphere was pervaded with ecstasy, bliss, and love. Ram Dass's father had generously opened up his estate to the forty or so young people who came together that summer. We all camped in the woods and made a communal center, meditation hall, and kitchen in the barn. Ram Dass pretty much left the organization of the *ashram* (spiritual retreat) to evolve by itself, although we followed most of his suggestions. This was my introduction to karma yoga, the path of service. Cooking, cleaning, and housekeeping, done as selfless service, could be a path to God. It was also my introduction to *kedgeree* and *chapattis,* gently spiced rice and lentils eaten with flat bread.

Ram Dass himself stayed on retreat but came down once or twice a day to give *darshan*—long ecstatic and insightful talks—interspersed with *kirtan,* devotional chanting, and just generally hung out whenever he felt like it. Ram Dass, dressed all in white, prayer beads in hand, blissful smile on his face, would sit under a maple tree, with all of us gathered around him and give darshan. The word *darshan* means "seeing and being seen" by an aspect, form, or gaze of the divine. Millions of Hindus visit temples every day for the darshan of the enshrined deity, or sit at the feet of the guru having his darshan. For Ram Dass in India, this meant hanging out with Maharaj-ji. For me, darshan meant sitting with Ram Dass under the tree, hanging out, listening, chanting, meditating . . . and bathing in the grace of Maharaj-ji.

We were all immersed in a gentle, luminous, loving atmosphere as Ram Dass talked of God and his guru, of the pitfalls of the ego, and the bliss of awakening, the discourse flowing effortlessly from his mouth and hands and eyes. Ram Dass was brilliant—eloquent, intelligent, enlightening, and entertaining—a sit-down comedian telling stories about himself. At times, we would all close our eyes and meditate together, resting in the peace. At times, we would chant the names of God in mantric repetition leading to ecstasy.

Ram Dass's talks that summer would form the basis of the book *Be Here Now,* which became a profound game-changer for many of my contemporaries.

This was all brand new to me. My mind eagerly soaked up the wisdom of India as my heart opened to the love flowing and the light of my soul began to awaken. Here was someone who could navigate all the levels of consciousness, from the most sublime to the most ridiculous. Here were people for whom God was a reality, a living reality! God was no more an empty word, a jaded concept, a lame excuse for authority. God is real and living among us and within us. God is the love that abides in our hearts. God is the light that shines in our eyes and in our souls. God is the knowing that knows itself as truth.

Every morning Ram Dass would come out dressed in yogi white

robes, sit under a huge tree, and hold forth endlessly on God, Guru, and Self; in this path, all are equivalent. He was like a TV talk show host whose perpetual guests were God, Maharaj-ji, and himself. But he was no pompous pundit perched on mounds of books and pontificating. He was continually telling illuminating stories of Maharaj-ji and divine wonders. Equally, he might be telling self-deprecating stories about the pitfalls and pratfalls of his own neurotic ego. Of course, we all have neurotic egos, so we could all identify with him, even though he didn't tell stories about anyone else but himself.

I would think, *Hey, if this schlub can love and be loved by God, maybe I can too. I feel bad about what a mess I am, but Ram Dass is no better off. Maybe there is hope after all.*

He would say he had the gift of Saraswati, the goddess of speech and learning. He also called himself Rent-a-mouth (Ram). "Out of my mouth comes the most sublime wisdom and the most mundane bullshit and the frightening thing is that I can't tell the difference between them in the moment."

Ram Dass had the most amazing ability to connect with soul. He was not talking to me or at me—he was speaking inside me, inside my heart-mind, answering questions I had not yet even asked. He seemed to be speaking to the inner questions and needs of each person present— not exactly reading our minds, but close enough.

On Sundays, people would come from hundreds of miles around, as well as from Franklin, to hear him speak. He would begin by welcoming everyone and talking about the most ordinary things, about the strangeness of seeing young people with long hair and beards, about social and political issues, telling jokes, and only gradually easing into spiritual matters, becoming more and more refined. I saw that he was *listening* to his audience rather than talking to his audience, speaking to the most basic concerns first, attuning and harmonizing the hearts, seducing us all with the sparkle of divine love and light.

Ram Dass's darshan talks awoke vast areas of subtlety and awareness in me as he told stories of Maharaj-ji and holy people, quoting sacred writings, touching on personal, social, political, and intellectual issues, always returning to the peace of silence and the bliss of love. His talks were always spontaneous, which was amazing enough in itself to an expert student like me, trained in research and the careful preparation of arguments, thoughts for presentation. In high school I had even gone as far as making extensive lists of what I wanted to talk to my girlfriends about so that I wouldn't be caught unprepared. Ram Dass was the first person I had heard who talked without preparation, directly from inspiration.

He never had any notes and seemed to have no fixed agenda, speaking from heart to heart, from mind to mind, and yet he could hold forth endlessly and brilliantly, keeping us enraptured until he led us into the bliss of kirtan and the peace of meditation. I was astounded that he needed no notes to speak from, no books to back him up, although his talks were peppered with pungent quotes from holy beings.

About the spiritual journey he said, "If it's not fun, I don't want to go."

*Dream . . .*

*Ram Dass comes on stage as Mullah Nasruddin, turban and patchwork robes, carrying an enormous pack the size of two double mattresses . . .*

*He falls all over himself, tells bad jokes, goes through slapstick routines with a donkey, and imparts real wisdom . . .*

Never once did he mention anything about money, about being paid for what he was doing, not even a "karmic exchange." In fact, he was giving us all a place to pitch our tents and make our meals for the summer. In the Indian spiritual tradition, spiritual wisdom is a gift freely given and freely received. In other words, you can't buy God and you can't sell God. God-consciousness is a gift freely given through grace— Maharaj-ji's grace, in this case.

Ram Dass always said that Maharaj-ji did everything, and Maharaj-ji always said that God did everything. So go figure. That's the way I got it to begin with. My soul longed to know something that my shattered ego didn't even know how to ask for, even *what* to ask for, and it was all given right in the beginning; it was all given by grace.

In the afternoons Ram Dass would retire to his cabin where he would continue to give darshan in the form of one-on-one meetings.

These private interviews were very popular and well-attended. Most people there eagerly pursued opportunities for private interviews with Ram Dass in his cabin. I thought I should get in on this. I wanted to have this experience. But I was very shy. If I was going to meet Ram Dass one on one, I thought I had to have questions to ask him, the way I'd prepared topics to talk about with my high school girlfriends.

I would assemble my list of questions, a minimum of three, and head off for the cabin, holding my questions in mind lest I forget them. And every time, as I was walking across the sunny green lawn with my questions firmly held in my mind, I would hear Ram Dass's voice answering each and every one of my questions briefly, eloquently, and completely, each and every time. All my questions were answered. I never even got halfway to the cabin. This must have happened a dozen times before I finally gave up on this strategy.

> *Blessed is the answer that uproots the question.*
>
>                                        HAZRAT INAYAT KHAN

Some of my friends on the spiritual path have had a strong sense of guidance. They have sought to find in this life the reflection, the embodiment, of something they knew to be true in the depth of their being: the divine presence. They had a burning love that drew them to seek God. I always admired their clarity and faith.

I lacked this inner certainty. I moved forward without knowing where I was going, motivated by the desire to relieve my existential suffering—although I lived so much in my mind that I was not in touch with my emotional suffering. I was all flavors of lonely, sad, and afraid, although I didn't pay much attention to my feelings because I didn't think I could do anything about them.

> *We are drawn to God through great suffering or great love. Most of us are drawn to God through great suffering because so few of us are capable of such a great love.*
>
>                                        RAM DASS

Ram Dass here echoes the Bhagavad Gita (7:16), which says that everyone worships God to get something from God (relief from suffering or to gain wealth or knowledge) except for the "man of wisdom" who loves God. But it doesn't matter, for all are drawn to God.

The essential methodology of the spiritual path that I received that summer was to quiet the mind, open the heart, and love each other: to quiet the mind through meditation, to open the heart through devotional chanting, and to love each other through serving each other. We were to love, serve, and remember God always and everywhere and in each being. This is not an achievement, something that can be accomplished and completed. This is a perpetual practice and an endless path.

∞∞

To judge a book by its cover, Maharaj-ji did not have the appearance of any guru I had seen in the media. He was lacking in movie star glamour: flowing white hair, long white beard, mellifluous voice, sweet incense, the whole nine yards. But what did I know? To judge by his pictures, Maharaj-ji was a fat, bald old man wrapped in a plaid blanket who sat on the ground and smiled or frowned or threw fruit at people. To judge by the stories Ram Dass told, he was enigmatic and unpredictable, appearing and disappearing at a whim. He could be as dense and still as a mountain or as light and swift as a bird. His body could change shape. Although he caused many temples to be built by devotees, he was not an institution in any way. He was totally free. He could not be confined by anyone or anything. Although he encouraged devotees to pursue meditation, chanting, hatha yoga, pranayama, holy books, and more, he was not a "spiritual teacher" in any sense of the word.

Apparently the main practice around Maharaj-ji was hanging out in his atmosphere of unconditional love, literally just sitting at Maharaj-ji's feet all day, witnessing and participating in his *lila,* his love play, conversations, and interactions with his devotees. He was the living embodiment of Hanuman, the all-powerful monkey god, the servant of Ram, of God. His diaries were filled with one word, "Ram Ram Ram Ram Ram Ram Ram Ram . . ."

Apparently, what was so incredible about Maharaj-ji was that he demonstrated time and time again that he knew everything about you, down to your most private thoughts. You knew that he knew everything about you, and he loved you anyway. He loved you unconditionally and hung out with you and played with you. No one had ever experienced this kind of love. It was this atmosphere of unconditional love that Ram Dass brought to us: the unconditional love that he knew through devotion to his guru, which he called the path of guru yoga.

*Love everyone. Feed everyone. Remember God always and everywhere.*

NEEM KAROLI BABA, MAHARAJ-JI

This may sound simple, and it is—but it is not necessarily all that easy. It is a life path.

This all was way beyond the ability of my little mind to comprehend, but the love that I could feel was very real: the love, the joy, and the peace. In the courses I took in comparative religions we were encouraged to practice a temporary suspension of disbelief, a temporary suspension of judgment, in order to appreciate the experience of another belief system. If, as Ram Dass said, "Judgment is the greatest block to unconditional love," I was ready to suspend my judgment, perhaps permanently.

It was a giant leap to occur in the space of a summer—from "God is a tautology" to "God is a living reality in each and every being." I was surrounded by friends who loved God, and I wasn't even sure God existed. This was way beyond my little mind. But my heart trusted the love I could feel and the light in their eyes, so I was happy to emulate and imitate this devotion to God and see what might happen. This, even as my mind remained skeptical and cynical. Maybe this was all just a contact high, just hype.

Maharaj-ji didn't live in an ashram or a temple. He hung out and stayed with ordinary people. He was a householder baba. Later on, devotees would collect remembered stories of Maharaj-ji's lila, his divine play, each one of which was remarkable if you really paid attention. He worked no big splashy miracles. But the impact of hundreds and hundreds of stories of everyday miracles demonstrated that this was no ordinary human being. Stories demonstrating "His Omniscience, His Omnipresence, His Omnipotence," recollected by hundreds of people, expand the possibilities of human potential for divine reality.

> *Man is divine limitation. God is human perfection.*
> HAZRAT INAYAT KHAN

Maharaj-ji was that perfection living among us as an ordinary human being. Maharaj-ji was, as Ram Dass wrote, a miracle of love.

Maharaj-ji specifically told Ram Dass not to encourage any Westerners to come and seek him out in India. Many of my friends that summer ignored his admonition and left everything behind to be with Maharaj-ji. I was not among them.

*Dream . . .*

*"Maharaj-ji is outside! Maharaj-ji is outside!"*

*I rush out-doors and come up behind an elevated stage. Great silence. I gather that his darshan is over and he is leaving . . .*

*And then I see him, that little old man, gliding rapidly and silently away from the stage. Tremendous rush of much, much higher energy than I have ever experienced. I am weak, overwhelmed with emotion . . .*

*He glides past me, looking upon me fiercely with total indifference and total compassion, total love. He says, "We keep meeting each other again and again," and glides away . . .*

*The words go straight to the gut center. He is saying, "Why keep chasing after me in this body when I am everywhere? Why keep refusing to meet me in everyone everywhere? When you see me in all and all in me, then I never leave you and you never leave me . . ."*

*Satsang* means keeping company (*sangha*) with seekers of truth (*sat*), hanging out in spiritual community. For me at the time, this meant sitting and singing. Kirtan (chanting divine names in satsang) was exhilarating and liberating for my heart and soul and voice. All of us were wide open to let the love in our hearts sing out in fullness. There was no inhibiting judgment or self-criticism because everyone was in it together. And if the chants were in Sanskrit, so much the better. My mind could not figure out what was going on. I could not relate to all the images of blue-skinned, green-skinned, multi-armed gods and goddesses, much less their mythologies. But I could definitely let all my vitality and longing pour forth in these ecstatic sacred chants.

The Sufis say that there are three types of music—vocal, instrumental, and dance—and that the source of all music is the voice because the voice is alive. I had not found my voice standing in the church congregation amid adults bellowing hymns out of tune. I had not found my voice pounding away on the piano nor strumming the guitar and trying to sing Bob Dylan songs. In singing to God, I was beginning to find my own voice.

One time we were chanting *"Sri Ram Jai Ram Jai Jai Ram"* with increasing fervor. I was getting carried away with enthusiasm, clanging away with fire on the finger cymbals. Ram Dass said softly between the lines, "I hear a little ego out there on the percussion." I knew he was speaking to me and pulled back into a softer space.

The first mantra I ever heard came out of the blue. I was deeply absorbed in listening to the glorious saxophone of John Coltrane weaving dizzying arpeggios when suddenly the music stopped, the beat went on, and a deep throaty voice chanted, *"A love supreme, a love supreme, a love supreme . . ."*

At first, I thought that this was inane, just repeating three words over and over. After all I had been brought up on Protestant hymns with four-square chords that changed with every note and impressively wordy lyrics too complex to remember (hence the hymn books) and the poetic eloquence of popular music from Broadway to the blues, with a predictable structure of verse, chorus, verse, chorus, break, or some variation thereof. I was insulted! And yet "a love supreme" found a place in my heart, and I remembered it in my darkest moments.

∞∞∞

I've always been a sucker for beauty, specifically for female physical beauty. The highlight of my adolescent Sunday school classes—where I would arrogantly prove to myself again and again that I had a sharper intellect than anyone else present including my teachers—was the sunlight glistening on the shimmering nylon caressing the inner thigh of Jane Hendrickson, a cute, petite blonde who never said a word and captured my full attention every time she shifted in her seat and pulled down her short skirt. I was never seduced by makeup or stuck-up beauty queens. Nevertheless, beauty for me had always been physical and always female.

Now I was absolutely blown away by the beauty of all the serene shining faces and glowing eyes of all the young people who had gathered around Ram Dass. I was opening up to the luminous beauty of the soul. I was surrounded by incredibly beautiful, radiant beings, many of whom, including myself, would not have been worthy of love by my conditioned standards. But the beauty of the soul that shone forth in every body just blew me away. The cage of my mind opened up. My eyes in my heart were seeing souls shining for the first time.

All these beautiful people were really quite ordinary if not homely according to my previous standards—society's standards—of physical beauty. There was one exception. Her name was Veda Rama. She had sparkling eyes, pale skin, long dark hair, and a playful, seductive manner. My little heart lusted after her though I did not dare approach. She was several years older, she had a young daughter, and I was a toad. While I lay down in a miserable pup tent, she camped out in a yellow Chevy van whose insides were draped in royal purple and gold. She was my carnal love fantasy that summer—but not a major obsession, as my mind was focused on liberation.

One of Ram Dass's teaching threads was along these lines: "Desire creates the universe. Whatever you desire will manifest, sooner or later. God will give you whatever you desire. So be careful what you wish for—because you will get it."

Well, this was news to me, especially as I was characteristically caught in a maze of frustrated desire. It was good news that I found very hard to believe. But since it came from such good authority, someone my heart trusted, I decided to give it a chance, put God to the test, and see what happened. Knock, knock, Mister God, are you real?

So, I spoke to the God I didn't really believe in but wanted to know better and said, "God, if this is true, I say to you that I want to be with this woman Veda Rama more than anything." Of course, my deeper desire was to know whether God was real. I allowed my heart to desire an impossible dream. My mind remained neutral and skeptical. *Humpf. This is just a test, nothing more. We'll see what happens. Or not.*

And nothing at all happened that summer. When I left, I forgot all about my wish until, improbably, it surfaced years later in another time and another place, and I got what I asked for—my karmuppance.

Years later I also learned that Ram Dass had been the object of desire of my object of desire, and that Veda Rama had spent the entire summer sitting as close as she could to Ram Dass, passing her prayer beads through her fingers and repeating her fervent mantra, "Mrs. Ram Dass, Mrs. Ram Dass, Mrs. Ram Dass. . . ."

But Veda Rama's desire never came to pass. Or it came to pass in some other form. Go figure.

I loved Ram Dass. I loved the satsang. I loved to chant and sing to God. I began to be able to touch a peace-filled space in meditation. I would like to think that God was becoming a reality for me the way it seemed to be for others. But part of me was still not sure that all of this was real. My mind was just too active and skeptical. Maybe this was all just a contact high, a popular delusion, the madness of crowds. Maybe they were just taking me along on their trip.

Despite all the love and light and joy and peace my soul drank in, my little mind was still holding its cards close to its chest, reluctant to surrender to the obvious. Maybe all this God and Guru stuff was just hype, a sales pitch for some whacky cult of soft-headed people. It was all right that they all believed in this, more than all right; but was this really my own experience? My little mind was stubbornly skeptical, unwilling to commit its votes, until. . . .

One evening I was sitting outside the barn on top of the green hill that overlooked the little valley with the three-hole golf course cut out of the forest in the fading light of summer twilight. Long cool shadows lay across the smooth grass. A girl followed by two dogs strolled down to an arched bridge over a little stream. There may have been fireflies winking in the waning light. It was all kind of astral, magical, spacey, that twilight time between day and night when appearances shift and things may not be as they appear. I closed my eyes, getting absorbed in formless meditation. . . .

Suddenly my mind was projected back in space and time, rushing through glowing golden hoops of light, via a time tunnel to when I was six years old in my magic glade in the woods. I was sucked through that time tunnel back to day camp at Beaver Dam, a twisting vortex of luminous hoops that deposited me in a little clearing on the edge of the forest and a field of young plants. That summer, I was sent away for the first time to day camp at Beaver Dam out in Baltimore County. No matter what activities were offered, I loved nothing more than to slip away to this little clearing on the edge of the woods where I could be alone with . . . an awesome, luminous presence that knew me and loved me intimately.

Somehow I had discovered this place, and every day I would steal away to be with my—what? My angel? My soul? Who knows.

That evening I wrote:

*Yesterday, gazing down the rolling lawns, trees, cool long shadow, girl and dogs strolling down to the bridge, I felt myself touch on an astral sphere that I often touched when very young . . .*

*In a subtle way I felt the existence of a psychic tunnel in the reality of sunlight and shadow and the girl and the dogs, waking some youthful fancy . . .*

*Déjà vu: touching an astral level that has been felt before . . .*

*It was a moment when I lost myself, lost myself in time and space, lost in the wholeness and the newness of that moment and place, whole in affirmation and mute bliss, so far beyond word or thought it has taken some sixteen years to touch again, beyond the senses but "sensed" almost solely through vision. There was a silence of the senses and an "other fullness," pure vision. I felt as if I glimpsed the pure geometry of every form and movement at the same time as the thing itself, as an astral trace just beyond . . .*

Clearly I am grappling to find language to describe this. Tuning back into that place over the years I have the impression that there was a presence, a being of light, there in that glade, for I would return again and again to that same spot throughout that summer long ago.

In the precise moment that evening in New Hampshire I knew for certain the wholeness I was experiencing now in satsang had been with me all of my life. It had been buried beneath the activity and drama of outer life. I had forgotten all about it until that moment. But in that moment, it all became real, I knew that this wholeness was not just a contact high but a reality I had always known within myself. My life was irrevocably changed.

In that moment, I knew that everything I was experiencing with Ram Dass I had known all along—and had forgotten. I had had no conscious thought of this luminous presence until this spontaneous recall. It meant nothing to me at the time. It simply was. But now I knew with certainty that I had always known this love and this light. My monkey mind surrendered its resistance and allowed itself to know that God is real.

Years later, a friend asked me when I first knew that God is real, and I told her this story. Then I asked her when she first knew that God is real and she said, "I knew it when I stood up in assembly at Bible camp and declared that Jesus Christ is my Lord and Savior."

I was astounded by her admission. I would never ever do something like that, let alone make a public statement that conformed to a social religious norm. And yet I could not deny the validity of her experience, or that God had revealed herself in this way. God is certainly not limited to or by my personal experience. And yet it is only through experience that I can know God.

*Recurring dream . . .*

> *I am very small, riding in an enormous elevator in a luxurious gold and maroon gas-lamp hotel, on a joy ride up and*

*down the elevator, playing hide and seek with people who aren't there . . .*

*On the upper levels we (the elevator and me) burst out into space in the ether of a glittering steel metropolis, shining skyscrapers, and pure blue sky: I go gliding off into the skyway . . .*

One bright sunny day that summer, Sufi dancing came into my life. An energetic Sufi master, Murshid Samuel Lewis, was teaching young people in San Francisco to hold hands, dance, and chant sacred phrases, the holy names of God in the multiple spiritual traditions of humanity, and through this, to experience divine love, joy, and peace in the body. He called it "getting high without drugs." He was called Sufi Sam and Joy on Legs.

Some of his disciples came to visit us in New Hampshire and invited us to hold hands in a huge circle out on the green lawn in the noonday sun and to walk to the right chanting, *"Allah, Allah, Allah, Allah . . ."* Other simple movements and phrases were introduced as the dancing went on, until I was whirling around, raising my arms and shouting *"Ya Hayy!"* (O Life!), then, lowering my arms, *"Ya Haqq!"* (O Truth!), spinning out of the circle and falling to the ground in ecstasy as the blue sky turned around like a prayer wheel. I was in bliss.

I immediately went back to my tent and wrote down every movement and chant I could remember, inscribing my first experience in the Dances of Universal Peace.

Part of this new life was a vegetarian diet and pranayama, building up the power of the breath. Prana, or breath, Ram Dass taught, is the most vital and refined food. He told us stories of yogis and saints who ate no food and lived only on breath. We practiced pranayama, breath exercises, to increase the vitality and radiance of our breath, primarily the controlled hyperventilation of the Breath of Fire.

Summer was coming to a close, and I still had not climbed the mountain I had originally come to New Hampshire to climb. So, I gathered some friends, Peter and Charlene and some others, to hike Franconia Ridge.

"Since breath is the most refined food," Peter said, "I suggest that we keep silence all day and take no food on this hike. Whenever we feel tired we will stop and recharge our energy from pranayama practice and nourish our bodies with breath."

We all agreed.

This was an all-day hike up gnarly rocky trails through the dense forest, until we came out above tree line. At first we were stopping, huffing, and puffing to recharge our energy, a lot. To my surprise, the pranayama worked, and we felt no lack of energy all day. Indeed, by the time we were cruising the rocky ridges from peak to shining peak, we were positively blazing with radiant life energy and high-altitude euphoria. Our vitality was not dissipated by talking nor densified by eating. We virtually flew down the mountain as the sun was setting and went straight to a steakhouse for a very un-yogic dinner.

My life changed suddenly and unexpectedly that summer. Spiritual community and a spiritual path through life opened up to me. I was blessed that both the love and the wisdom that opened me up came from a very pure source. But that fall, I went back to work in the world—to earn enough money to buy a used Volkswagen van that would be my magic carpet.

In the middle of that winter, I went to hear Ram Dass speak at a theater in New York to find out when I could go to yoga camp again. To my disappointment, Ram Dass said that he was not going to do the same thing twice and there would be no yoga camp next summer. But if anyone was interested, he had some friends who were starting a spiritual community in the mountains of New Mexico, and they might need some help. I took that as a directive and wrote to Lama Foundation asking if I could work there for the summer. I later found out that the guys at Lama thought that I was a "wuss" and didn't want to let me in, but one of the gals there thought I was cute and persuaded them to let me come. Go figure.

# 2 RESTLESS, 1947–1970

Before all of this I was not what you would call a happy camper. I roamed alone in my car up and down New England from the ocean to the mountains and back and forth across the country in restless, unblessed wanderings, totally driven by feelings that I was totally out of touch with: unease, discomfort, disorientation, dissatisfaction, depression, anxiety, fear, panic, and terror, to name a few. These strange and unsettling inner motions were scarcely covered over by the nonstop motor mouth of my mind babbling sense and nonsense to my delight and dismay.

I was hearing voices all the time. Often it was just automatic scholastic word play. Sometimes it was what I called the singing voice—a quiet but authoritative incantation that whispered to me what seemed to be the most exalted poetry, chanting in slow resonance, repeating the words often enough that I could write them down. Sometimes it was pure, disembodied poetics. Sometimes it was the ranting of an angry, frustrated little boy locked in his room and left to his own devices, the plaints and complaints of infant sorrow so deeply ingrained that I paid them no attention as they had no new information for me. Sometimes the vague murmur of indistinct voices holding indeterminate conversations lay just beyond the threshold of comprehension, talk show subways roaring by each other in the night, radio music fading in and out of hearing, murky movie theme music submerged in the landscape, escaped elevator muzak with no strong emotional or rational content, just a never-ending tide of voices pounding like surf in my head.

*Restless, unblessed wanderings through glorious summer days in New England forests, green and gray mountains, mind spinning, whirring, buzzing, voices swarming like bees around a hive, mind opening, reaching, grasping, collecting thoughts, phrases, impressions, reflections, central switchboard swamped with calls from above, beyond, all around, red lights blinking—much noise, little signal, no direction known . . .*

*Fascinated with homelessness, fugitive status, life on the run, run out of time, driving miles without meaning in a rusted-out VW bus, counting the hours in dead heads of cigarettes sucked into the slipstream, driving up nameless country roads to crash out at dead ends beside streams, bogs in the road, nowhere to go, to escape, hopeless hitchhiking on wooded turnpikes as afternoon fades to dusk and dusk to night, absorbing the headlights of hundreds of cars passing me by . . .*

My story starts with my parents, Jack and Mary, who grew up in Towanda, a small town on the Susquehanna River in upstate Pennsylvania. They came of age during the Great Depression. They were married in 1942, just before Jack went off to the war in Germany. After the war they moved downriver to the big city, Baltimore. I was born there on June 23, 1947, at 4:04 a.m., soon followed by my sisters, Lucy and Katherine.

My parents bought a large house in a leafy neighborhood just over the city line to accommodate three rambunctious children. My father had a good job and would rise to become president of the Baltimore Bank for Cooperatives, a branch of the Federal Farm Credit Bank. We children went to the best private schools: Gilman, Bryn Mawr, and Roland Park. I grew up a golden child with all the material advantages.

I have memories of the primal state of unitive consciousness, the infant bliss and wonder that pervaded my early childhood.

*I spend endless afternoons in the sky*
*suckling the light*

*I am a baby crawling*
*to sit in the robes of any being of light*
*who happens to come in through the window*

But my actual first memory of this life on Earth is of a being in a lonely, fogged numbness, isolated in a crib in the newborn nursery in the hospital. Either this was residual trauma from previous lives or I was born in the twilight sleep of drugs given to my mother to ease the pain of birth, although she denies it. At any rate, in the beginning there was numbness, loneliness, and abandonment.

I was supposed to be the well-loved golden child. Only after my own son was born, a peaceful happy baby, did I ask my mother what kind of a baby I was.

"Oh, you were a horrible baby," she said. "You were howling and screaming for the first three months of your life!"

Apparently, my mother was doing her best to be a modern mother, 1947 model, feeding me formula from a bottle on a rigid schedule. When she finally brought her unhappy baby to the doctor to see what was wrong with him, the doctor said, "Mary, your baby is hungry. You're not feeding him enough. Feed him whenever he wants."

She began feeding me on demand and I morphed into a chubby, happy baby.

When I was six, I had a sledding accident and smashed my nose up, resulting in a deviated septum and diminished breath in my right nostril. My mother took me to a Dr. Broyles, who took a lump of radioactive radon, stuck it up my nose, and held it there. He struck a tuning fork and held it to my skull to distract me from the radon disintegrating cartilage and God knows what else inside my head. That was the beginning of my profound distrust of the medical establishment.

Fifty years later I would read that the government at that time was encouraging doctors to treat patients with radioactive materials so that they could study the results.

My mother, for her part, always trusted the good doctors. When she began putting on weight after her children were born, her doctor told her, "Mary, you need to stop drinking beer and start drinking whiskey. Then you will stop putting on weight."

Grandpa Patterson, my mother's father, had discovered and patented a chemical that was to become the standard emulsion for X-ray screens until the digital era. He turned this into a business, the Patterson Screen Company, that brought prosperity to his family and his home town, Towanda, Pennsylvania.

When I went to the shoe store as a kid, I could stick my feet into a live X-ray machine, gaze down through a viewer, and see the bones in my feet move as I wiggled my toes. It was a radioactive era.

The fifties were economically burgeoning, psychologically repressive, and boring, even to me as a child. Remember when the air was clean and sex was dirty? Remember when everybody smoked and nobody was gay? That was the fifties, the era of Betty Crocker home cooking, Ivory Soap to wash your mouth out with, and the Breck Shampoo girls, all very squeaky clean and tidy whitey. I thought the grownups were controlling, repressive, and most of all, tedious. I mean, how long can you talk about road conditions and the weather and people I've never heard of and expect me to sit still and listen?

*Sit still. Don't squirm. Little children should be seen and not heard. Little children are blank slates to be written on, little savages to be tamed.*

My parents grew up in the Great Depression. I grew up in the Great Repression. Even as a child, I knew I didn't fit in. I knew I was someone and they thought I was no one. My mother Mary was indulgent and permissive, while my father Jack could be harsh and punitive. My father had just gotten out of the army and liked to run his household in a military fashion. Discipline and obedience were primary virtues.

When we were little children, Lucy and Katherine and I would play all day, building all sorts of forts and castles in the backyard or in the basement and playing all sorts of fantasy roles. If they were Bugs Bunny and Porky Pig, I was Elmer Fudd. If we got too loud or wild or disobedient, my mother would always say, "Just wait until your father gets home. You'd better behave yourselves when your father gets home." And sure enough, the minute we heard his car pull into the driveway, we knew we had to quiet down or face the wrath of Jack. We were terrified of his angry outbursts.

If I was too energized to settle down, if I was too enthused and out of control, I would be locked in my room to cry and rage, yell and scream, protesting the unfairness of the way I was being treated, until I calmed down enough to join the family for dinner. Eventually hunger won out over my offended dignity.

Our family table was formal, polite, and cool. Hot food but no heart warmth. Everything was chill enough to make you shudder. My enduring image of childhood in the fifties is a huge, gleaming white, quietly humming Frigidaire refrigerator. As I would later sing to some faraway lady:

*With your cocaine eyes*
*and your misty twisty hair*
*your soul grows like an orchid*
*in this frigid air*

*Your laughter flows like warm wind*
*through these gardens under ice*
*I'm falling through the mirrors*
*that are buried behind your eyes*

My father sat at the head of the dinner table and commandeered the conversation. He would ask each one of us about our day at school and then hold forth on economics, politics, history, business—all the things children need to know. No doubt it was well intended, but dinner time was like being trapped in a lecture hall. We three children would grow restless and fidgety, exchanging nudges and glances and kicks under the table. Sometimes we would start giggling, simmering with repressed mirth, and we just couldn't help it—we all burst forth in gales of laughter, my mother included, that we could not control. My father would get very angry, grow red in the face, get up, and leave the table.

As a teenager, I became sensitive to all manner of historical undercurrents that had no place in the family conversation. Sitting in the backyard and sipping cocktails with the family on a warm summer evening, bored out of my gourd, I slipped into the sunlight glittering behind the shady trees and dreamed of the blood of the native people drenching the land, slaughtered so that we might possess it. I smelled the sweat and blood of the enslaved people whose labor made this land fruitful. I was aware of all the human beings who had been sacrificed so that my family could sit here, sipping cocktails.

> Maples pale and blouse full with twilight
> Leaves like white waters cascade green
> above the cocktail hour
> (our glacial smiles cracking melting and mixing
> in this deep narcotic dream
> this purple rose of the deeps beyond the beach)
> Eyeless fish shimmer in the leaves
>
> Gossip embers in the grass and dusk lurches
> ash away with us
> Home through the falling blue shacks
> where crazed slaves prophesy blood and molasses
> Home through the call of a toucan sundown
> Home to the mountains of the moon
> where blacks strip down distance in shadows of sunfish
>
> where with jubilant hands drugged as flamingos
> we dowse for lovers in the drums
> three rainy suns

That's me and my sisters: three rainy suns.

Prep school in the early sixties. I was saturated with all sorts of stimulating information, ideas, and images I had no idea what to do with.

Transcendentalism, existentialism, surrealism—what was that all about? The history we studied was nothing but an endless succession of battles, conquests, dynasties, and empires—what was that all about? I excelled in the study of ancient Greek and Latin—but what was that all about? I shared my enthusiasms and confusions with my father, who shook his head and told me I was crazy.

I did my senior research paper on Friedrich Nietzsche. Getting into the spirit, my senior speech was brilliant exhortation and expostulation, yelling about the coming superman before a placid auditorium of bored boys in coats and ties. What was that all about?

My first hint of the generation gap came when my father was driving us up through sleepy rural Pennsylvania on the way to visit the grandparents. He was driving his brand-new black DeSoto sedan. It must have been 1956. I must have been nine years old. Here I am, nodding off with my sisters in the back seat when this song comes on the radio like a house on fire:

"Rat tat tat, tat tattat, ta—You ain't nothin' but a hound dog, cryin' all the time. . . ." It was Elvis!

Click! My father turned off the radio, muttering, "Work of the devil!"

And that was that.

I went to see the Beatles in the Baltimore Civic Center (basketball arena) in 1964. The hysterical pandemonium of yelling and screaming girls was so cacophonous that I couldn't even hear what songs they were playing, the little ants on the stage. What was that all about?

Baltimore had seven radio stations, three of which played white pop music, bubblegum music, and four that played black soul music. I loved the soul music and the jivin' DJs. I fell in love with passionate, ecstatic, heartbreaking soul music, full of rampant emotions that had no place in my actual everyday life. I would listen to soul music turned up loud while playing pool with myself in the basement of my parents' house. It was like I was stranded on a tiny desert island with no way to reach the brightly lit party ships cruising by.

I excelled at academics, sucked at sports, and had no idea what I wanted to do when I grew up. I kept looking at my father, trying to understand what it was to be a man, what a man did in the real world.

I knew my father was the president of a bank. I knew he lent money to farm cooperatives, but I had no idea what that meant. He would take long business trips away from home, visiting orchards and vineyards and mushroom farms, coming home with cartons of applesauce and grape juice. I always wondered if he had some other woman he was seeing in those long times away from home. Although I eventually concluded that he lacked the passion necessary for love affairs, I still wonder.

But what I really wanted to know was what he did every day while we were in school. I kept on pestering him, demanding to see him at his workplace, until one day he took the whole family down to see his office on the second floor of a gray downtown bank building. He led us through the workplace where a dozen men and women worked away on handwritten ledgers with mechanical calculators, and into his private office. He shut the door and all was quiet. His desk was completely bare, with nothing but a telephone and a family picture on it. I was astounded. Was this what my father did—sit at an empty desk all day while everyone else did the work? What was that all about?

My musical heritage was limited. There was one blessed week when I was three years old and had to stay with my Welsh grandmother who delighted in singing nursery rhymes and lullabies like a bright yellow bird in the morning of my life. Other than that, no one in my family ever sang a note except when standing and singing Protestant hymns loudly and out of tune in a congregation that bellowed like a barn full of distressed cattle. I never could find the right note to sing because no one else could. I became convinced that I could not sing anything other than "Ninety-Nine Bottles of Beer on the Wall" with the boys at summer camp.

My mother did insist that my sisters and I take piano lessons, starting me at age eight. It was invaluable to learn how to read music and how to play piano from sheet music at an early age. It was an intellectual exercise in hand-eye coordination. Rhythm was mechanical adherence to a metronome. I was not taught how to listen or how to hear. It was strictly the reproduction of written music.

After the introductory exercises, I was taught to play simple classical piano music, including Bach, Beethoven, Brahms, and Mozart, and then more complex classical piano music. Next came piano recitals and then I rebelled. I hated this music. I had not been taught to listen to music, so the only music I heard were the notes coming out of my fingers. I hated this music.

I persuaded my mother to find a piano teacher who would teach me to play pop music—our church organist, as it turned out. He did teach me to play pop songs, stride bass, and boogie-woogie. The high point of my time with him was a rock-and-roll passion play staged in the church sanctuary with me happily pounding away on the piano while Jesus suffered.

Unfortunately, the piano at home shared a wall with my father's den, and my passionate pounding away on the piano was a source of constant irritation to him. He would repeatedly storm out into the living room and demand that I quiet down or quit playing, which set up a passive-aggressive dynamic. Passionately pounding on the keyboard, doing what I loved, was a way of getting back at my father. But ultimately his wrath prevailed and my musical testosterone was repressed. Hermetic, I would only play music if no one was listening.

I came to feel as contained by song structure as I had been by classical sheet music. I was like a hamster in a wheel running through the same songs over and over again. I wanted to sing but I didn't know how and didn't think I could. I wanted to be free to improvise on song structure.

My last piano teacher was a cocktail lounge jazz pianist, who taught me the basic elements of jazz improvisation. This was liberating at first, but ultimately also confining, as the written course material we were using soon plunged me into endless complex harmonic chord progressions that I had to learn. It was all mind and no heart, like the rest of my life.

The piano keyboard became a prison. I wanted to be free of confinement in all these musical forms. I wanted to play the music I loved. I blamed all my teachers.

At age sixteen I stopped playing piano and got a nylon-string classical guitar. I vowed that I would never let anyone teach me anything about playing guitar. That was how I felt I had to do it. I would come to my music on my own or not at all.

Slowly, slowly, I taught myself how to play basic chords and practiced enough that I could keep up some simple rhythms. I croaked away, singing simple folk songs like "Blowin' in the Wind" to my lame accompaniment. It wasn't much, but at least I was on my own, free of the learnin' prison.

I always had a lot of energy of a certain kind. There were times when I was a child that my energy was too much for my parents to take, and I would get shut up in my room. I loved to escape into the woods and realms of fantasy. At kindergarten, when it was nap time, I could never go to sleep. I was restless and fidgety. The teacher said to me, "If you can't take a nap like everybody else, then I have an activity for you to do." She took me into the boiler room in the basement of the school next to the kindergarten and showed me a big pile of newspapers. She said, "You can rip these up until you are exhausted." I really enjoyed ripping those newspapers to shreds day after day.

At summer camp, I could never go to sleep when it was nap time, so I lay on my bunk and wrote in my diary and read my books. My counselor identified me as an intellectual.

I began keeping a diary as soon as I could write, at age five or six, in a little brown five-year diary with a teensy lock on it. I always started out "Today" with a colon. At first, at least half the time, it was "Today: Nothing happened." I recorded only external events, nothing about my feelings. But I was very devoted to writing every day.

By the time I was in high school, I was keeping a daily journal with many pages a day devoted to the agony and ecstasy of adolescence, all my burning feelings enhanced with mild profanity and all the things I would never ever tell my parents. I even went as far as filling a notebook with the narrative of my first love, in which Laura herself wrote the middle portion.

This all ended abruptly one day when I came home to find that my father had gone into my room, read my diaries and journals, and confiscated and destroyed them all. He was shouting, livid with anger. I was livid with anger. But in our family only one person was allowed to shout and yell and express anger, and it wasn't me. So I took the verbal beating in silence. I knew that if he had done more than just skim the surface of my colorful language, I would have been in much more trouble. This gross violation of my privacy destroyed any trust and respect I had for my father, and drove me deeper into hiding.

There was a lot of adolescent uproar going on in our house, which resulted in a lot of tension between our parents. My mother was very distressed with my father for "treating you children so horribly." I would go into the kitchen and wash dishes with her every night after dinner. I would listen to her complaints and her desire to leave my father. I would sympathize with her and support her desire to separate, but divorce was not an option in her world.

The development of intelligence was highly valued in my birth family as a means of survival, if nothing else, so that we could make a living with our intellect and not face a life of manual labor as my father had, growing up on a farm.

After repeated violent encounters on the playing fields with such Anglo-Saxon uber jocks as Pitts Dockman, Rocky Ober, and Tinsley VanDurand, I forgot about sports and devoted myself to homework. In the eighth grade I achieved the highest grade-point average in my most excellent school and was given a silver plate with my name inscribed to prove it. By the time I got to college I could maintain a high grade-point average like walking a treadmill—with minimal effort and enthusiasm.

But all work and no play make Jack a dull boy, as my mother used to say. And my mother, somewhat subversively, gave me and my sisters ample space and encouragement to indulge in creative play, fantasy, and self-expression. I never had invisible playmates like my sisters, but I would be absorbed in daydreams of epic grandeur and play out all sorts of fantasy dramas while walking alone in the woods.

At the crossroads of intellect and imagination I discovered I had a gift for writing poetry and turned to word crafting with introverted enthusiasm and the ambition to express a unique identity beneath my quiet mask.

As my first published poem, "Inspiration" (1962), suggests, I have always experienced creativity as a gift that is given, not an achievement that is earned, and the muse is unpredictable.

*Behold St. Elmo's holy fire—*
*A hovering luminescence of cold green beauty*
*Clinging to the foretops, prefacing a terrible blessing*
*On those beneath.*

*Watch as the frigid fire descends.*
*The airy lava scampers about the taut ratlines,*
*Setting ablaze the sails, but not singeing*
*The sloshed canvas.*

*Now look—the sparks spatter*
*On the bowed, toiling heads, missing one man,*
*Setting another aglow, but rarely touching*
*The same man twice.*

While in high school I generated a lot of poetry and short stories. These writings were full of adolescent angst and ennui, cynical and sarcastic, heavy with vague sentiment and frustrated longing, reflective of the oppressive environment that was my experience growing up. It was not until I went to college that something approaching a true poetic voice began to emerge.

## Fall 1965

Wesleyan University, Middletown, Connecticut

As a nineteen-year-old virgin college freshman far away from parental oversight, my hormonal goal was to get laid as soon as possible. Despite being intoxicated with beauty and nurturing all sorts of romantic longings, I was ignorant of sex, how to get it, and how to do it. Sex Ed was not part of my school curriculum in the sixties.

I invited a bright, sexy Vassar girl down to Wesleyan for the weekend in hopes of some sex education. Amy was slender and petite, with a pert, cat-like face, green eyes, pale white skin, and long black hair. She was a music major, training her voice to sing classical music. We spent a cramped, uncomfortable night squeezed together on my single bed in my dorm room. I was getting all hot and bothered, but didn't know what to do about it.

The next day we were sitting at a big round table having lunch with a bunch of my friends and their weekend dates when Amy announced in a very loud voice, "Frank, when are you going to make love to me?"

In an equally loud voice I shouted, "Just as soon as you show me how to do it!"

We lost no time going back to my room where Amy opened up the heavens of sexual pleasure for me. She took me inside her and held me and stroked me with her velvet glove. Naturally, we had lots of sex. Naturally, I fell in love with her and wrote lots of mannered poetry to her and wanted to be with her every weekend.

I found out that her sexual activity was quite expansive and in no way confined to me. She was screwing one of her professors ("Older men last longer"), exploring lesbianism with her roommate, and so on. So, the archetype of Amy as my one true love could not endure for very long, even though I still love her for being my first lover.

But the most astonishing thing was . . .

After Amy left that first weekend, I sat for hours that night under a streetlight, trying to imagine my parents making love, having sex, to conceive me. I knew now for a fact that I had to have been conceived in this way. But I could not for the life of me imagine my parents being so tender, so juicy, so passionate, so intimate with each other. My parents were always cool and distant with each other, physically and emotionally. They never touched. My mother would cringe and withdraw on the rare occasion my father tried to put his arm around her. I don't know what went on in their bedroom behind closed doors except that they had two huge separate beds. It was inconceivable that they were or had been hot and horny, warm and loving sexual beings. And yet it was a fact. I was astounded. I had been conceived through sex.

It took me much, much longer to know that I had also been conceived in love.

*With your cocaine eyes*
*and your lips like yellow mud*

*you left your five-year diary*
*dissolving in my blood*

*You left your one-time lover*
*between here and Omaha*
*You're trying hard to discover*
*whatever it was you saw in him*
*You're leaving him one more time*
*my friend*

We came of age in the sixties as the winds of change were sweeping away the illusory quiet of peace and prosperity. The Vietnam War, sometimes violent anti-war protests, civil rights movement, non-violent resistance and civil disobedience, women's liberation, sexual revolution, influx of Eastern spirituality, explosion of psychedelics, rock and roll, and sweet soul music—all were exhilarating and confusing, terrifying and liberating. The tectonic shift that took place in the sixties was a mass movement that I fully participated in. My personal journey is a gleam on a bubble in the foam on the crest of a huge wave of generational change, a speck of dust in the tsunami of transformation.

I participated in protests in college. I chanted and held up signs as others held up pig heads on stakes in front of a police station in Manhattan. I bussed out to Fort Dix, New Jersey, and joined the waves of people who invaded the army post there and were turned back by waves of tear gas. I shouted down Dick Nixon at a campaign rally in Hartford. But my heart wasn't really in it.

I wasn't identified with the issues. I couldn't relate to the anger and the passion of the protestors. I thought it was a good thing they were doing, but it wasn't my thing. I decided that social activism, righteous as it might be, was not for me.

Being an introvert, I was drawn more to the psychedelic movement, though I found that my body could not tolerate psychedelic drugs very often, and cocaine and speed not at all. I wanted to break free of the manacles of my mind. I knew that there was more that I could see, feel, and be, if I could just ditch the academic headset. So, when Timothy Leary put out the word, "Turn on, tune in, and drop out," I did, along with so many in my generation.

*We shamans loose on silver cycles*
*We runners of blue Apache snow*
*We hush electromagnetic lovers*
*We all crazy anyway*
*rain-faced crazies with crazy hair*

*We volts we heads of hurricane slumber*
*We seekers along electron streams*
*We star-fuckers of Mama Sutra*
*rain-faced evolutionaries*
*dragon shadows lost under the sea*

*Dharma wheel unleashed like laughing gas!*

It is said that, "If you remember the sixties, you weren't there." The first time I smoked marijuana, time stopped. I was sitting with a group of friends passing around a joint in a college dorm room. I inhaled deeply. Immediately all thought stopped, time was suspended. I was aware only of the golden light spilling from a floor lamp. For the first time in my life, the perpetual mental chatter just stopped. I was fully conscious but without cognitive commentary. I simply *was*—for a moment, a split-second in eternity. Then it all started up again just as suddenly as it had stopped. All of us started talking at once, excited about our new experience, talking and eating popcorn, popcorn, popcorn, feeding a hunger unlike any other.

Drugs played a major role in the awakening of consciousness in the sixties, or at least a shift in awareness away from conventional, conditioned mentation. At the beginning, getting high together was a sacrament that opened the doors of perception to a vaster more cosmic consciousness—or so it seemed—and totally displaced the alcoholic bacchanalia we had grown up with.

∞∞

I was investigated by the FBI for threatening to kill presidential candidate Richard Nixon. One evening, I was driving a bunch of guys from my college up to Smith and Mount Holyoke to connect with some girls. This was back in the day when boys and girls were educated separately. We decided to stop in Hartford to participate in an anti-war demonstration at a campaign rally for Nixon. As we were getting out of the car, a retired naval officer leaning out of his window heard one of us say, "We're really going to fix Dick Nixon tonight," and reported this threat to the authorities.

The FBI first knocked on my parents' door in Baltimore before sending a special agent to take me down to the police station and interrogate me. Naturally I didn't know anything about anybody. But I did use this as an opportunity to inform the government that I was a homosexual drug addict, thereby getting on the record books as totally udersirable cannon fodder for Vietnam. Such was the depth of my scorn and contempt for the status quo.

I didn't understand why we were in Vietnam fighting a war. I didn't know that Lyndon Johnson had signed a declaration of war based on an outright lie. I knew that it was wrong because so many people said so. I participated in anti-war protests and was tear-gassed without really knowing what I was doing. But I did know that the government wanted to draft me and send me to Vietnam and get me killed. And I wasn't going to let that happen.

I heard of a psychologist in Boston, Dr. John Perry-Hooker, who was helping young men get declared mentally unfit for the army. I drove up to Boston as soon as I could. Dr. John interviewed me, had me take four hours of standard psychological tests and, based on this, wrote a letter to my draft board. He said, "You will read that I've written about your religious convictions and suicidal tendencies. Don't worry about that. It's just for the draft board." But he was spot on. And he saved my life, along with the lives of thousands of other young men. We were the lucky ones who found out about Dr. John and could afford to pay for the tests. He didn't charge for his services, but we had to pay an institution to administer the tests. I never told my father why the draft board refused me.

This was the moment I took my life into my own hands and, by trusting in the beneficence of others, kept myself out of the killing machine.

Psychedelics were rolling across the campus. Comparative Religions was the hot course everyone was taking. Judaism and Christianity were dry, overworked history, but Hinduism, Buddhism, and Islam were juicy, exotic mental destinations. Our professor was young, personable, and user-friendly. He eschewed dry lectures and encouraged class discussions. At the beginning of the semester on Buddhism, he asked us what we wanted to know about Buddhism, and of course we all said, "Enlightenment! Yeah, enlightenment! We all want to know about enlightenment!"

So of course we all went straight into multiple metaphors for enlightenment, merely brushing over the Four Noble Truths, missing entirely the First Noble Truth:

*There is suffering. Suffering exists. Suffering is real.*

If we had spent even a week on this First Noble Truth, we might have gotten on the ground with the reality of Buddha's awakening. I might have had to look at my own suffering. What a difference it would have made if I had become aware of my own suffering, let alone the suffering of humanity. But I had no language for emotions. I was conditioned not to express my feelings. My environment was masculine and intellectual. I had brilliant mind friends but no heart companion. So, my mind pursued the ideal of enlightenment—and getting high, which seemed to give a taste of *satori* (sudden awakening), however temporary.

In fact, I was suffering like crazy from loneliness, depression, and all sorts of developmental trauma. But the reality of suffering was not part of my narrative, not in the pack of identity cards I answered to. The First Noble Truth was just another idea to be memorized and shelved. Freedom from suffering was, at first, dissociation and self-medication.

The most significant influences on my emerging poetic voice were surrealism and marijuana. The French surrealists showed me the potency
of bypassing the rational linguistic mind and getting directly in touch
with the flow of irrational imagery in the unconscious mind.

*Ominous blue printed page*
*Runic blue virgin rage*
*Piano solitude fat like a pig*

*Aspirin door suns in flight*
*Storms curdle in cellar light*
*Incense blue cylinder night*

*Crossroads falling on the shacks*
*Blue bottle sunk in golden wax*
*Blue lava spike my angel axe*

Like the surrealists I felt limited, oppressed, and imprisoned by my
mind—my intellectual, rational, language-based mind. I felt the urge
to explore and express deeper levels of feeling and perception than my
intellectual acculturation permitted, to stop making sense, to unleash
the turbulent flow of imagery just below the façade of the conscious
mind, and to be liberated from the tyranny of the rational. Of course,
the risk is imagery that makes no sense at all, to oneself or to others.

*Black corpuscles fill the trees*
*Volcanic spores drift down the scarp*

*Protozoa glitter guts*
*Proton shocks*
*Stars*
*rift*
*Arclights hiss*
*Scimitar expressway swerve*

*Steel ruins breathing like seaweed*

*(tall white government of voiceless nerves)*

But the reward can be a much richer expression of feelings in their own language, the subconscious flow of images. For feelings are not thought, nor are they thoughts about feelings.

Writing down the traces of irrational images below the surface of my mind allowed me to express primary emotions such as anger, rage, anxiety, fear, loneliness, and grief—emotions that I was culturally conditioned not to permit myself to feel, let alone express. At times, this flow of images allows the expression of feelings that are so subtle you can barely put your finger on them but are very real nonetheless.

*Stars shout in the soaring borealis*
*sucked-up intellectual teeth*

*The domino of night crashes down*

*Screaming mice stitch crystal in bone*
*The huts of my blood are falling*

*A horse stands shackled on a flatcar*
*The sun drifts up in a blown flute bone*

Smoking marijuana was my preferred technique for bypassing my hyper-active rational mind and getting in touch with the deeper flow of lyric imagery. Smoking marijuana was mostly a solitary pursuit for me, always associated with creativity and later spirituality, in contrast to the dense competitive alcoholic culture I grew up in. Smoking marijuana affected a shift in consciousness much like getting into an elevator and riding it a few floors higher to a much broader, freer, and more enjoyable perspective.

*When the day closes the rose closes*
*Where the miners end the fire begins*

*I swim under water deeper than breath*
*breathing my cells steering by sirens*

*and keep on swimming until it begins*

*Sails lean like stars against the fort*
*Rags of fire in the dark above*

*Over the rocks see my bones flow*
*A white mare clambers up from the sea*

*Dinosaurs gather cars into the sea*

I always equated marijuana with creativity, although not cre-ativity with marijuana. In fact, many of my best poems were writ-ten while *not* under the influence of marijuana. Smoking marijuana was at first a liberating expansion of consciousness. Later it became a modality of mind play and only much later, a debilitating limitation.

It was only with the rise of the medical marijuana movement that I became aware that marijuana is one of the most powerful natural pain-killers known to mankind. Only later could I acknowledge that the reason I got so addicted to marijuana is that I was in so much mental and emotional pain. Getting high relieved the pain—temporarily. I was so intellectual that I wasn't even aware of how much emotional pain I was in. Nonstop mental chatter masked that pain, and then marijuana stopped the mental chatter—temporarily.

By self-medicating I could not really feel the pain. By not feeling the pain I could not acknowledge it. By not acknowledging the pain I could not recognize its cause. By not recognizing the cause of the pain, I could not get to the root of what caused the suffering, and so the root of suffering remained, no matter how much I self-medicated.

I have no regrets whatsoever at this time in my life. But if I were to have regrets, my one and only would be that I wasted so much time smoking so much dope for so long.

I was drawn to the exuberance of creativity and the exaltation of poetry, resonating with Blake and Yeats and Neruda and Bly, but mostly exulting in the songs that were singing in my soul, the magical singing voice that came from within.

I was essentially inspired by the methodology of the French sur-realists who sought to bypass the structures of the rational mind and connect with the language and imagery spontaneously flowing from the unconscious mind and to express an aesthetic that was more real and vivid than ordinary everyday consciousness. They sought to shock awake the rational bourgeoisie mentality of their time by writing and painting irrational dreamlike imagery.

This was a liberating inspiration to break free of the hamster wheel of my rational mind and to get in touch with my own deeper feelings by allowing the flow of images to speak. Of course, some of the resulting poetry was beautiful language that was literally incom-prehensible even to me, let alone to the reader. The initial goal was to liberate the imagination, the image nation of my inner life. The desire to communicate something to someone would come later on. And some of the resulting poetry was indeed musical language and exquisite imagery that expressed exalted emotional experiences as nothing else can. The key was to rise above the nitpicking censor of the critical mind, to surrender to the flow of feeling and let whatever needs to be sung in the moment come forth: the good, the bad, and the ugly.

I had a lot of self-identity wrapped up in being a poet.

When I went to hear Robert Bly talk, I paid close attention when he said, "If you want to be a poet, you must go and be alone for a time."

Being alone for a time will nurture you as a poet, he promised. I took him at his word. As a country boy, he had gone to be alone in New York City. As a city boy, or at least a suburban boy, I would go to be alone in the mountains.

I got the key to my college's ski lodge in Franconia, New Hampshire, and drove up to spend the summer alone in the woods. I didn't write a decent poem all summer, but I was alone for the first time in my life, removed from all the socio-cultural influences that had molded me. Every morning, I climbed up the hill to sit on a ledge and watch the sun rise over the eastern woodlands. I didn't eat all that much, and what I ate was simple. In the afternoons, I would go running along winding roads through the sunny green forest and through red covered bridges. In the evening, I watched the sun set from my rocky ledge. I fell into a rhythm with the landscape. I read little and wrote even less. Mostly I just sat and listened.

Nothing happened all summer. But for the first time in my life, I was sitting and breathing and touching a place deeper than my mind, although I didn't even have that concept at the time. I just didn't know who I was away from all the stimulus and impetus of parents and teachers and friends and newspapers and magazines and radio and television. I came away with none of the poetry I went to get, but sitting in the silence, in the stillness, quieting the mind, awakened something in me. I thought I was going to be by myself in order to do something, to write poetry. In fact, I was going to be by myself in order to be something— to be myself.

An ethnomusicology program at Wesleyan University had a Balinese gamelan orchestra and a family of South Indian musicians. I was privileged to study *veena* (a stringed instrument) and *mridangam* (a two-headed hand drum) for a semester. There were also monthly curry concerts with spicy Indian feasts cooked by the musicians followed by long, free-form concerts of classical Indian music.

This all came together one rainy spring afternoon when I had taken some LSD and was tripping away in my dorm room, listening to George Harrison play sitar music. I thought, "Hey! I can do that!" I put my guitar into open tuning, just like the veena, broke free of the tyranny of playing chords, and spent all that rainy afternoon playing soulful ragas.

The open-tuning guitar became a resonant ocean of sound from which simple yet exquisite melodies freely emerged under my fingers. I was improvising free of structure and form. I just had to stay in the *raga,* the scale, and let the melodic line rise and fall, appear and disappear, in harmony with the gentle spring rain and the fading gray afternoon light. This was my liberation and the beginning of really making music. No one ever taught me about open tuning on guitar. I had never played melodies on guitar strings let alone improvised. But somehow, I just knew to do it. In a flash of insight I broke out of the prison of three-chord folk songs. I kept my guitar in open tuning for the next ten years.

I grew up in a segregated all-male (all-Christian, all-white) environment, going to boys' schools and summer camps from kindergarten through college. My peer group was smart, bright, aggressive, judgmental, cutting, elitist, disciplined, and highly accomplished. Expression of feelings, let alone sympathetic listening, was not in our vocabulary. The standard reaction to emotions was "Don't have a cow!" Our conversations were constantly sharpening the swords of our intellects. Writing poetry was a way of getting in touch with feelings I didn't even know I had.

*I put my head inside my blood*
*where lay the tents of babble*
*where the sands slur with cellular headlights*
*and wet weeds of obscurity*
*where stray the tattle of mad violin solos*

*Grief! you dark and siren foam!*

Intellect was highly valued where I came from, along with good behavior, good grades, and a certain kind of stoicism. *Keep your head down, keep your nose to the grindstone, don't question authority, put up with the abuse, don't speak unless you're spoken to, if it hurts it's good for you, this hurts me more than it hurts you but it's for your own good. . .* all that sort of rot. Disciplined mental effort was highly praised. Emotional displays were frowned upon.

I consistently made the best grades at the best schools, although more and more often, the course material was meaningless. The only vocational ambition I ever had was to be a teacher, to continue being good at what I was good at. But when I went to cocktail parties with my college professors they all seemed like vapid, narcissistic drunks, bathing in the attention of the undergraduates, so I lost that ambition.

*Flecked gray stones*
*in the folded cloister*
*The ice in your glass*
*is melting insane*

*Our abbess just so*
*in Tibet on the phone*
*bursts into measure*
*loose gray feathers*

One evening I went to the university library, resolved to directly experience the knowledge and wisdom that was accumulated there. It was a grand building fronted with huge white columns. The entry room had marble floors and a ceiling forty feet high. I went behind the front desk and back into the stacks, which comprised twelve stories of metal shelving with wooden planks for walkways. Peering along the sides of the shelving I could see the stories above and below me, hundreds of thousands of books.

I sat in a corner and let my mind expand to embrace all the books of knowledge that were in the library. I realized that even with a lifetime of reading I could absorb only a small fraction of the words housed there. It felt like an abstract, airless vault filled with billions of words, facts, ideas, and opinions that would only absorb and suppress my life force. I gave up faith in intellectual knowledge that night.

In fact, I lost all faith in the institutional knowledge I had been brought up in. Getting high became my religion: getting stoned out of my mind, plunging into new worlds of sensation, perception, ecstasy, and delight, and entering into cathedrals of beauty in the ordinary that I never knew existed.

> *If the doors of perception were cleansed every thing would appear to man as it is, infinite.*
>
> WILLIAM BLAKE

☙❧

The first time I saw my natal horoscope, my astrological birth chart, I got angry. I saw red. At first glance I knew this chart was wrong. I couldn't say why. I knew nothing about astrology, but I knew it was wrong.

My college roommate, Walt Odets, who was always lit with some new revelation, told us all we had to have our astrological birth charts done. It was the greatest thing! It would reveal the cosmic secrets of the universe and the map of destiny! I was game.

I received in the mail a dot matrix printout of the astrological representation of my birth time. It said I had a Cancer Sun, a Virgo Moon, and Gemini rising. It didn't make any sense. Where was the Leo? Don't ask me how, but I knew, I just knew, I had Moon in Leo or Venus in Leo, something good in Leo, not heavy Saturn and Pluto in Leo like the chart said. I was quietly outraged. Hey, dude, where's my Leo?

And I could not relate to Sun in Cancer—sensitive, emotional, nurturing—say what? I knew and had known all along that I was an intellectual, a brain. My achievements in life so far had all been academic, the highest grades in all subjects in the best schools. As for my feelings, they were all in my head.

Nevertheless, I was profoundly impacted by my first darshan with my natal horoscope and irresistibly drawn to discover everything that astrology could tell me about myself. I was smart enough that I could make what it was telling me work for me, even though in my heart of Leo hearts I knew that it was not quite right.

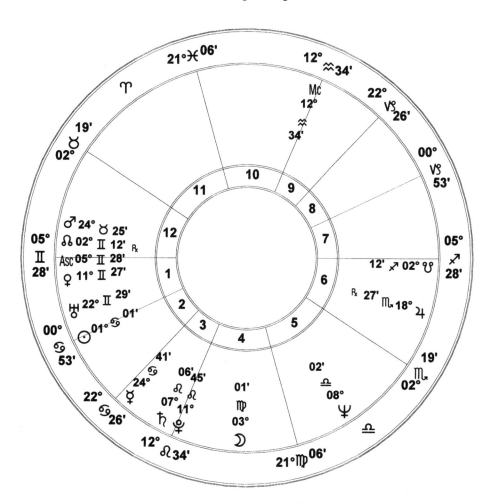

Natal horoscope, Frank Cobb.

I read everything I could find to read, which was not all that much at the time. Isabel Hickey's *Astrology, A Cosmic Science* was my guidebook and cookbook for the first ten years. Dane Rudhyar's *The Pulse of Life* was particularly useful to me as it blended the specific significations of the twelve signs of the zodiac into a symbolic drama representing the continuous and cyclical evolutionary journey of spirit in matter.

Why would I pursue astrology so assiduously when I knew that something was not quite right about my own chart? I was definitely drawn to this awesome ancient wisdom tradition in and of itself. I didn't know much, just that there was much more to learn and that maybe in time my chart would make sense to me.

On a deeper level than I could recognize at the time, I didn't know bupkis about myself, who I was, what I was going to do with my life, and most of all, what my relation was to all these other people. In fact, I was downright existentially terrified, like a caveman who didn't know what to make of all these dinosaurs pounding around outside the cave. I was like a child hiding under the dinner table, not knowing what to make of all the big scary grownups talking so loudly, afraid that if I came out and revealed myself I would be eaten up. Underneath all the smart talk and hormonal torment, I was a scared little child without a clue about what to do or whom to do it with.

I found out that I couldn't understand myself in my chart without understanding everybody else in their charts. I couldn't comprehend Cancer in and of itself without knowing its opposite, Capricorn, its squares, Aries and Libra, the other water signs, Scorpio and Pisces, and so on. In fact, I had to comprehend the whole cosmos to know where I fit in.

From the start I would sit with people and their charts and give them a reading, at first literally reading from an astro cookbook, gradually gaining the confidence to repeat what I had learned, hoping that some of this information was useful to them, but mainly hoping that this process would give me insight into other people and what makes them do what they do with their lives.

☙❧

## Summer 1969

The end of my college education precipitated a major identity disin-
tegration crisis. I was kicked out of the womb of school with no idea
where to go or what to do. I had come to the end of the line. I kept
hearing those words, *at the end of the line, at the end of the line* . . . and
seeing images of standing on an empty railway platform, *at the end of
the line*, in winter, after midnight, *at the end of the line* . . .

*Snow drifting down in the night, thick silent snow falling through
the aureole of a single light up high, bright snow angels swirling,
sifting down through the trees, filling the forest, covering the
embankments and the railroad tracks in deep cold white, silence
in the snowy fields . . .*

*I'm in a deserted waystation next to the rails,
just a wooden bench against a board wall, peaked roof overhead, half
walls on three sides, a platform to pick up and discharge passengers,
barely a shelter, open to the snowy night drifting down, the empty
spaces beyond the light . . .*

*White upon white upon white, snow
drifting down into the night, silence folding into silence. No where to
go. No thing to do. No one to come. Fear on the run. Run out of time
at the end of the line . . .*

College graduation was the opening of the abyss: pure terror, nowhere
to go, nothing to do with my life. My classmates, stoned on acid, saw large
silvery beings of light in the air presiding over the graduation ceremonies. I refused to go to the ceremonies but graduated nevertheless, totally
unprepared for life outside the educational institutions that had sheltered
me, whose limited games I had doggedly mastered for the last sixteen
years. I had no picture of life in the real world, no life after institutional
life. Having no idea what to do or where to go, I hit the road.

*Restless unblessed wanderings
measured in the dead heads of cigarettes
chucked out the window*

*plunging down*
*headlight hallways of corn and concrete*
*manic beyond the applause of sunsets*

*A ringing of crickets throbs in the window*
*sucked in the vacuum of a red star:*
*blind muskrat motor car*
*A moth creams a cheer on the windshield*
*In lidded towns the darkness sits like beer*

I did have exemplars: Blake, self-taught genius, solitary inspiration; Yeats, beloved song; Rilke, angelic voices; Van Gogh, art for art's sake; Hart Crane, against the tyranny of philistine commercialism; Robert Frost, the road less traveled; Robert Bly, light around the body; Pablo Neruda, surrealistic images of deep feelings; Allen Ginsberg, rave; Gary Snyder, meditate, go against the grain, follow the muse, fuck the world, in the music lies the truth. . . .

I had opened myself up to the collective unconscious and I was hearing voices—not the voices of entities or multiple personalities, but the indistinct murmur of the voices of humanity.

*I sit up all night in tense lotus, stoned on snow and hashish, tuning in to these rhythm and blues I hear in my nerves, this jumpy jazz organ out on the prowl, my body like concrete shaken by subways, soul out for a little stroll, pounding the pavements of this endless Harlem TV melodrama, standing on the corner of the desert, rocking back and forth on rubbery legs, doing up the numbers, the dirty dozens, dealing out jive smooth and senseless, freaked-out stoned jungle yogi, man, tuning in to the acid blues in the basement steam pipes, toilets flushing upstairs, people fucking in hot showers, cold cellar, vast electromagnetic fields of night, sea of static, radio idiot submarine telephone babble, Tiamat, no signal, all noise, ruins, everyone talking, no one listening, nervy, horny, grabby, desperate gossip, distance, no one weeping . . .*

This ongoing hum of voices was a phenomenon I experienced for several years until I learned to quiet my mind with meditation practice.

I called the gift of the muse given to me the singing voice. I would hear the voice within giving me a verse to write down. I might hear the prompting to write at any moment. It would persist throughout the day until I got to it. When I was finally able to pause and write, the voice would continue to give me verses, which I would continue to write until the voice was finished. It was not rapid-fire, distinct dictation, but more like catching the drift of a conversation in the wind and writing down what I heard. Or hearing a melody and simultaneously remembering the words, as if the song was singing itself. Or listening to the soul sing its own song in its own time, like witnessing the timelessness of my being interacting with the present moment.

What was needed from me, from my ego, was patience, receptivity, and attentiveness. The minute my mind started to get involved, to editorialize, to criticize, to speculate, to diverge, to search for better words, it would block the flow and try to take control. Imagine that: my mind wants to take control of my soul!

*First thought, best thought.*

ALLEN GINSBERG

There is always ample time later on to tinker with the words, but usually the first thought is the best thought.

I was writing poetry as I am writing these memoirs, not for recognition or appreciation or career or income, although my ego would love all of these, but because my soul has a song to sing and a story to tell.

Mind moves on, relentless flow, endless monologue, sketchy dialogue, pervasive polylogue, vast as the Amazon, full of flotsam and jetsam, observations, expectations, frustrations, judgments, worries, and anxieties. In the village, the music never ends. . . .

I always enjoyed my mind. It was a source of entertainment, enlightenment, and distraction from the tumultuous, tortured feelings I definitely did not want to feel and was habituated not to feel as a stoic little Cobb. What's more, the intellect was the one area of life experience where I could accomplish, achieve, and be recognized for my good grades, so I devoted most of my youth to polishing my mind and suppressing my feelings.

The goal of meditation, as I understood it, was to quiet the mind, or, as I thought, to stop the mind, or at least to go beyond the mind, leaving all those thoughts behind like the radio chatter of yesteryear. But I was largely unaware of the tortured, emotional complexities that lay behind and churned much deeper than my thoughts and that generated a lot of off-the-wall mentation and undermining, subversive behavior.

Emotional expression was conditioned out of me at an early age. I had feelings, but I could not recognize my feelings for what they were. I was unable to make such simple statements as "I feel sad" or "I am angry." When powerful emotions did arise, I was conditioned to repress their expression and to cover them over, to conceal them even from myself, with the dashing, flashing word-play of my mind. My mother called this stoicism. Don't complain. Suck it up and soldier on.

The first time I felt my father's belt on my behind, I cried. At all other times I would not give him the satisfaction of hearing my pain. I would take it like a man.

My father loved us and supported us in a generous manner. He could also be angry, explosive, authoritarian, controlling, sarcastic, invalidating, and punitive. He had a fixed worldview that permitted no other. There was only one person who was permitted to be angry in the house I grew up in, and it wasn't me.

I had no idea how much repressed anger was simmering beneath the surface. I grew up to be a brilliant sword dancer, wielding incisive thought forms to define, master, create, and destroy realities. The hand I was dealt did not have many cups of emotion or wands of enthusiasm. Meditation could quiet my mind, but I could not deal with my emotions until I could acknowledge that I *had* them.

After college, I was suffering like crazy, sure enough, but I was also having the time of my life, roaming free of all the control structures of family and school. I had no idea where I was going—but then again no one else had any idea where I was, including myself. I was finally free to be crazy.

Before long I had diagnosed myself as schizophrenic, with a little help from a book by R. D. Laing entitled *The Divided Self,* which, as I read it, promoted the idea that schizophrenia is a stage in the process of coming to wholeness.

The core of his ideas is that most of us are caught up in and identified with the outer world: normative consensual consciousness. But there is another world within us, the inner world, which is just as real as the outer world and of which most of us are blissfully unaware. When we awaken to the world within us, it is so compelling and so real that we become completely caught up in and identified with our inner world, its voices and visions, emotions and spaces. We find ourselves cut off from the outer world of normative conditioned consciousness and isolated in the magnificence and terror of our inner domain and unable to come out and relate to the outer world.

The inner world is completely real but not the only reality. To get isolated in the inner world is schizophrenia. To come to wholeness and sanity, one has to discover that the inner world and the outer world do overlap and interpenetrate. One has to establish communication between the inner world and the outer world.

These ideas came as a saving grace to me and allowed me to trust in the reality of my inner experiences, to know that eventually there would be a way to live in the outer world without being totally dominated and controlled by it, the so-called normative consensual social reality.

"Boom! Boom! Ain't it great to be crazy? Boom! Boom! Ain't it great to be nuts like me?"

These ideas were very liberating for me at the time. Later on, when someone I loved very much turned out to have actual, incurable, congenital schizophrenia, I found out how tragic this disease really is. What I experienced was only "metaphorical" schizophrenia.

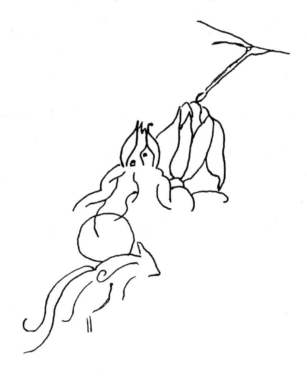

The inner world that had opened up to me was not all love and light and bliss, although that, too, was present. My mind was a beach on which endless waves of unfamiliar thoughts and emotions surged and withdrew. Elation, depression, inspiration, confusion, comprehension, unknowing, voices, images, and feelings would all break into awareness and then draw me back into the depths. I was not trained to deal with this, but my quest for lyric and image kept me open to receive.

> *The world within you is reflected in the world without, and it is the action and reaction of the two upon one another that constitutes your life.*
>
> HAZRAT INAYAT KHAN

After leaving Ram Dass's yoga camp, I spent the fall and winter working in the theater department at Sarah Lawrence College. I worked in windowless concrete rooms and lived in the cold, cluttered storage area in the basement of an off-campus house. I spent the winter underground. I was very alone, assiduously pursuing meditation and a simple vegetarian diet, eating the same thing every day: yogurt, muffin, kedgeree, chapattis, vegetables, coffee. . . . I longed to be in the love again.

Sitting in meditation, I experienced heightened awareness of my environment as my hearing imagination extended far and wide. I also became aware of a continual murmur of voices babbling just below the level of comprehension. Meditation opened me up to the inner life. The boundary between the inner world and the outer world was blurred and porous. I was entering into unknown territory.

I was given clear and distinct poetry to write, one line at a time. It was as if a text were being read and dictated to me. The voice would wait patiently until I wrote down the line before speaking the next line to me in a definite flow that needed little, if any, revision. This singing voice was very different from all the subconscious laughter submerged in the sofa and chatter that was dissolving the ceiling. The process of creative self-expression—seeing something emerge from nothing in my mind—was thrilling and liberating and life-affirming. I pursued self-witnessing through poetry, more absorbed in process, less oriented to product.

That winter I read *In Search of the Miraculous* by P. D. Ouspensky, a narrative of his work with George Gurdjieff, an enigmatic mystic and spiritual teacher. I found his philosophy challenging and harshly awakening. Was ordinary man an automaton, just food for the moon? Was I caught up in automatic reactive mentation with no real "I," no true individuality? What was self-remembering? What was the self and who remembered?

I recognized that I had an automatic behavior pattern—smoking cigarettes—and decided to subject this automatic behavior to self-remembering and see what might happen. Every time I lit up a cigarette, I would stop and be completely conscious of what I was doing. A stop exercise. I became aware that I always smoked in association with something else. I would finish a meal and have a smoke with a cup of coffee. The phone would ring and I would light a cigarette before picking it up and talking. And so forth. I would never just sit and smoke. Now I forced myself to just sit and smoke. Now that I was focusing on nothing but smoking, I became aware of how disgusting the habit was, how awful the smoke tasted. After a while I would just watch the cigarette smoking away in the ashtray and not even touch it. My desire for smoking fell away. I didn't try to give up smoking. The behavior just stopped, for many years.

In the spring of 1970 outrage against the Vietnam War swept the nation, and college students rose up in protest. The students at Sarah Lawrence College occupied the administration building and shut down the campus. The occupying students began forming committees, generating agendas, issuing manifestos, and so on. I did feel some guilt about not participating in this righteous social activism, but this was not my battle.

Ram Dass had said: "The most basic social institution is the individual human heart." That was where I needed to start.

I wanted to travel, but I didn't want to pay for motel rooms to stay in. I took my earnings and bought a used 1968 Volkswagen bus with twenty thousand miles on it for $2,200. I took out the rear bench seat, built a simple plywood bed platform in the back of the bus, put a foam mattress on it, and drove west to go to Lama Foundation.

I stopped to visit a friend who was working in Yosemite National Park. She was staying in a staff dormitory. I slept on the valley floor near the river. I was lying in my sleeping bag looking at the stars glittering in the night sky and drifting off to sleep, when a huge black shape hovered over me, blotting out the sky, huffing and snorting and reeking of bear breath. I was being sniffed out by a bear looking for a snack! Fight or flight? I froze. I kept perfectly still, mentally repeating my new mantra: "Bears are vegetarian, bears are vegetarian, bears are vegetarian. . . ." After several intense minutes the shadow moved on, and I breathed easy again. A little later I heard some surprised shouting and yelling in the distance—some unlucky campers who did not know my new mantra.

# 3 EARLY LAMA, 1970–1972

Just after my twenty-third birthday I drove into New Mexico for the first time. I was driving east on I-40 from Flagstaff. I had just smoked my last joint. I knew no drugs were permitted at Lama Foundation. That was one of the reasons I was going there. A nice high rushed into my head as I saw the welcome sign bathed red in the light of the setting sun, the yellow sign with red letters that said: "Welcome to New Mexico, the Land of Enchantment."

*Whoa!* I thought, *What am I getting myself into?*

At that moment I caught a glimpse of a wild man with long black hair hitchhiking on the side of the interstate. I whizzed right by him. It took a moment for this impression to register, to remember the kindness of the people who had picked me up when I had no car to get to where I had to go, to intuit that this brother was somehow a part of my new life. I turned around and picked him up.

Wrapped in a serape, with a shaggy black beard and a gleam in his eye, he was a firebrand blend of Mexican outlaw and Moroccan pirate. He had just been released from jail in Flagstaff, where he had been picked up for vagrancy, and was headed for Albuquerque, spouting off the radical anti-establishment rant of the day. Although I was glad to serve the cause of brotherhood, this brother made me a little uneasy. There was violence just beneath the surface. I was happy to drop him off on the night streets of Albuquerque. I slept in the back of my bus next to an ancient kiva beside the Rio Grande.

The next morning I drove up to Taos. At that time the highway to Taos took me winding all the way downtown to the Santa Fe Plaza, where I stopped for breakfast at the Plaza Café, before heading north through Española, through the Rio Grande Gorge, and up onto the glorious Taos Mesa. To this day, when I come out of the gorge into the vista of the vast mesa cut by the gash of the gorge, with massive mountains in the north under the vast blue sky, I feel like a traveler arriving in Tibet for the first time, so pure and pristine is the atmosphere.

As I drove north of Taos across the mesa and through the valleys of Arroyo Hondo and San Cristobal, I felt like I was entering another country. Little brown houses with metal roofs were scattered among the green alfalfa fields. A few cows or horses grazed here and there. Tall cottonwoods drowsed near the waters. An old culture living peacefully on the land. I was entering a different time zone.

I found the turnoff for La Lama, an old village on the western slopes of the Sangre de Christo Mountains. La Lama had provided rich summer pastures until it was virtually abandoned in the drought of the 1950s. Now it was being resettled by young people moving back to the land. I drove through the village and up the mountain along five miles of gnarly dirt road until I came to a stop at the closed gate of Lama Foundation.

### July 1, 1970

My first impression of Lama Foundation was vast silence. . . .

Cool, pure mountain air, ponderosa fragrance, wind breathing through the tall trees and rustling the scrub oak on the forest floor, random birdsong woven in the wind, the whisper of wings. . . .

Vast silence was not the absence of sound but the cessation of mental chatter, a spontaneous, astonishing stopping of ordinary mind, leaving nothing but the deep quiet of the silent world within. Vast silence was and still is the most profound gift Lama has for me. As with many essential experiences, this was taking place in a timeless dimension, awakening my soul even as my body was walking up the road to the community.

Situated at 8,600 feet on the western slope of the Sangre de Christo Mountains, surrounded on three sides by National Forest land, old growth piñon and pine, fed by a spring, situated in a meadow, Lama Foundation looks out over upper Taos Mesa. The mesa is a flat ancient seabed, split open by the Rio Grande Gorge, populated by the mounds of ancient volcanic hills, and stretching away to blue mountains a hundred miles away. You can see weather coming from far away in the 180-degree panorama of the Lama mountain cloud observatory—white puffy clouds, huge white thunderheads, massive gray storm fronts, the walking rain, the shadows of the clouds rolling slowly over the plain, a pristine blue vista of spaciousness, emptiness. At night only one or two distant lights are visible for hundreds of miles. The stars at night are very bright, very many, and very close. On a dark night the starlight faintly illuminates the landscape.

As I was walking up the road through the meadow, which was mostly sagebrush and chamisa with a few tall stands of old scrub oak, two domed buildings came into view, with evergreen forested ridges and the gentle peak of Flag Mountain in the background. The nearer, larger dome had two wings extending from it, making it seem like an adobe airplane. The smaller dome farther up the hill sat on top of a two-story octagon, with the kitchen on the bottom and the dining room on top.

Everyone must have been working, but they were working in silence, and I could see no one. I went up behind the kitchen and was greeted by a tall woman in muddy clothes, Barbara Durkee, who stopped what she was doing, looked deep into my eyes for a long, long time, and welcomed me to Lama. She told me about the basic structure of community life (meditate, eat, work, meditate, eat, work, meditate, eat, sleep) and gave me a place to sleep in a double A-frame dormitory.

I soon found out that the Lama community was not governed by a set of rules and regulations dictated by hierarchical authority. Rather, the community was held together by a network of consensual agreements and decisions. Everything was decided by consensus, by unanimous agreement of participating members. Participating membership was a status that had to be earned and granted by, you guessed it, consensus of all participating members.

"We" was the operative word for everything from "We keep the spices on this shelf" to "We meditate three times a day in the prayer room." So, while we might say, in the old way, "No drugs are allowed," what we actually mean is, "We have agreed that no drugs of any kind are allowed on the land. But if you do have to smoke a cigarette, it's okay with us if you go over the fence and off the land to do it."

If we all agree to everything then theoretically everyone is 100 percent behind, committed to, and engaged in everything we do. And no one can complain. This was a very refreshing change from authority-based society, where parents, schools, corporations, or government is the authority. Consensus process was and is Lama's bedrock education in making and taking responsibility for collective decisions.

The Dome, or more accurately the Dome Complex, was almost complete by the time I arrived. The Dome itself is actually a zome, an eight-sided polyhedron. The octagonal adobe walls of the Dome were surmounted by the diminishing diamonds of the zome roof. It was always left empty and unadorned, ready to hold whatever form of activity wished to use it. The Dome had two wings. The northern wing held the library and the prayer room, with a separate entrance. The prayer room, a square room with concentric circles of seats sunk in the earth around a square altar, was likewise unadorned, save for a candle in the center. The southern wing held the bathhouse, the bathroom, and the "only room." (It is now the music room but at first it was the *only* room at Lama.)

Work at Lama had begun in the summer of 1968. Amazingly enough,

Lama Foundation Dome and Flag Mountain.

most of the central structures and residential cabins had been built in the first two summers. As in the development of an embryo and then a newborn baby, the most intense growth takes place during the first days, months, and years of life, the formative years.

In July 1970 the community work was focused on making adobe bricks to build the fire house, a cubical room with a kiva fireplace in the center, which would be the east-facing outside entrance to the Dome. The adobe field was on the flat land to the north of the Dome.

About sixteen men and women worked in silence, making adobe bricks in the glorious mountain sunlight every morning and afternoon. They made the mud, formed the bricks, and delivered them to the men from Taos Pueblo who were laying the bricks and building the room. There were piles of dirt and sand and barrels of asphaltum, which is added to the mud to make the adobe water resistant. The raw dirt would be screened to take out the rocks. A big pit had been dug in the ground and huge batches of mud were made there with shovel and hoe, mixing dirt, sand, water, and asphaltum. The wet mud would be shoveled into wheelbarrows and then poured into ladder-like brick frames on the ground and left to dry in the sun. A week later the dried bricks would be stacked, leaning on their sides.

This was the longest, hardest, most intense physical work I had ever done. I hated every minute of it. My mind was moaning and groaning and complaining all day long as I broke my back hoeing mud, until suddenly a mud-spattered, bare-breasted amazon would come barreling down the hill with a wheelbarrow full of mud and a "Here, Frank, catch this!" I had to get a grip, literally and instantly.

(The women at Lama only worked bare-breasted for a short while. They began to cover up out of respect for our neighbors who would come up the road to check us out.)

Up to now I had been a blue-ribbon intellectual living mostly in my head. My family values disdained physical labor as beneath our economic status. But this was, I told myself, Gurdjieff's method of awakening through conscious labor and intentional suffering.

One afternoon I had satori. I was in a line of men unloading bricks from a pickup truck in front of the fire house. These bricks were very heavy, at least thirty-five pounds—some genius had made the brick frames much too large, so the bricks were very heavy and studded with small sharp pebbles, despite the screening. These nasty, heavy bricks just kept coming one by one by one into my hands all the hot, blazing afternoon until my hyperactive, ever-inventive mind was reduced to *grab, brick, pass, grab, brick, pass, grab, brick, pass* . . . and then just *brick, brick, brick, brick, brick, brick* . . . until finally my intellect just stopped, vanished, and there was nothing but sensation, nothing but heat, movement, and weight. My mind had gone away. I was totally present to *brick, brick, brick, brick*. . . .

I looked up and saw two contrails crossing each other in the sky high over Flag Mountain. I thought I'd had a vision.

"Look! Look!" I said, "There's a cross in the sky!"

The Pueblo men gently teased me. "Hey, he says he sees a cross in the sky! How about that? A cross in the sky. . . ."

There wasn't much night life at Lama Foundation, maybe an occasional chanting gathering when the moon was full. The night sky was astonishingly clear and real for a city boy like me, the black dome of space pinpointed with stars and planets, so near and so far. The sun went down and we went down, to deep sleep and vivid dreams.

At 5:00 a.m. the wake-up bell would ring while it was still dark, another bell at 5:30 a.m., and a last bell at 5:45 a.m. By 6:00 a.m., the light was just beginning to show behind the mountain, and we were all sitting in the prayer room, at that time called the truth room.

We took off our shoes, entered in silence, and walked clockwise around the circle. There were two circular levels of seating around a square altar in the center. A simple candle sat in the center surrounded by four bowls for the four directions. We began with a Tibetan invocation to the four directions: *Ah Nu Ta Ra Hung.*

And sometimes with the Essene Invocation:

*We enter the infinite and eternal garden with reverence to the heavenly father, the earthly mother and great masters, with reverence to the holy, pure, and saving teachings, with reverence for the brotherhood of the elect.*

Lama Foundation prayer room.

There was one hour of sitting three times a day. It was silent sitting—there was no instruction, no guidance whatsoever, no structure, simply sitting. You just came in and you sat. There was permission for and openness to spontaneous prayer in the meetings. The model was the Quaker meeting, when people would sit together and wait upon the Lord and if the Lord moved them, they would speak. This rarely happened. Sitting in the utter stillness of the prayer room was, and still is, the central experience of Lama.

Sitting in silence, being aware of breathing in and breathing out, breathing into the silence behind the mind, the stillness, the presence, is a practice of utmost simplicity and utmost profundity. Regular daily meditation in community instilled in me a discipline I was not able to achieve on my own.

> *Meditation is a solitary practice best done in a group.*
> JACK KORNFIELD

Regular daily meditation was a very hard practice. My attention wandered. My mind went wild. My body rebelled. No one told me what to do. I had no idea what I was doing. And despite my best efforts to sit upright and alert, my body would slump over, I would doze off and jerk myself awake again and again. I could not get it right. But I kept on trying.

> *The sun pitches to the zenith*
> *the solstice*
> *high light spinning in the wind*
> *flooding the dry forest piñon*
> *Digging a cellar hole in sandstone*
> *we pitch up rocks and earth*
> *and the wind rips rolls of dust away*
>
> *Dust devils spin high in the valley below*
> *SAC vapor blades peak the blue*

*At midday we are all sitting together*
*nodding off*
*in shafts of light*
*in the cool prayer room*

Just the experience of touching something deeper than my mind, a bright, alert awareness, unbounded, spacious, dependent on nothing, was enough to keep me going. Group meditation is a very egalitarian practice. We were all in it together. We had to have compassion for our shortcomings; otherwise we could not function. Meditation is not an achievement. We were not in competition. There was no judgment nor evaluation, nor better nor worse, unlike the last twenty-three years of my life. Meditation is daily practice, free from any ideas of liberation or enlightenment—it is simply sitting and breathing. . . .

After a while, three hours a day was not enough. Whenever I could get away in the afternoon, I would climb up through the scrub oak to the south ridge, find a seat underneath a tall solitary ponderosa, sit, and open myself to the sky and the light, the blue sky and the sunlight, the gentle high wind and the birdsong. I found my home in the sky and the light and stayed there as long as I could.

Sometimes, after working all morning in the sunlight I would walk back to my cabin, exhausted, feel the warm sunlight filling my body, nothing but sunlight, knowing that *I am sunlight.* My body, mind, and soul are sunlight.

> *What is transmitted is the quality of sunlight*
> *of a particular hour of our dream:*
> *awakening*

But there was a shadow side to my meditation.

One of my jobs was taking care of the goats. One cold fall evening in my second year, I was meditating in my cabin, the Aspen A, just as the sun was going down. The sky was ruddy and fading. After a while I could hear the goats bleating down in the valley. Their teats were full. They needed to be milked. I was acutely aware of this and yet I could not get back into my body to go milk them. I was aware of their pain but I could not do anything about it. I was in some kind of dissociative state, unable to get back into my body. This had happened several times with marijuana, but now there were no drugs to blame. This was scary. I did not like this.

One time in particular I had been walking alone at night in Cambridge, down the sidewalk beside the brick wall around Harvard. I had just gotten stoned. I was licking a strawberry ice cream cone. I was out of my body, watching my body from above walking under the street lights licking my ice cream—and I could not get back into my body. I was exteriorized. Try as hard as I could, I could not get back into my body for a long time. This was very scary, and not an uncommon occurrence, which was even more unsettling.

What impressed me was the high degree of vision, intelligence, and motivation of the core members of Lama Foundation, the dedication to spiritual practice and awakening in every aspect of life, not just in the prayer room. This was no love-and-light festival—and certainly not a drug-and-sex commune. There was no central spiritual teacher or teaching, no fixed dogma nor belief system, no fixed practice other than meditation and silence. We called it a Buddhist concentration camp. Every one of us was dedicated to forging a new individuality, both personal and collective. The mountain morning cold was as harsh, bracing, and invigorating for my soul as the dawning light was warm and illuminating.

There was silence on the land until the morning meditation was over, and we went up to the kitchen for breakfast. We took our silence with us throughout the day. Idle chit-chat was not encouraged. But in the early morning, upon occasion, we did tell each other our dreams, as is the custom among many indigenous peoples.

*The variety of astral experiences people here at Lama have witnessed leaves no doubt in my mind as to their reality and vitality . . .*

*The walls of Haki's Cambridge apartment dissolved and a glorious angel manifested, heralded in German and Spanish . . .*

*During hermitage Tu Fu appears to Zim and gives him the Word, speaking Chinese . . .*

*Both Haki and Zim understand these languages they have not learned . . .*

*Basira is living on Mount Shasta and one night sees a tremendous beam of light burst forth from the summit. Soon Mother Mary manifests and explains it all for her . . .*

*Caroline sees shafts of light coming from the pastor preaching at St. James in Taos . . .*

*When Lama was first being built, now and then Steve would see Meher Baba quietly laying on adobe bricks . . .*

*endless, endless . . .*

Stimulated by this dreamtime sharing, I began writing down my own dreams, the dreams that were big enough and vivid enough to impress me. I wrote down my dreams because I loved the imagery and the drama that were given to me at night. The surrealists had sought to bypass the rational mind through automatic writing in half-awake states. Recording my dreams was my own form of automatic writing, taking dictation from the unconscious, writing down everything without questioning or evaluation. I wrote down my dreams for their sheer aesthetic value.

*Dream . . .*

> *Two people and a black bear in an old convertible sedan are rolling down the road to the Rio Grande Gorge . . .*

> *When they reach the bottom, the car plunges into the river, and the bear swims away free . . .*

We took ourselves very seriously. We were not at Lama to get high or to get laid or to "win friends and influence people." We were dedicated to the possibility of the awakening of consciousness, not just in meditation and prayer, but in every aspect of everyday life. Some of us were oriented to what we knew of Mr. Gurdjieff's methodology: work on oneself, work in silence, self-remembering, the stop exercise (stop what you are doing and remember your self), conscious labor, and intentional suffering. We had no living teachers at that point, only each other.

Some people took it upon themselves to mimic Gurdjieff's practice of what he called "treading on corns"—in other words, busting other people's ego trips for their own good. Because we were so immature, this practice ended up being more hurtful than helpful. But we were trying, trying in every way we could to wake up.

> *At Lama Foundation people practice, practice, practice what others only preach, preach, preach.*
> MURSHID SAMUEL LEWIS

Lama Dome overhead.

At the center of the community was the family constellation of Steve and Barbara Durkee, the founders, and Hans and Frances von Briesen, their in-laws, Hans being Barbara's brother. Steve and Barbara had four daughters, and Hans and Frances had a daughter and two sons, seven children among them.

There were many back-to-the-land, down-to-earth people who would join us: builders, carpenters, gardeners, craftsmen and women, as well as many avant-garde intellectuals. I was drawn to the artistic and creative types, especially Surya Bhakta, a fiery yogi minstrel, and Joshua Zim, a very refined mystic poet.

At first Lama was a closed community. Random visitors were definitely not welcome. As the saying went, we had a very strong gate—both to keep external influences out and also to keep the people on the land. Only invited visitors were permitted on the land. Contact with the outside world was very limited. There was no coming and going. There was no telephone. We had to drive half an hour to the San Cristobal post office to pick up mail or make a phone call. People rarely left the land.

Everybody did everything together. Everybody worked together, everybody meditated together, and everybody paid two dollars a day for room and board, no exceptions. You paid your own way, you worked your fair share, but no one was expected to sign over their assets to the foundation. That said, there was a still good deal of sharing of personal resources within the community.

That first summer I noticed my toothbrush was always wet. Someone was using my toothbrush! My mother would be horrified! I announced this disturbing observation at a community meeting. Barbara responded:

"Oh, is that the purple toothbrush? Purple is my favorite color!"

There was a work wheel, a seven-petaled mandala outline painted on a green chalkboard, where people would sign up for daily chores like cooking and cleaning. Meals were of the utmost simplicity—I'd like to say rice and beans and veggies, but I really can't remember. What I do remember is scarfing down tortillas and cheese late at night with other hungry campers, talking animatedly as finally some protein and fat hit the bloodstream.

One evening after a long day of work we were all sitting around the octagonal upstairs dining room waiting for dinner. Steve Durkee was the cook, and we all knew how he hated to cook. Steve came up the stairs with a huge soup pot and announced that he was going to feed us all the most refined food in creation. Tonight's fare was air soup! He went around the table and ladled out scoops of air from a pot of air into our bowls that, truth be told, were already full of air. And that was it. We all went hungry, except those who were nourished by the teaching. It was one of those Gurdjieffian fuck-you moments where you don't know if it's a real teaching or just nasty behavior. We all showed up for tortillas and cheese that night.

Steve Durkee was tall and lean and strong as a whip, crackling with energy. He had the vision for the sacred geometry and architecture that was the blueprint for Lama Foundation. He had a tremendous ability to inspire people to work together to realize this vision, both outer and inner, of a new life of conscious communal living and spiritual awakening and to inspire other people to donate money to further this purpose. He drove us all to work long, hard hours in the sun, and he worked harder than anyone.

Barbara Durkee was equally the driving force and the inspiration behind Lama Foundation. She was a tall, masculine, and assertive woman with a big heart and big emotions. The mother of four children, she was maternal and sympathetic, but she had a commanding voice that constantly directed tasks, and she worked equally long and hard on construction and in the kitchen.

We had business meetings in the only room to make consensual decisions. But we knew that most of the decisions had already been made at home between Steve and Barbara. They were larger-than-life figures to me. I was not yet a participating member. I could only sit and listen (and learn) at business meetings, my mind bursting with things to say, my lips sealed.

Consensus process was not always harmonious. Steve and Barbara needed to build a new home because she was pregnant with their fourth child and their A-frame in the garden was too small. Steve proposed to build their house on a site directly below the Dome. However, when this came to consensus, Surya opposed this proposal, saying that to build a house on this site would obstruct the awesome view from the Dome and make Steve the de facto "king of Lama."

The fatal flaw of consensus process is that one person's "no," no matter how irrational it may seem, can block any decision. Surya's opposition generated tremendous animosity, but Steve had no choice but to abide by the rules he had dreamed up.

Within a week, lightning struck a tree on the north ridge above the garden. Fortunately there was no wind and the fire went straight up in the air as our bucket brigade put out the embers. Steve took this as a sign to build his house here, which we all agreed to. He built the Tower House for his family, a two-story house with a zome on top, overlooking the garden and all of Lama.

One day I did the town run, leaving the rarefied sanctuary of the mountain and driving into the dusty town of Taos to do laundry and errands. Doing the laundry meant taking over half the Taos Laundromat with a dozen loads of muddy clothes. Errands always included Randall Lumber for hardware and tools. And doing the town run always included stopping for a treat on the way home.

I had finished my errands and was walking out of the 7-11, having scored my little box of Good and Plenty, feeling so pleased with myself that I was whistling a happy tune to the blue sky, when out of the shadows stepped a big, burly, dark, clearly drunken man, who snarled at me in a menacing voice, "Hey, you, what you so happy about?"

As he hulked toward me, I felt a little fear.

Mr. Gurdjieff talks about developing external considering. Ordinary man, he says, is absorbed in internal considering, thinking of nothing but one's self. External considering is the ability to see reality from another person's point of view. I had read that. Now I applied it.

I saw that this person was unhappy and that my happiness was making him more miserable. I slipped into a sympathetic mode, saying, "Hey, man, I know what you mean. Life down here is so hard and us poor people are suffering all the time," and so forth.

I matched his mood and diffused his anger. His hostility fell away and he wandered away. I had protected myself, but more importantly I had stepped outside my massive self-absorption and taken another person's feelings to heart.

That fall I sat my first and only Zen *sesshin*. We had invited Zen teacher Joshu Sasaki Roshi to come from Los Angeles and lead us in a sesshin, a week of sitting meditation (*zazen*) alternating with walking meditation (*kinhin*), all in silence.

Sasaki Roshi was known as the Laughing Roshi. When we asked him why he was called the Laughing Roshi, he threw his head back and laughed—for about twenty minutes straight—a big relentless belly laugh that was genuinely funny, until we were all out of our mind laughing with him.

And then there was the Zen *koan,* the trick question, which I could never quite take seriously but was determined to ace anyway. You get one one-minute interview every day in which to answer the koan. Finally, I thought, *What the hell. . . .*

When Roshi asked me, "Ah, so, what is your face before you were born?" I bleated out loud like a goat.

Roshi was unfazed. "Very good! More zazen!"

That was the answer to everything—more zazen.

I naively asked Roshi what he had done while riding in the car all the way from Los Angeles.

He answered, you guessed it, "Zazen!"

At that moment I knew that Zen Buddhism was not the path for me.

This was the hardest practice I had ever done. When the week was over I felt like I had ingested major psychedelics. My mind was wiped clean, my perceptions totally altered, everything was just so . . . so . . . so. . . .

One cold November night, I was awakened by the fire bell ringing and came down to see a wall of flames climbing up the south side of the Dome. Earlier there had been a party and chant in the adjoining room, the only room, celebrating the completion of the only room. A new gas heater had been installed and it was the first time we were cozy. There had been a lot of psychic tension between Steve and Surya (who was saying no to Steve's desired location for his new house) and the chanting was very intense, especially chants to Shiva, the god of destruction. Our best guess was that the fire in the fireplace had not been put out completely, that an ember had popped out onto a rug, which caught fire, setting the room and then the Dome on fire. Or perhaps the gas heater had been left on and gas had leaked into the room. We will never know.

It was terrifying to see our temple consumed by flames. With bucket brigades and hoses we managed to extinguish the fire. The only room was destroyed. We rescued the Dome from destruction, but the black scorch of the fire can still be seen on the inside panels of the roof.

That fall I had been living outside in a teepee, but it was getting really cold, just about to snow, and there was not enough indoor housing at Lama for me to spend the winter inside, so by Thanksgiving, I was on my way down the road. They said I could come back in the spring.

I stayed a week in a cell at Christ in the Desert Monastery in Abiquiu. I crashed with some friends in Santa Fe. Then I got a two-month housesit in La Cienega, just south of Santa Fe. My plan was to spend December and January in La Cienega and then drive out to San Francisco and be with Murshid Samuel Lewis, who led people in Sufi dancing, the Dances of Universal Peace. Many of my contemporaries were already gathered around Murshid Sam, as we called him. He had visited Lama Foundation twice, in the summers of 1969 and 1970, and, in fact, had left Lama the day before I first arrived. I felt my time had come to join Murshid Sam and his *mureeds* (disciples).

The house in La Cienega was a one-room shack on a ramshackle ranch at the foot of a long, black, east-facing mesa. When I climbed up the mesa, I found ancient white petroglyphs etched into the black volcanic rock just under the top of the mesa and extending for a mile or so to the north. I was very charmed with my little retreat on an old ranch straight out of the movies beneath the singing petroglyphs. I was very lonely, but I was getting used to it. And I was still suffering mental storms like crazy. I took some LSD and saw the light.

Extreme cold hit northern New Mexico in January 1971. Four feet of snow fell, up to the windows of my VW bus, and the temperature plunged to twenty-three degrees below zero. I was frozen in place. I could not move. The only heat in the house came from burning wood in a compartment the size of a long shoe box in the iron cook stove. I could feel the heat no more than three feet from the stove. Since I had no choice, I had a week-long meditation intensive. Wrapped up in my sleeping bag, down jacket, hat, and gloves, there was nothing for me to do but watch my breath. It was a good thing I could take this forced immobility as an opportunity for spiritual practice. Just don't ask me if anything happened, because it didn't.

When I finally emerged from the deep freeze and made it into Santa Fe, I found out that Murshid Sam had died suddenly. It was not my destiny to meet Murshid Sam, whose Dances of Universal Peace and Sufi transmission are now my love in life. I drove back east and thrashed around the east coast until I could return to Lama in the spring.

Meanwhile, back at Lama, major changes were happening. The previous summer, a book production project based on material from Ram Dass had been happening in the library, resulting in the publication of *From Bindu to Ojas,* a brown cardboard box containing a motley assortment: a large string-bound square book of brown paper, several booklets, an LP record of chanting, and pictures of holy beings to cut out and put on your *puja* table. Incredibly enough, this publication was paid for by Ram Dass's lecture tours. Everyone who signed up at the lecture received a copy. Now they were being mailed out.

At the same time, Lama Foundation was making a deal with Crown Publishers in New York to publish this material as *Be Here Now* by Ram Dass, a book that would shape a generation. Although it was a group project, Steve Durkee was the aesthetic director and hands-on producer of both the box and the book. *Be Here Now* would put Lama Foundation on the map for spiritual seekers and provide a significant income from royalties, which Ram Dass had generously assigned to Lama Foundation, and which would allow the residents a certain amount of financial stress reduction for a time and even a few tiny luxuries.

(How about some avocados with those rice and beans?)

Murshid Sam, who had lived and died in San Francisco, chose to be buried at Lama Foundation for reasons best known to his soul. The casket containing his body came to Lama in the middle of winter. A grave was dug five feet deep in the frozen earth in a clearing in the forest above Lama. He was laid to rest with a high mound of white quartzite over him. Murshid Sam's *maqbara* (gravesite) would become a place of pilgrimage for Sufis from all over the world. The Lama Dome would become a central location for the Dances of Universal Peace.

Finally, some time that year, well-hidden at first, an affair began between Steve Durkee and his sister-in-law Frances von Briesen. Their love affair would break up their families and rock the core of the young Lama community.

## Spring 1971

The first thing I did when I returned to Lama was drive down the road with Surya to get stoned with Jim Fellowes and Veda Rama, who were staying at a ranch in San Cristobal. There were still no drugs at Lama, but they were getting closer. And Veda Rama, the object of my desire two summers and two thousand miles ago, was now just down the road.

This was a very Sufi summer at Lama. Many of Murshid Sam's mureeds came to visit his maqbara and blessed us with lots of Sufi stories, songs, practices, and dancing in the Dome. One of Murshid's intentions was "to get fifty thousand Americans to say and repeat 'Allah' and believe in Him. . . ." That was happening this summer in the Lama Dome, with Frances leading dances, Abraham playing guitar, drummers, and people holding hands, walking, and chanting, *"Allah, Allah, Allah, Allah. . . ."* Once again I was scribbling down dances and chants in my notebook.

We would gather in the Dome on Sunday afternoon, young men with long hair and beards, ponytails, and muddy work clothes, earthy young women in India print summer dresses and flowing skirts, not exactly dervishes in rags, but close enough for America. Maybe forty souls, we held hands in a circle and recited the Sufi Invocation given to us by Hazrat Inayat Khan:

*Toward the One,*
*the Perfection of Love, Harmony, and Beauty,*
*the Only Being,*
*United with All the Illuminated Souls*
*who form the Embodiment of the Master,*
*the Spirit of Guidance.*

Still holding hands we walked to the right chanting *"Allah, Allah, Allah, Allah,"* raising our arms, *"Er Rahman,"* and lowering our arms, *"Er Rahim,"* supported by guitar and drumming. As the dance progressed, the leader prompted us to drop hands and spin on *"Er Rahman, Er Rahim,"* then come back into the circle holding hands for *"Allah, Allah, Allah, Allah,"* then spin again. The one spin became two spins became three spins became free turning until all were caught up in a

Dancing in the Lama Dome, summer 1971.

whirling ecstasy. The music stopped and the dancers came to rest, to stillness and silence, all facing center, amid beams of sunlight streaming through the diamond windows of the Dome.

The dance began again. This time we took partners, holding hands and circling around to the right with our partner, greeting each other in peace, *"Shalom Aleichem, Shalom Aleichem,"* then dropping hands and spinning individually to the right, *"Shalom, Shalom."* We joined hands again, circling to the left and spinning to the left, singing the descending melody, before progressing to our next partner.

*It can't be taught; it can only be caught.*

JOE MILLER

*Where on the rim of midwinter spring, where the scimitar of the old moon drifts down into dawn, where the lake still, where the sun sleeps in a chill daffodil of dawn just under the horizon, the long white lake breathless, where rimmed with black fir, dawn is always coming on, we are dancing in the longhouse, we are dancing forever into the dawn, dancing to the old songs with the magic words, in the white robes of the saved, singing God's names—Adonai, Yahuvah, Shiva, Rama, Allah, Allah—chanting with tamboura, with saxophone, flutes and conga drums—Jesus, Christos, Hallelujah—clapping hands, laughing, singing, jubilant faces moist and streaming with light, clasping hands to hips in a conga line, weaving in and out of ourselves—Om Sri Ram Jai Ram Jai Jai Ram . . .*

*Sensualists, some of us, heavy eyes and moist wavy hair, caressing, arousing, groin into rock and roll, sweet jelly roll, moaning, while elsewhere among us lyrical melodramatic courtships surge flower and collapse at a kiss, couples poise breathlessly in swirling waltzes, while singles writhe hypnotized, each in his own longing desire . . .*

*The music is memory and desire. We are what we are what we have always wanted to be: dancing forever into the dawn to the old songs with the magic words, radio blues and old movie themes fading in and out of the din, centuries of folk music reverberating, still reeling and tumbling where we are . . .*

*We are never each with just one and only other, but always with some one, the same one. We never change partners, but we partners change from within, like gulfs of light moving through a pasture . . .*

Meditation and hard work were still the bedrock of Lama Foundation, but love had come to town with Murshid Sam and everyone was getting on the love train.

The particular love train that had my interest was sparkling, sexy Veda Rama, who was moving out on her latest man ("I'm in love with him, but he's not in love with me") and into a teepee in a glade under the cottonwoods by the river in Arroyo Hondo. Somehow between becoming a voting participating member and serving as kitchen master at Lama (Saturn transiting my Ascendant) I found time for romantic dalliance in the teepee by the river. Veda Rama was very light-hearted and charming. I was instantly in love with her and wrote lots of poems to her. She showed me her sex diary. I was number fifty-seven. She was number two for me. We played around for about a month and she moved on. I awesomely acknowledged that God had fulfilled my impossible desire.

Steve Durkee, who had always kept his distance from me, began to invite me over to his house, the Tower House, in the evenings and would draw me into mystical conversations, visions, and imaginings. The fierce taskmaster opened up luminous inner worlds to me and I was enraptured.

Long before finding the land for Lama Foundation, Steve had created the blueprint for a sacred school he called Solux. It was a constellation of apartments surrounding a twelve-sided initiation temple. One level was underground, a huge sunken hall based on the major arcana of the tarot. In the center was a ladder that reached all the way to the top of the central dome. Solux was a precursor vision of Lama.

Steve took me for a ride on the light train of the mystics who pull prayer around the globe at three in the morning while the world sleeps.

*Who is aboard the hour 3 a.m. as it travels round the globe?*
*Who knows? Do you?*
*Who are you?*
*Hu are you. Hu knows.*
*Allah Hu.*
*Hu Man.*
*Hu Man Being.*
*Breath Man Being.*
*Breathe in AH.*
*Breathe out HU.*
*If you want to*
*slip down river into the sea, that's fine with me. The wind will carry*
*you back into the sky eventually . . .*
*But I want to swim upstream to*
*the source, to the eye of heaven where the cold water of life comes*
*from . . .*

I really loved the man and he became, for better and for worse, a second father figure for me. He was spiritual, visionary, mystical, artistic, romantic, inspiring, and illuminating—all qualities that I emulated, all qualities I found lacking in my blood father.

*Dream . . .*
*Sunday at Lama in Maryland, crowds of people thronging*
*through white Mt. Vernon buildings . . .*
*I am down with the chickens*
*when Lomax tells me that Little Joe wants the youngest soul to carry*
*the last pole to the teepee for a peyote meeting. This means me, and*
*I do so, actually straddling the pole and floating down a grand interior*
*staircase . . .*
*Outside people are gathering for Sufi dancing, thick*

*colloidal masses of all sorts of people under the white noontide. I am silent and feel marked, special, suffering. I am with some strange blonde lady who is shakti for me. Surya leads the dancing, begins the chanting. Some New Buffalo people turn the words around to bawdy. Finally two bagpipers come to unify us with their wild drone and lead us on, away, masses of people moving over rolling green afternoon hills . . .*

*Released, I begin to somersault, cartwheel on the grass, losing gravity, reality, getting more and more ecstatic until I find I have lost the Earth and am flying, soaring, gliding above the pine trees, wheeling above the mass scene, beautiful and invisible, dipping and turning above the deepening twilight, phosphorescent gloaming, touching the tree tops, drinking in the crazy rocking perspectives . . .*

*Beginning to lose altitude, I grow a little scared of crashing and dying, but regain confidence in the illusion and actually gently touch down on one foot, then leap up again, throwing one arm straight out like Superman . . .*

*I feel this powerful rainbow peyote energy channel through me and take me away, exalted, intoxicated, rejoicing, very much between two worlds and never coming down . . .*

*Later we are all in one of the white buildings for a big dinner, everyone sitting around everywhere with plates of food. I hear Surya putting down someone, says he has met him and he is much too proud for where he really is. I am suddenly sharply aware that I have no powers at all, that I have been shown a function I have as a messenger between the two worlds and a guide for those in the fearful narrow passageway of the bardo. The two worlds are in all ways simultaneous and interdependent, and if I am clear and humble, I serve as a channel . . .*

## September 1971

Pir Vilayat Khan came to Lama Foundation and initiated many of us, including me, into the Sufi Order. Pir Vilayat was the son and successor of Hazrat Inayat Khan, who brought Sufism to the West from India in 1910, and who brought the transmission of the Chishti *silsila* (lineage) in a mode that was universalist rather than Islamic. Murshid Sam was also a direct mureed of Hazrat Inayat Khan and many of his mureeds were also initiated into the Sufi Order, although they had their own Sufi Islamia Ruhaniat Society as well. It was all one big, more-or-less-happy family at the time.

Pir Vilayat was a striking and exotic person of noble bearing with a shock of white hair, aquiline nose, and piercing eyes, his body wrapped in a brown Sufi cloak. He spoke in a very educated British voice with very precise diction, while giving us very refined Sufi practices with breath and light.

Pir Vilayat gave us the practice of *zikr*, of divine remembrance, the chanting of *"La ilaha il Allah Hu."* The literal meaning of this phrase is "There are no gods but God. There are not many gods, only God. There are no (*la*) gods (*ilaha*) except (*il*) God (*Allah*)."

From time immemorial in Sanskrit, Sumerian, Hebrew, and Arabic, *ila* has meant "god" in one form or another and Allah is simply The God, *Al Ila*. And *Hu* is the sound of the divine breath. The literal translation of the words is the least dimension of the effect of the repetition of the sacred phrase, which opens up experience beyond the mind.

Pir Vilayat gave us the form in which to chant this zikr. Sitting down (or standing up), sweep the head down across the chest in a crescent from left to right, sweeping the heart clean of all impressions—*La ilaha* (There is no god)—ending with the head held high; then plunging the head down into the heart, piercing the heart with light from the third eye, like a sword—*il* (except); and finally, raising the head as the heart affirms the reality of divine unity—*Allah* (God)—while the lips gently breathe—*Hu*.

There are thousands of ways to perform zikr. This is how I received the zikr in the early times.

Pir Vilayat initiated me into the Sufi Order and gave me the initial practice of kneeling on one knee like a knight and pledging myself to the service of the spiritual hierarchy while intoning *"Ya Fazl"* (Oh Blessing). I tried this a few times, but it made no sense to me, so I dropped it. But I kept up with the practice of zikr.

CROCO

All summer long I had been living in a teepee high on the north ridge above the garden, above the Tower House, in the gentle breeze. Some mornings I would be singing in the dappled sunlight, and the birds would sing along with me, and the squirrels would be part of the conversation. Now that it was getting colder, I moved into the yellow school bus surrounded by mature scrub oak, way below the Dome. This was called the Ram Dass Bus. Legend had it that he drove up the road in the yellow school bus with a statue of Shiva dancing on the roof. It was cold inside that metal shell, although there was a small woodstove. I sang a lot of songs and wrote a lot of poems at night in that yellow school bus.

### ON THE ROOF OF MY HOUSE
### IN THE WIND WITH GOD

*The moon is blowing against the wind*
*The wind is blowing against the stars*
*in my face*
*Behind my back*
*I can see*
*the half-moon coming conjunct with Mars*
*pale blood-star*
*The wind blows through*
*the Milky Way*
*the meadow of ashes*
*flows and flashes like river fish*
*through the cellular stream of scrub oak leaves*
*the moonlit thickets boiling up*
*the mountain*
*roiling in the wind*
*The clouds crawling up from the south*
*look huge and dark and are full of bright holes*

### MIND BLOWN HEART BONE
### STARS SOWN IN THE WIND

## November 1971

Steve Durkee disappeared. This was when he was the Coordinator, the head honcho of Lama Foundation, and no one knew where he was or how to reach him. His love affair with Frances had created a deep level of uncertainty and anguish in the community. During one business meeting in the dining room, all of a sudden everyone was on their feet shouting at each other as a massive hailstorm hit the land and broke through the plastic windows on the dome. Hail came spiraling down into the room, sending everyone off to rescue the livestock. There were fistfights. At one point, Steve had left the land and pitched his tent on the other side of the Rio Grande gorge to fast and pray and try to figure things out. And now he was gone.

Things got very lonely.

On Christmas Eve everyone had gone down to the feast day at Taos Pueblo, except me. In my stubborn isolation I refused to have anything to do with parties. A poet has to be alone, right? And I got really, really lonely walking around in the dark, cold snowy forest. There was absolutely no one anywhere. I was all alone. Absolute panic seized me. The dark forest started to throb like my heart. I got in my bus and drove to Taos Pueblo.

I wandered among the bonfires blazing in the plaza by the river. I found my way to the home where my friends were being feasted. I went inside. It was hot and crowded and loud and bright. I couldn't take it. I fled outside. Frances saw me go and came out after me. She didn't say a word. She simply stood before me, a compassionate presence, a tall Madonna with a shawl drawn over her head, the pueblos and starry skies behind her, her face and body in shadow—and then the shadow opened up into outer space and I saw all the stars and all the galaxies inside her form. Something settled down inside me.

Thank you, Frances, for your Christmas presence.

## December 28, 1971

I trudged through the snow to the small Upper Dome to do a seven-day hermitage. I took all my food with me. I saw no one and did nothing for seven days, nothing but meditation and zikr and reading *The Tibetan Book of the Dead*. I never could comprehend this book, but now in the utter quiet of retreat I did.

On the seventh day I fasted and took LSD. I had never had a spiritual experience on LSD, even though it had that reputation. Soon the psychedelic was coming on and iridescent peacock eyes were streaming up the walls of the cabin and I started doing zikr—*La ilaha il Allah Hu*—to pray my heart out, to keep it all spiritual. . . .

I did zikr practice all day and into the night without a break, and everything but everything in my psyche came up and into my face and was swept away by the zikr. All day it kept on coming and I kept on sweeping, until nothing was left but the evening star bright above the sunset glow in the west.

*Venus is setting. The wood stoves are ruddy. Welcome home to another night beyond the planet Earth . . .*

*The affairs of men are monkeys howling and peeing at the limits of territory, dogs baying at the moon . . .*

*There is an ancient place, just before the womb we left, behind the stars . . .*

*an ancient face whose veils are eyes. . .*

*an ancient race which thinks with the heart. . .*

*La Ilaha Il' Allah Hu*

## January 1972

Steve contacted me and asked me to come work with him. I drove Frances in my van to Wickenburg, Arizona, outside of Phoenix, where we joined Steve, Barbara, and his four daughters in the guest house of a wealthy patron. The guest house was simply two rooms with a bathroom between them. I found myself in one room working with Steve while the two women and four children were in the other room. Much to my dismay and delight, Steve was smoking weed again.

Based on the success of *Be Here Now,* Crown Publishers had given Steve carte blanche to produce another hopefully wildly successful new age book. Steve had brought me down to brainstorm this new book with him. His inspiration was that the book would have a game board and a deck of cards of archetypal images that would give people a mind game to play. He did the brainstorming and I did the listening. Actually, I did little but listen. I wondered why he had called me to work with him when I was doing nothing. If it was my project, I would do all the work by myself.

Another person would be a distraction. It became evident that Steve was a person who needed to work with somebody or, more accurately, needed somebody to work with him—and that would be me in this moment.

I was excited about working on a book project. I loved books and making books, although my poetry books had not yet gone beyond the Xerox-and-staple stage. I slept outside in my van for two nights and then drove east to crash at my parents' house in Baltimore.

The first day home I walked into the new age bookstore on Charles Street just a block north of the Washington Monument in downtown Baltimore. I asked to see the manager. I had a set of four postcards that Steve had produced to sell—duotones of old images, a teepee, a cave, and so on. The one I loved was a golden duotone of a vast Tibetan plateau, chorten and prayer flags in the foreground, with the motto, "Emptiness endangers compassion."

The store manager was a beautiful young woman with long dark hair and a quick mind. She took me back to her office. She looked at the cards and said sure, they would buy a few of them, and that was that. I was browsing through books out front when suddenly, between me and the books, Wendy, the store manager appeared, looking into my eyes with wonder and amazement. I must have had quite the atmosphere, coming so soon from hermitage at Lama to downtown Baltimore. We stayed there entranced, gazing into each other's eyes for the longest time, one of those merges where all the boundaries disappear and nothing remains but light. We kept coming in and out of mingling souls. I had no idea what was happening, but I absolutely loved this beautiful woman who had apparently loved me at first sight. She invited me to come home with her.

*Hours flicker falling through your face*
*pods dropped from the sun through windless day*
*vague round children at recess*
*births falling through birthless flame*

*At last your future child swims up*
*out of the vast blue breath of your skin*

*All there are in the room are your eyes*
*at rest in solar winds*
*unborn where love is always*

I called my parents and told them that I would not be coming home that night. I knew that my going home with Wendy would be a definitive and final break with their values, especially as my grandmother, my mother's mother, was also staying with them at the time. Their values were simple: no sex before marriage, no sex outside of marriage, and, by the way, don't even mention the word *s-e-x*. I had broken with their values in so many ways already, including long hair, smoking dope, liberal politics, spiritual aspirations, failure to get a job, living in a hippie commune. Not coming home and spending the night with a strange woman was the last straw. My father refused to speak to me for the next seven years. At the moment I could not have cared less.

Wendy took me home and fed me and took me to bed. She loved me and I loved her. It was very sudden and very pure. If I had been more mature, we could have had a beautiful life together, for she was the first woman who really loved me.

As it was, I was deeply conflicted about spirituality and sexuality. As brilliant as my mind might have been, I was out of touch with my feelings. My hormones were raging, lust was overwhelming, yet, somehow, I had the mistaken notion that sexuality was antithetical to spirituality. My dreams reflected this deeply embedded conflict. It didn't help that I couldn't communicate any of this other than by acting it out. Every morning I would get up at five and do my zikr practice at great length and volume, plunging the sword into my heart exclaiming, "Il Allah!"—right next to the bed where Wendy, who had to get up and go to work in the morning, was sleeping. In retrospect it was extremely rude and inconsiderate—and I thought myself some kind of holy man!

In addition, with my smattering of astrology, I had concluded that our charts were wrong for each other, and I had to get away from her. In hindsight I was right. Our natal charts were not compatible. However, it was our mutual secondary progressions to each other's charts that had brought us together and opened my heart to love.

∞∞

After six glorious nights of love I left and drove up to Bronxville, New York, where I would stay while commuting to Manhattan to work with Steve on his new book project, *SEED*. Steve and I met with Bruce Harris at Crown Publishers to seal the deal. I spent the next week in "glitter flickle image search," to use Steve's riff, at Crown, combing their archives for images to use on the cards that would be torn out of the *SEED* book.

Steve directed me to engage in constant prayer and continual remembrance of God in all circumstances with the practice of *fikr,* which is silent zikr on the breath.

I had already experimented with the Jesus Prayer, written about in *The Way of the Pilgrim,* as a way to pray without ceasing. *Adonai Yeshua Hamasheach Ben Elohim Rachim Chanenu Hayim.* This translates as "Lord Jesus Messiah, Son of the Merciful God, Have Mercy on Us the Living."

But there is a big difference between picking up a practice from a book and having a practice given to you by a living spiritual teacher—and that difference is transmission. Steve was giving me not just an outer practice to do but an inner bestowal of blessing and potency (*baraka*) to vivify the practice as well. Remember, God always and everywhere. This was the way to do it. Breathe in—*La ilaha,* negating and wiping away all subjectivities. Breathe out—*il Allah Hu*—affirming the reality of divine unity. Always and everywhere.

I remember clearly at this time riding the commuter train into the city, riding the subway underground, walking the city streets, surrounded by the world, immersed in Allah. I felt I was in another dimension, more real than apparent reality, not separate from but rather permeating and underlying apparent reality. The bubble knows that it is the ocean.

Then Wendy came up after me. She took the train and showed up in Bronxville. She would not take no for an answer, not that I resisted too hard. When love comes to town you better catch that train. My walls came tumbling down. We wandered around New England, visiting my friends and dancing with the Sufis in Cambridge, before returning to our love shack in Baltimore.

In mid-March I elected to have my four wisdom teeth extracted at once against the doctor's recommendation and then refused to take any painkiller out of some notion of retaining purity of consciousness. So, I lay on the bed in Wendy's apartment while she was at work, writhing in incredible, unending agony, unimaginable suffering for hours on end, until suddenly I was out of my body, floating near the ceiling, looking back at my body writhing in pain. I began to explore the apartment, moving into the kitchen and down the hallway to the living room and out the front door and down the stairs and—I panicked. What if I got lost outside and couldn't get back into my body? Immediately I was back into my body in all the pain all over again.

I had found myself out of my body before. There was the time I left my body when I was walking around Cambridge, stoned, while eating a strawberry ice cream cone. There was another time, too, much earlier, when I was nine years old at Camp Red Cloud on Lake Champlain in upstate New York. I had been thrown off a runaway horse and broken my arm. I was taken to the hospital in Plattsburgh where they put me under anesthesia to operate. I found myself flying back to Camp Red Cloud and cruising up and down all the familiar forest paths before going to my bed in my cabin. I was astounded by the literal, physical reality of the landscape. This was no dream.

Meanwhile, Steve had been traveling in India with Pir Vilayat. Now he was back and staying with Wendy and me in Baltimore so that he and I could go down to the Library of Congress in Washington, D.C., and get as many free images as we could find for the book. He was smoking a lot of dope and so was I, right along with him. But it was not good for me. One evening I started shivering uncontrollably, and they had to wrap me in a blanket to warm me up.

Wendy did not like this dope smoking at all. None of my girlfriends ever have. Wendy was a Meher Baba devotee. Baba must have heard her cry because one morning the stash vanished from the drawer it was kept in. We turned the house upside down but could not find it. Steve raged at Baba for taking it away. We spent the day in D.C. miserably un-stoned. When we returned in the evening there was the stash right where he had left it, in the drawer under the smiling picture of Meher Baba. God keeps playing tricks on us.

## April 6, 1972

Wendy and I were packing up to leave Baltimore and go back to Lama together. It was her birthday, and we were lying in bed together. She was sleeping, and I was weeping. I was crying my heart out for the first time since I was five years old and had refused to cry when my father strapped me with his belt. Now I could not stop sobbing and weeping. I knew what a good woman Wendy was, how much she loved me, and how much I loved her—and yet deep down in my soul I knew that I was unable to love her, I could not love her as she needed to be loved, as she deserved to be loved. I just did not know how to love her, or anyone for that matter, and my heart was breaking because I knew that I would lose her some day. And I was right. This was the first moment in my twenty-five years that my heart broke open to love.

*Dream . . .*

> *Wendy and I are driving through hilly English countryside in a VW convertible: rolling green hills, winding road, blue sky. I am driving full throttle, hair in the wind, rapping away gaily, careless . . .*
>
> *I see a car leap into the air from the crest of the next hill but have no care, hit the hill at full speed and go flying into the air, into ecstasy, sexual and emotional, writhing in each other's eyes, bewilderment in eternity, not knowing if we'll ever come down nor how violently we will crash into earth when we do . . .*
>
> *After an eternity the car touches down smoothly on the road and we cruise along as before . . .*
>
> *Wendy is mildly freaked, but I am careless as ever and before long the same thing happens again: we are hurled into violent ecstasy and bewilderment. This time when we come down we roll to a stop against a sports car, barely touching its fender . . .*
>
> *Wendy is mad now and says there are tickets we must pay for this, that we must go to the police and get the tickets. I say this is ridiculous, but she takes the wheel . . .*

*We are cruising slowly around the shores of a Florida lake lined with palm trees, a broad smooth road, the evening sun behind the trees . . .*

*We get to the waiting room of the police station where Wendy raps to me that I put on too much beauty too often like a woman with too much makeup . . .*

Wendy loved being at Lama that summer, loved the community, loved the practice, loved the work, and loved me—for a while. We were living in the yellow school bus. Lama was more relaxed and open. We danced with the Sufis. We laughed with Ram Dass. We celebrated Shabbas with Reb Zalman Schachter. I was kitchen master again. I threw away my dope again. We were young lovers, fresh as a peach, until everything started to go downhill fast. She began drifting away from me, falling out of love with me, and there wasn't a thing I could do about it. Maybe it was the inherent incompatibility of our charts coming out. Maybe our progressions were moving on. I had tried to run away from her, and she had pursued me and captured my heart. Now I had brought her home to Lama and she was withdrawing from me. Maybe her ticket to freedom had turned into her new jailer. Who knows? Whatever the reason, it hurt like hell, losing the love of the first woman to really love me, and there was nothing I could do about it.

In the midst of all this, I managed to type up a book of poems and gather a motley assortment of pictures to send to Richard Grossinger, who published my first book of poetry—*Love Minus Zero* by Frank Zero—as Issue #24 of his *Io* magazine. Richard's writings were my model for contemporary intense imagination liberated in poetic prose. It was an honor to be published by someone who was an inspirational genius to me. And I loved the way he blended the images with my poetry.

Things were getting very freaky with Wendy. Her former lover (and owner of the bookstore) came to visit and she left with him for a few days. Next she fell in love with a Sunday visitor named Hobbit, who came and went and occupied her romantic imagination. Then she moved out of the yellow school bus and into a nearby blue school bus and refused to sleep with me anymore.

I was freaking out. I was angry and abandoned and agitated and panicked and desperate. It felt as if a great big scab on a very deep wound on my forehead had been ripped open and blood was flowing into my eyes. I couldn't see what was happening or where to go. I was trembling all over, in really bad shape.

I went to see a man named William Lesassier who, it was said, had the ability to read the akashic records. He had a school of natural healing in Taos and lived on the edge of the forest in Arroyo Seco. He was a young man who looked like an old Swiss doctor with a wispy blonde goatee and wire-rimmed glasses. I was frantic to unload my situation on him, but he invited me to gather clover with him instead. We spent an hour gathering clover in a sunny meadow under the blue sky. That calmed me down a little bit. Then we went inside his house for the reading.

He closed his eyes and described entering a huge hall of records, going down corridors of filing cabinets, searching for and finding the right one, pulling open the drawer and sorting through the index cards until he came on. . . .

"Oh, yes. I see that you and Wendy were brother and sister during the French Revolution. Aaah, hum . . . I see no problem here."

No problem, I thought, that's what I want to hear.

I went back to Lama and all hell broke loose. I was obsessed with Wendy and pursued her all over the land like a hungry ghost. I realized that I was totally out of control and that the only remedy was to leave Wendy at Lama and put a lot of space between us.

I went to see William Lesassier again on the way out. I said to him, "You said there was no problem with Wendy and me and—waaah! It's nothing but impossible. It's a big problem!"

He shrugged, and responded, "When I said, 'I see no problem,' I meant that there is not a lot of karma binding you two together. You don't have to get married or have children or run a business. . . ."

That's what he meant by no problem—no life together! I couldn't relate to this. I had to leave.

# 4 OVERSEAS, 1972–1975

I left Lama Foundation and drove straight through to San Francisco. Barbara's brother Hans was kind enough to let me stay in his apartment while he was elsewhere. He had also left Lama, unable to stay in the face of his wife's infidelity. Once again, I got very lonely very fast.

I wandered around the city streets, picking up cigarette butts out of the gutter and smoking them while gazing wistfully at airplanes taking off over tall buildings. I was heartbroken, agitated, restless, and depressed. I had gone from living on the mountain under the big blue sky to existing in a room in a big city full of noise and pollution and, worst of all, an amplified heavy bass line throbbing away downstairs night and day. I could not meditate. I could find no peace.

In desperation, I called Lama and left a message: I have to come back so that I can meditate in the prayer room. I knew this would have to go to a business meeting for consensus, and that it would be a while before they got back to me. So I kept on trying to meditate.

One morning I woke up and got out of bed, determined to meditate until I found peace. Peace, I reasoned, cannot be dependent on being in the Lama prayer room. If peace is real, it is inside me and not dependent on external circumstances. This is the peace I want!

I assumed the lotus position, closed my eyes, became aware of my breath rising and falling, rising and falling, and kept my attention focused on my breathing through the morning, through the traffic noise, through the noontime, through the bass line thumping, through the hunger, through the afternoon, gradually coming to a solid bedrock of internal peace and quiet. The phone rang around three o'clock in the afternoon. It was Surya, calling from Lama.

"We think you're crazy, but you can come back if you want to."

"Thank you all for putting up with me," I replied. "I've just been meditating all day, and I've just discovered that the prayer room is inside me. Thank you all very much for being willing to take me back, but I'm going on. I'm not coming back."

In the Bay Area, I went to massive dance meetings, two or three hundred people in the huge Sausalito Art Center, all the urban hippies decked out in their finest rags, holding hands and swaying, praying, meeting waves of ecstatic lovers in the circles, or going into the center in pairs, joining hands and turning, chanting *Allah Hu, Allah Hu.* I was transpersonally meeting one ecstatic lover after another in the circle, dancing in glory while chanting the holy names. I was connected with the love.

I went to small classes with Wali Ali, Murshid Sam's secretary, in the Mentorgarden, Murshid Sam's home in San Francisco, where we would learn the Wazifa Walks, the embodiment of the divine attributes. I studied Murshid Sam's Astrological Walks and Breaths with Pir Moineddin, Murshid Sam's successor, at the Khankah in Novato. I joined the Early Choir, an offshoot of the Sufi Choir, to sing the music of Allaudin Mathieu.

I took classes with psychic guide Frida Waterhouse, who channeled the Lord God of Israel and cared for the psyches of the Sufi community. "Pir Vilayat," she would complain, "comes to town and gets everybody high. Then he leaves me to deal with all their garbage."

Murshid Sam had only been with his young disciples for three years before he died. He left a group of young people in their twenties, impressed with an awesome bestowal of blessing, baraka, vision, and initiation. Murshid Sam's transmission was held by a group of brothers and sisters who collectively cherished and nourished the seeds of the Dances of Universal Peace that he had sown. At the beginning though, the dances were held by the small group of Murshid's direct mureeds and could only be led by Sufi Ruhaniat initiates. Forty plus years later, the dances have spread around the globe, from Europe to Russia to New Zealand to South America, with thousands of dances and over a thousand dance leaders.

Meanwhile Steve's book *SEED* had been published to no great acclaim. It was a square book, like *Be Here Now,* with a sunflower mandala on the cover. The all-caps text, printed in yellow-green ink on dark brown kraft paper, was virtually unreadable. Even those who made the effort to decipher the text, like me, found a mystic rant and ramble with no clear story line or message. The enclosed game board mandala was artfully done, but it was unclear exactly how to play the game. And the perforated playing cards themselves, which you had to tear out of the book to use, for which I had helped find the imagery including some of my own photographs, were a chaotic mishmash of disparate images from all eras. In short, you'd have to be really stoned to get off on this mess, and even then, *SEED* was a big disappointment.

I rented a room, first with some friends in San Francisco, and then at a Sufi house in Novato. My emotional state went from worse to even worse, including suicidal imagery. At one point my body was literally throwing itself around the room.

> *These days cyclotrons of eternity*
> *whirl me around and around:*
> *can't eat can't read can't*
> *think can't sing can't sleep*
> *can't go can't stay*
> *ain't no way*
> *All my psychic mechanisms*
> *so recently and vaguely formed in cryptic twilights*
> *explode*
> *and I am thrown around like a rag doll*
> *in raging pranic void*
> *until I can slump in a corner in the sun*
> *and nod senseless*
> *as everyone in eternity tramples over my somebody*

The first three years of life are the formative years. These first three years of my spiritual life brought into formation all of the elements of my spiritual path for the rest of my life—meditation, Ram Dass, Maharaj-ji, chanting, Lama Foundation, Dances of Universal Peace, Murshid Samuel Lewis, Pir Vilayat Khan, zikr, fikr, Sufi Order, Sufi Islamia Ruhaniat Society—and, above all, the spiritual community of brothers and sisters, friends, and lovers. My spiritual life has been the growth of seeds planted in these first three years.

## October 1972

Steve Durkee had spent the summer heading the work crew at Pir Vilayat's meditation camp in the French Alps. He was now a sheikh in the Sufi Order. Pir Vilayat had given him a new name, Noor, which means light. Noor contacted me and invited me to join a group work project to produce a book for Pir Vilayat Khan. We would live together in Marin County. We would study with Pir Vilayat. I would transcribe the recordings of his talks. Others would edit and illustrate these teachings. The book and the communal household would both be called Toward The One.

We all moved into the Toward The One household on Hillside Avenue in Kentfield—that is, Noor, Frances, Barbara, their seven children, myself, Quddus, Latif, and Raqiba with her daughter Zadie. It was a big, three-story house built into a steep hillside. When the rains came it was Hill-slide Avenue. The entrance, living room, dining room, and kitchen were on the top floor. The adults had bedrooms on the second floor and the children lived in one big room on the bottom floor. Under the bottom of the house was a little open-air platform next to the furnace—that's where I stayed, in a hermit hut in the rain forest.

As at Lama, we ate together, worked together, prayed together, and studied with Pir Vilayat together.

My workstation was a drafting table in the corner of the living room where I transcribed Pir Vilayat's talks for the book. It's a good thing that I was writing down his speech word for word, because when I listened to Pir Vilayat in person at the many seminars we attended, I couldn't understand a word he was saying. His speech was refined and articulate, his sequence of thought very logical, and yet his presence communicated something beyond my ken. I could follow what he was saying at first, but soon I went into what I called "the white space." It was like white noise without the noise. It was like my head was full of etheric cotton—no thoughts, no emotions, just presence. It was neither pleasant nor unpleasant. It was not like the utter stillness and clarity I sometimes touched through protracted meditation. It was very pre-dictable though. No matter what he was talking about, I went into the white space, or the white space came over me, and I was gone. I couldn't figure out what was happening. I still can't. But I trusted the process. His words, when transcribed, were brilliant expositions of spiritual-ity and Sufism. But I never could relate to Pir Vilayat on a personal level, the way I could relate to Ram Dass or Noor. He was too elevated, remote, and distant.

Noor's zikrs were the heart of the Toward The One household. We would get up at five o'clock in the morning and gather together, stand-ing and holding hands in a circle, and begin chanting very softly, just whispering—*La ilaha il Allah, La ilaha il Allah, La ilaha il Allah . . .*—gently rocking from the waist up, dipping to the left and back up, to the right and back up, bodies swaying, soft in the knees—*La ilaha il Allah, La ilaha il Allah, La ilaha il Allah . . .*—invoking the name, polishing the heart, opening to the presence, blooming light upon light. As the daylight grew stronger, so did the intensity of our practice, the chanting gradually becoming louder, more vocal, more animated, the movements freer, until we were almost shouting with glory—we were shouting with glory, love dogs at dawn.

These zikrs went on for a very long time, driven by the light in Noor's heart that ignited the fires in our hearts . . . and they were very tiring and tiresome. There was no singing zikr, no change of movement, just rocking in place with increasing or decreasing intensity. Typically, it would reach a place that, for me, was very dry and boring, my body weary, emotions drained, mind flat (*When is this going to get over with,*

*enough already, very dry and boring, just keeps on going and going)*—
*La ilaha il Allah, La ilaha il Allah, La ilaha il Allah*—until the whole
group with one heart broke through to a luminous blazing love presence
that goes on forever, divine bliss, kiss of the beloved. . . .

And just when you never want to leave, everything started quieting
down, settling down, returning to whispering and breathing and then
silence. It was only after the *Hadrat* (Presence) was over that the dervishes we had become would sing their love songs to the One. Mystical
love poetry is best comprehended from a place like this. This was our
practice morning and night for nine months. It built up tremendous
magnetism and unity in the group and attracted many souls to join us.

There are twelve levels of initiation in the Sufi Order and certain
esoteric papers of Hazrat Inayat Khan's teaching that are designated for
each level of initiation. Noor wanted to read to the group a certain set of
esoteric papers that were restricted to the seventh level of initiation. So, he
initiated everyone in the household to the seventh level of the Sufi Order.

Late one night, Noor came down to my little open-air sleeping platform underneath the house. It was raining heavily outside. Noor had
three joints between the fingers of one hand. He said, "We're going to
smoke these joints and I'm going to initiate you to the seventh level."

"It's past midnight," I protested. "We have to get up at five o'clock
in the morning. There's no way I'm going to get up at five o'clock in the
morning if I smoke all that dope now."

He said, "Look, either you smoke all these joints with me now *and*
get up at five o'clock this morning, or I'm not going to initiate you."

I acquiesced. We smoked the joints. He gave me a very high verbal transmission, of which I can't remember a word since I was totally
blitzed, and he initiated me into the seventh level of the Sufi Order.
And I got up at five o'clock in the morning for zikr.

One evening, Veda Rama danced into my life again. She just appeared
as my next partner in one of the dance circles. God was not through
satisfying my desire for this woman. Try to put God to the test and
God will put you to the test. Veda Rama and her daughter, Vickie,

were living in Santa Venetia, down behind the Marin Civic Center. We resumed our love sex dance play.

She made no secret of her promiscuity. ("You're lucky you came over tonight. I was thinking of calling Jerry.") There was no pretense of loving me. ("It's a karmic reversal. I was in love with Jim and he wasn't in love with me. Now you're in love with me and I'm not in love with you.") I was a return entry in her sex diary, maybe number sixty-four, and I was still hungry for her love.

Fortunately, Veda Rama was also a Sufi. In early December, despite Noor's misgivings, Veda Rama and Vickie moved into the Toward The One household. Veda Rama and I had a corner bedroom, high in the eucalyptus trees, in which we put her big heated waterbed. Vickie joined the eight other children downstairs.

I learned a lot of things about living with a mature older woman who is not in love with me. She likes lots of presents for herself and her daughter. She likes to have her feet rubbed in the morning. She likes to have sex when she likes to have sex and not otherwise. If you go to sleep all wrapped up in your lover in an accommodating hot waterbed, you wake up in pain, all bent out of shape.

There was a party on Christmas Eve that, in a bizarre replay of last Christmas Eve, I refused to go to. Everyone went to the party, and I stayed home alone. I felt secure in solitude and insecure at parties. Everything was fine for a while until I started to fantasize that Veda Rama was having sex with another man and I panicked. I called the party house but no one could find her. I drove over to the party and eventually found her passed out in a bedroom on top of a pile of coats. I shook her and pulled her awake. I was very agitated and upset. She said she had gone into ecstasy and left her body. She was really pissed at me for bringing her down.

I kept on going to Sufi dance meetings and learning the Astrological Walks and Breaths. These walks and breaths are practical esotericism, giving one the ability to be aware of and to change at will one's vibrational state and affect the environment. I put this to the test one evening. I was trying to concentrate on working even as the children were raising havoc next to me in the living room, laughing, screaming, having a great time. Without saying a word, I stood in the middle of them and got into the Saturn breath—a strong exhalation in both nostrils, very sober—and began very slowly turning to the left, chanting a very deep Huuuu . . . . To my amazement they all cleared out of the room and went downstairs.

Veda Rama and I had a great time for a while. But as winter moved into spring, she began getting restless. She started going away for the weekends, spending the weekends with other men, and I started to feel heartsick all over my body. Once again there was no way to deal with my emotions, no cure for love but to leave.

I flew east, leaving my van with Noor, who would use it for the next year. I would join the group at Chamonix in July. I saw Wendy again in Baltimore, but the fire was gone. We were distant and wary of each other.

I was asked to lead Sufi dancing at Savitria, a commune in Baltimore County. I had no training in leading dances, but I knew the music and the movements, so I gave it a whirl. I had everyone hold hands in a circle. I gave the instructions and got the dance going and went into bliss. I did not know that the dance leader had to stay grounded and monitor the dancers and especially bring the dance to an end. So the dance went on and on and on and on and eventually just kind of petered out, leaving everyone diffused and confused about what had just happened. It would be a dozen years before I would lead another dance.

Come June, I drove up to Pir Vilayat's Sufi camp in Woodstock. The culmination of the camp was the outdoor staging of La Messe Cosmique, The Cosmic Mass, a celebration of the cosmos, which included all the angels and archangels and all the masters, saints, and prophets, dozens of Sufis in gowns and robes. The Cosmic Mass was staged in a green valley laced with white birch trees with the spectators high on the hillside that overlooked the valley. The appointed afternoon was sunny. But as soon as the pageant started, rain started pouring down amid tremendous claps of thunder. The show went on with Pir Vilayat sitting on a rock and shouting through a bull horn, angels and archangels sliding down muddy slopes, prophets drenched and inarticulate. You couldn't hear a thing above the storm. It was a cosmic mess, but it was a glorious show, a triumph of the ideal over the real.

*Dream . . .*

> *I go visit Lucy in Brighton and find that Poppa and Momma are also visiting her. They are sitting around in her room, all smoking dope . . .*
>
> *Poppa gets really high for the first time. He doesn't know how high he is. He is sailing. As they are going out the door, he turns and says to me: "He is in the traffic light!"*
>
> *I reply: "Yes, and in the tiny anklets jingling on the feet of crickets!"*
>
> *We embrace warmly . . .*

## June 1973

I flew from JFK to Amsterdam, took the train to Paris, stayed two nights in Paris with friends—there were always friends on this Sufi path—then took the train up through Haute Savoie to Chamonix in the French Alps, took the bus up the valley to La Flegere, rode the *telepherique* (cable car) up above tree line, and then hiked forty minutes straight uphill to the old sheepherder's hut that anchored Camp des Aigles. My personal life was now reduced to the backpack on my back, a guitar in my hand, and a blue tent I had shipped over, which I pitched on a platform down by the stream.

Camp des Aigles was a stunning location for a summer meditation camp, a rocky meadow on the south-facing side of the steep, east-west L'Arve river valley. Several big white circus tents stood on platforms in the meadow. The stone sheepherder's hut served to house the work crew and the kitchen. Individual tents were scattered around. Directly in front of us, when not shrouded by clouds, were the serpentine Géant Glacier and the Aiguille Verte. Farther to the right in the distance was Mont Blanc. Behind us were craggy granite peaks and pristine lakes, home to eagles and marmots. In the winter all was buried in snow.

Most of the work crew—Noor and his family, Quddus, Latif, Michael, and Abbey—lived in the sheepherder's hut. I was fortunate to have my own tent and my own personal space. We put up and took down the big tents. We did all the cooking and cleaning and maintenance work for the camp and still had time for Pir Vilayat's meditations.

The Toward The One crew had a strong group dynamic. We had worked together for a year now. We still got up at five in the morning for vigorous zikrs led by Noor in the central tent. But Pir Vilayat soon put a stop to the zikrs. Too much ego, he said. Noor was not happy with that.

Pir Vilayat was a falconer. His soul soared to the heights. His highest roost was Camp des Aigles. He lived in a cave fashioned between some massive boulders above the camp. Every morning and some afternoons he would sit on his perch, his throne, a huge boulder like an egg standing on end in the meadow, with the stunning vista of the Alps and glaciers across the valley behind him, and lead us in meditation. Pir Vilayat was a master of meditation who brought people into *samadhi* (absorption into unitive consciousness) all the time. I went into the white space for hours on end—whether it was samadhi or not, I just couldn't say.

Camp des Aigles, above Chamonix, France, summer 1973.

At Chamonix, Pir Vilayat emphasized light meditations: "Feel your body flooded with light, like you are standing in a bright spotlight. . . . Let yourself be transported into realms of light. . . ."

The only problem I had was that I simply could not see the light, no matter how hard I tried. I wanted to see the light, longed to see the light, but somehow I lacked the capacity to see it. Maybe I could sense the light, sense a change in vibration.

But if seeing is believing, then not seeing is. . . .

Even though I couldn't follow what was going on, even though I couldn't see the light, I persisted in meditation, keeping my attention on my breath. "Take time for the timeless," Pir Vilayat would say.

The whole summer at Chamonix was time beyond the world. Sometimes we were swathed in clouds and drenched with rain. Other times we were surrounded by blue sky and high clouds gliding over steep snow peaks.

Noor offered a class in cloud watching: lie on your back and open your eyes to the sky.

There was warm kinship and Sufi dancing to balance the austerity of constant meditation. One night, Pir Vilayat played recordings of his favorite classical choral music, such as Monteverdi, and encouraged us to turn to the music. I whirled into ecstasy for what seemed like hours on end, centering myself in the still column of breath at the center of the spinning world.

Pir Vilayat, Noor, and all the retreatants left at the end of August. The core group stayed to take down the camp during September. I worked with the crew, but during that time, I also did a retreat in a tiny hut high above the camp for the ten days leading up to the full moon. One room, one door, one candle, one zikr practice, and one book—Rumi. I immersed myself in the ocean of the Mathnawi, copying down long passages in green felt pen in my Clairfontaine notebooks: "But this tale has no ending. . . ."

I was studying the sacred texts the old-fashioned way, by copying them into my personal notebooks. I filled two Clairfontaine notebooks with green-penned passages from R. A. Nicholson's translations of Rumi's Mathnawi. I had discovered the most divine poetry of humanity in Rumi, and for a time I thought it was my destiny to pen modern versions of Rumi's verse.

View from Camp des Aigles, above Chamonix, France, summer 1973.

Allah Hu Ahad
Allah Hu Allah Hu Samad
Ah Camp des Aigles
God bless!
Gone are all the summer's hermits
living like marmots
in your caves and A-frame retreats
though their faint breath remains in your sunlight
ultra blue        shimmering
We have struck the splendid white tents
of Vilayat Khan
The prayer flags are now the pure wind
of the eternal snows
en haut
Ah Tahir
Gone are the angelic medieval choirs
echoing Magnificat in the granite
all phantom now

*Only the song of the hard-working people*
*the Helveti Dhikr*
*remains*
*Subhan Allahi w'al Hamduli'llahi*
*La Ilaha Il Allah Hu*
*After such ecstasy*
*peace*
*ripe as your blue berries*
*Oh bliss!*
*Everywhere I walk I hear*
*astral sheep bells in your luminous mist*
*Ah morning brightness!*
*Now you know why I say*
*Hu Allah Hu Allah Hu Allah Hu*

## October 1973

I had grown very close to Quddus, Latif, and Yahya, all young British Sufis. We decided we would travel together to Turkey to meet the dervishes. But first, we needed to earn some money for our travels. So, we took the train from Chamonix over a narrow mountain pass into French-speaking Switzerland, to Martigny, and then to Fully (pronounced "Fweee") in Valais.

Valais is the broad green upper valley of the Rhone River, hemmed in by high mountains on either side. Well-watered and sunny most of the year, it is an excellent region for growing grapes. We came to Valais, to a family winery in Fully to seek work in the *vendange,* the grape harvest. There was plenty of work to be had. We joined seasonal workers from all over the Mediterranean for the month of vendange. Although we did not drink alcohol, we had several glasses of the local vintage in their wine cellars to seal the deal.

But first I had to go to London. Under strong Uranian influence I had decided that the stuffy academic translations of Rumi, although totally correct, were too difficult to read and were hiding too much of his light. What was needed was a passionate contemporary voicing of

Rumi that spoke to the heart—and I was the person to do it.

I went to London to speak to the publisher of the translations, Luzac, and get authorization to base my versions on their translations. I got to London and Luzac wouldn't give the time of day to this raggedy hippie. I did purchase the three hardbound volumes of R. A. Nicholson's translation of the complete *Mathnawi* to lug around. Coleman Barks must have had the same idea at the same time, but he followed through and I didn't. He did have the blessing of his teacher, and he probably didn't ask for permission from Luzac.

After this detour I was back in Fully to work *dans le vendange,* in the grape harvest. I worked picking grapes in *Le Combe d'Enfer,* the Valley of Hell, a steep conical vineyard of ancient Roman rock terraces stretching up the mountainside. We would go to the worksite via a platform on a cable and spend all day bent over among the vines, clipping off clusters of grapes, piling them up in plastic cartons, and sending them down on the platform. The grapes would go to the winery where they would be crushed, strained, filtered, and then fermented in casks in the wine cellars.

It was hot, sweaty work for honest pay. Three times a day we would stop for wine, bread, and cheese, although as non-alcoholic Sufis we settled for soda pop to drink. We also missed out on getting drunk at the village fetes and raclette and wine parties we were invited to. Reality intruded when several Arab states started the Yom Kippur War and all the young Egyptian men, seasonal workers in the vineyard, were suddenly called home to fight in their army. After they left there was much more work for us to finish the harvest.

At the end of October, I boarded the Orient Express at Martigny and rode the train for two and a half days to Istanbul, where I stayed alone in the Otel Ömür for two weeks until the others came. Istanbul in winter seemed a dark, brooding, smoky city, and very, very old. The atmosphere was dense with coal smoke, tobacco smoke, exhaust, and fog. The masses of men on the street, bundled in grays and browns, trudged along in muted intensity.

I don't remember much from my time alone in Istanbul except that I played my guitar a lot in coffee shops and in my hotel room. When Yahya and Latif and Quddus and his girlfriend BlancheFleur came, we all moved into the Marmara Hotel.

We made contact with the Helveti-Jerrahi dervishes, first of all with Sheikh Muzzafer in his bookshop in the bazaar, where he warmly greeted us. He generously gave me two books of Turkish *ilahis,* songs to Allah. Dervishes were still a semi-endangered species at this time, having been outlawed since 1924 in the modern secular state of Turkey. Dervishes still flourished, but they had to keep a low profile and hold meetings in private.

We were invited to several Thursday night meetings at the Helveti tekke, joining the dervish circle for long, *jalali* (masculine) yet very sweet zikrs, followed by *sohbet* (spiritual conversation) with the sheikh in a crowded room with everyone smoking and drinking coffee. Women prayed separately from men in Turkey, but BlancheFleur was allowed to join us out of respect for her status as a liberated Western woman.

Many times we went out to dinner with dervishes at restaurants. What most impressed me was the way the dervishes would argue over the check. Every one fought over who would pick up the tab for the whole table every night. This global and obviously customary generosity blew my

Helveti Dervishes, Istanbul, Turkey, December 1973.

mind. I had never paid for dinner for anyone in my life, except when I was taking a girl out on a date. Pretty soon, I joined in the gregarious competition for the honor of paying for everyone. This alone was worth the trip.

We were invited for dinner at the house of a young Sufi prince. Priceless Ottoman calligraphy was displayed on the walls. What impressed me was the housemaid who served the dinner. Dramatically wringing her hands, she said, "Every day I weep for Allah!"

We went to visit Hasan Shushud (pronounced "shoe-shoe"), a sweet old man with wispy hair and lustrous eyes who was an enigmatic Sufi master. He was sitting in his parlor playing with some Matchbox toy cars, a red London double-decker bus and a yellow fire truck. He greeted us and continued playing with his little trucks.

"I'm a very old man now," he said. "I just got back from London and I'm playing with my trucks. If you want some teachings, you're going to have to ask me for them."

So, we asked, and he gave us three very potent "secret" practices. The only one I still recall is an inhalation and breath-retention zikr: invoke Allah with a sharp inhalation three times and on the third time hold your breath for as long as you can. It seemed like a simple meeting, but when we came out onto the street, it was as if we had taken a hit of sunshine acid. The world seemed altered, shimmering, and radiant.

At the end of November I took the bus to Konya—the home of Rumi, the Mevlana Museum, Rumi's tomb, and the Mevlevi dervishes— for the annual Mevlevi Sema, the ceremony of the whirling dervishes, which culminated on December 17—the Urs, the celebration of the death day, the wedding night of Mevlana Jalaluddin Rumi. Although the public Sema was tolerated by the government as a tourist attraction, dervish activities were still very restricted. We would stay up late at night, performing zikr quietly in people's kitchens, because public dervish gatherings were prohibited. Konya was a very quiet place at that time.

The Sema was held on a basketball court with the spectators in the bleachers. The haunting sublime Mevlevi music was played by an orchestra of stringed instruments, kudüm (kettle drums), and neys (wooden flutes), and sung by Kani Karaca in the most amazingly sweet and resonant bass voice I have ever heard. The semazens (whirl-

Mevlevi Sema, Konya, Turkey, December 1973.

ing dervishes) in flowing white robes and tall conical hats came slowly out on the floor and bowed to the sheikh in black robes and then to each other. Soon the entire room was full of white-robed figures turning counter-clockwise, arms spread out, heads thrown back, turning like atoms, like whirlpools, like cyclones, like planets, like galaxies. And among them all one black-robed figure, the sheikh, was turning very slowly clockwise, the pole of the whole assembly.

The Sema is not ecstatic, shamanistic trance dancing. It is a very sober yet sublime testimony to the glory of God by the semazens revolving in harmony with all creation.

> *The work that a Sufi considers his or her sacred work . . .*
> *is only this simple thing which I have just said: to be in*
> *rhythm with life's conditions and in tune with the infinite.*
> HAZRAT INAYAT KHAN

☜☞

In Chamonix, Istanbul, Jerusalem, and beyond, I continued to fill Clairfontaine notebooks with sacred scripture, poetry, and teachings; transcriptions from Arabic, Hebrew, and Sanskrit; as well as my own songs, dreams, poetry, color wheels, prayer banners, all written in multi-colored felt pens, along with photographs and exotic travel postcards. This was before the days of direct internet access to downloadable text and imagery, audio and video, cut and paste. When writing sacred song and wisdom on the pages of my notebooks, I was also writing them in my soul.

My poetry up to this point had tended to be murky, metaphysical, cosmic, surrealistic, and sometimes whimsical, but I had also written genuine love poetry to my beloveds. My heart had opened to love and now this love kept singing in my soul, even though I had no external beloved, no love object. So, I kept singing and writing mystic love poetry to an impersonal "you" and began to model my poetic voice more after Rumi. I went from crafting brilliant inscrutable word gems that had a dream logic of their own to genuinely wanting to say something to somebody and to be heard by that somebody.

I always had the sense that poetry was sacred, that preexisting and eternal word formations were being inscribed on my mind and on paper as if being chiseled in stone, and that their poetic beauty would endure through time, independent of their author. I thought I would be content for my poetry to be discovered after my death, like Emily Dickinson. I had faith in the truth of the beauty of my poetry. As time went on, I began to realize that I had been writing for myself and for eternity, like Emily, but I had not been writing for other people. I came to desire to communicate something to somebody, some thing to some body.

I had always written love poems, which might more accurately be called poems of hormonal frustration or fulfillment, poems of relationship function and dysfunction. I came to recognize that I was always writing these poems to mourn or celebrate my own experience.

*Whales are rolling beneath the pasture*
*The sea is breathing again in the Earth*
*lifting up its crocus ribs*

*Small streets are flowing dark with answer*
*My waters have burst in a rebel dancer*

*We tumbled one night like satellites*
*mites borne on a germinal gust*
*There in her maw I held her paw*
*and reached us right through that ember onion*

The only thing I got out of my love experiences was the poetry I took away. I began to suspect that I was using my love experiences to generate poetry rather than actually focusing on loving the other person.

I had a dream that I was standing in a long line of men going up a staircase and across a dark room to where Joni Mitchell lay on a couch smoking a cigarette in the light of a single table lamp. When my turn to be with Joni finally came, she pulled me down into her embrace with one hand while with the other hand she was checking off on a piece of paper the effect that her various verses had on me. Then my turn was up. She let me go and embraced the next man. Was this what I was doing? Using life to make art?

Increasingly I wanted to say something to somebody, to sing of my love for you to you. But *u* were fairly ephemeral in my life. My soul needed to express greater and greater love for a *you* that was only *Hu,* that was only *Allah*—and that was totally goddess, in every form *you* come in. I maintained no distinction between the personal and the impersonal beloved in my verse.

*I found you everywhere*
*You were beneath the stairs*
*You were out driving in your car*
*when all the stars were gleaming*

*Now there's no need to run*
*for I have seen the sun*
*It was hidden in my heart*
*where right there from the start*
*it was beaming*

*Aah . . . I lost every thing and every one I thought was you*
*Aah . . . all my loves impassioned vanished like the dew*

*I even lost my prayers*
*out in the evening air*
*down in your long black hair*
*now there is nowhere else*
*I can seek you*

*Your sun it never sleeps*
*It's shining through my dreams*
*It's smiling in the streets*
*when every morning sweet*
*I greet you*

## January 1974

I flew back to the States after the final Sema. The next eight months were a whirlwind of taking trains, visiting friends, driving cross-country, making connections, dancing, and singing. The lovers of God were in celebration mode and I was in travel mode—New York, Baltimore, Amagansett, Santa Fe, Talpa, Lama, San Francisco, Santa Cruz, Guerneville, San Francisco, Talpa, Lama, Boulder, Lama, Baltimore, New York, Amagansett, before finally flying to Europe again in August.

The spiritual path was opening up into many journeys into many dimensions, unending travel, always alone and always with friends. I sought out and embraced the wholeness of aloneness in solitude and retreat *and* there were always friends to stay with, friends to pray with, friends to travel with on the path in the company of seekers of truth, satsang. We are all related *and* we are all one.

I renewed my connection with Rameshwar Das (Jim Lytton) and the Ram Dass satsang, most of whom had gone to India and spent time with Maharaj-ji before his *mahasamadhi* (death) in September 1973. I was with a group of devotees as they were playing a ninety-second film clip of Maharaj-ji's last days nonstop for several hours, the same loop over and over, whooping and hollering, laughing and weeping, totally rapt and in love with his physical presence. "Oh look at his feet! His hands! His skin! He is so beautiful!" This was all still new to me, but I loved the love that loves to love.

In March I went to an all-night *puja* (ritual worship) at Winterland Ballroom in San Francisco—Ram Dass, Krishna Das, Bhagavan Das, and others leading a huge crowd in all-night kirtan. In July I attended a smaller all-night Shiva puja under the full moon on a golf course in Boulder. The all-night ecstasy was maintained by the fresh green peyote that was freely circulating. I found that I didn't really like the effect peyote had on my body. The all-night high is sublime, but then I feel brain dead and drained for the next three days.

I took classes in Indian vocal music with Bhagavan Das, a wild soul with whom I felt a lot of resonance. He gave me the darshan of the *sargam,* the experience of the inner meaning of singing the Indian scale until each note of the scale became like an objective place in space for me. This freed up my voice to sing my own improvised devotions.

I continued dancing with the Sufis and attending dharma nights in San Francisco, which were given by Wali Ali, who had been Murshid Sam's esoteric secretary and carried his transmission. I opened myself up to Wali Ali.

"I find myself wandering aimlessly around the city streets, kind of spaced out and vaguely paranoid," I told him. "This makes me feel very uncomfortable."

"Just repeat *Allah Ho Akbar,*" he replied. "That will take care of everything."

And it did.

My time at Lama was a midsummer's night dream of getting high and singing in the Dome. Marijuana was now freely used at Lama Foundation, which was now offering retreats with spiritual teachers as part of its summer program. The pace of construction was way down. The dance of hosting the guest was in full swing. With income from retreatants and the added income of royalties from *Be Here Now,* the livin' was easy—for the moment.

❀❀

*Dream . . .*

*Lama is more a magical kingdom like Tibet than a commune: long buildings and big stone plazas. Ram Dass and Bhagavan Das and Zim are all flying up in the blue sky like kites, arms spread-eagled, looking like flying squirrels in their white robes, like magical prayer banners . . .*

*We are on a rooftop, and I try to show Wendy how to fly—I say just lay back let go and the flow of cosmic forces will take you away, just let go, just let go . . .*

*I wander down to the sea, which is magnificent and overwhelming, cold winter seas, armies of white combing breakers rushing from the horizon to the shore. A palace in ruins is standing on the shore, the czar's summer palace, for there are tattered brown banners for the fiftieth anniversary of the people's republic floating in the wind . . .*

*Some young men there direct me farther down the beach to where there is an enormous gathering of people sitting on a gigantic green air cushion singing kirtan with Bhagavan Das. A very wild magnificent kirtan, like the sea, but also very tender and loving, for they are all waiting to have darshan with Maharaj-ji who is in a small ruined outbuilding of the palace in a little room with a big grated window so you can see him giving thirty-second darshans to people individually. They come in, and he throws a lei around their neck or hits them on the head or something and that's that . . .*

*From each person you can see the instant release of their psychic entity or soul form, usually a very astral dynamic form in vivid etheric colors that leaps right up out of the room into the clear blue sky . . .*

☙❦☙

I found my voice while chanting kirtan with Ram Dass and the satsang and, later, dancing with the Sufis. Before, I had been trying to sing folk songs, pop songs, all of these songs with all of these words that just kept me wrapped up in the mental world. My heart wanted to open up and sing the love, the pure raw burning, sweet soothing, exhilarating love of all that is, the love that is all that is, call it Rama or Allah or Kali Ma. Singing in satsang made it safe to open up and let the heart sing and be fully human, as divine as I could be.

Just as white light contains all the colors, so heart love contains all the emotions: joy, bliss, tenderness, sadness, grief, anger, rage, courage, desire, delight, detachment, serenity, peace, affection, compassion, and on and on. . . . All are part of heart love. To let heart love sing in its purest form to God, or really, ultimately, in any form, is to allow all the feelings of our humanity to pour forth in love. I found my voice in heart love, singing to God in all her forms, with all his names. My heart voice can also sing my own songs or the songs of others now that I have found it, although mostly I sing pure sound or divine names.

Bhagavan Das introduced me to singing sargam, singing the Indian scale of *shrutis* (notes) against the background of an instrumental drone: tamboura, shruti box, or ektar. Each shruti is an overtone of the fundamental sound, the tonic note, the *Sa*. The practice for the voice is to find union with the tonic, and having found that union to then sing the notes in the scale, *Sa Re Ga Ma Pa Dha Ni Sa,* hearing them as overtones emerging from that ocean of sound. Vocal practice done in this way is spiritual practice. *Nada Brahma*. Sound is God.

Hazrat Inayat Khan says that there are three forms of music: vocal, instrumental, and dance. He says that the human voice is the most fundamental, the source, of all forms of music.

Now that I had found my voice, I was singing all the time, singing with my guitar or my ektar. I would sing in the morning sitting outside my tent above the Lama garden, sing until the birds and the squirrels were celebrating with me. I would sing for hours in the resonant Lama dome, singing alone with my eyes closed, chanting the heart love, until my eyes were watering, my mouth drooling. And if people sat down and sang with me, so much the better. I would sing and play with all the beautiful musicians coming through Lama, sharing their chants and songs. I would chant and dance zikr with the group until late in the evening in the Lama dome.

In private I began to sing my own songs, songs that came flooding through me, singing my own versions of Blake and Rumi as well. I would open my heart and sing songs in a place where no one else could hear me, conditioned by my father's shutting me down so often. I was a paranoid poet, the opposite of a performance artist. Singing to an audience brings out the best in many singers. Not me. I would sing in the shade at the edge of the meadow. I would sing in secluded glades in the woods. I would sing late at night in my cabin by kerosene light. But if anyone came near, I would shut down. My best songs were published in my poetry books but were never sung in the presence of another person.

There is a story told of the reclusive Spanish poet Juan Ramón Jiménez. Should someone come a knocking on his door, the visitor would hear his voice floating down from the second-story window: "Juan Ramón Jiménez is not at home." That was me.

I had put extra thick nylon strings on my classical guitar to make it louder and more resonant. I took my guitar with me when I traveled overseas. Staying alone in a seedy hotel in Istanbul for two weeks, I played my guitar ragas for hours in my cold winter room. Thinking that I was all alone I began to sing:

*Now that we've come back again*
*won't you tell me where we've been*
*my darling*

*We flew all night on wings of light*
*beyond the seas and the silent trees*
*of morning*

When I was through, enthusiastic applause, two hands clapping, burst out in the adjoining room. That was the closest I came to a public performance.

*The angels told us many things*
*too strange to sing far too intense*
*to remember*

*We flew on a swan beyond the dawn*
*the morning star gleaming far off*
*in December*

In Mickey Hart's book *Planet Drum,* there is a full-page picture of a hoary Siberian shaman clad in skins holding a large drum and a beater. The pull quote says, "For the shaman the drum is not so much a musical instrument as a means of transportation."

I stayed in contact with Noor, who was living with Frances in Talpa, south of Taos. He told me he had funding for a new book project in Jerusalem, the holy city of the three major faiths of Judaism, Christianity, and Islam. The book, he said, would demonstrate the essential unity of these three faiths and so contribute to peace in the Middle East. He invited me to come to Jerusalem and take part in this project.

Somewhere along the way Noor gave me the Sufi name Ahad, which means "One" as in "Divine Unity." It could have been while he was living in Talpa, where he was experiencing increasingly illuminated states. I had been going by my pen name, Frank Zero, inspired by a verse from "Keeping Things Whole" by Mark Strand:

*Wherever I am*
*I am what is missing . . .*

*We all have reasons*
*for moving.*

> *I move*
> *to keep things whole.*

I was engaged in the dissolution of false personality, the emptying of the personal self, and zero seemed the appropriate cipher to replace my unloved patronymic—the poet as empty mirror.

"I was wondering what Zero could change into," Noor told me. "And I thought of the song by Leonard Cohen":

> *You know who I am*
> *You've stared at the sun*
> *Well I am the one who loves*
> *Changing from nothing to one.*

Noor said, "What can Zero change into but One? Your name is Ahad, the One."

I immediately accepted this name. I had never felt that my birth name, Frank, was my own. In fact, Frank was the name of my mother's younger brother, who had been killed by a sniper in the war in Italy two years before I was born. It never felt like my own name.

Ahad Cobb,
passport photo, 1974.

Everything exists in the divine unity. The *ahadiyat* (unity, oneness) is beyond all qualities, even light, and yet all qualities exist within the One. Interestingly enough, *ahad* is also the indefinite pronoun in Arabic, as in "one walks down the street." Everything moves in the stillness of wholeness.

I went to Israel with the name Ahad, traveling with Maryam, a fiery sister in the faith. I flew to Brussels and spent ten days at Camp des Aigles before taking the train to Venice, where Maryam and I boarded a ship for Haifa. We cruised down the Adriatic and through the Gulf of Corinth before stopping at Athens, where I walked around the interior of the Acropolis hearing echoes of ancient citizens and peripatetic philosophers.

### September 10, 1974

Maryam and I got off the boat at Haifa and took a *sherut,* a taxi, to Jerusalem. It was a bright, hot sunny day. We drove south down the coast, breezing by lush, green orange groves and kibbutzim, passing along the outskirts of Tel Aviv, which seemed like a cut-rate Miami with low, white apartment buildings. Then we turned east into the Judean Hills. We drove up the steep narrow road that was the theater of bitter battle in 1947, the year I was born. We emerged to a view of the ancient walls and modern high-rises of Jerusalem.

At my first sight of Jerusalem, a cascade of cold electrical trickles of recognition rushed through my body, like when a limb has fallen asleep and is waking up. I knew I had been here before. I knew this on a cellular level. My body knew I was coming home. And yet not only had I never been here before, I had not the slightest notion of the modern history of Israel. All I knew about Jerusalem were some Bible tales from Sunday school long ago. I was just coming to work with my group. Never before or since have I had such a sensation.

The sherut let us out at the bus station near the Damascus Gate of the Old City, where we took a bus to the Mount of Olives. The Old City of Jerusalem is built on top of Mount Moriah, which drops off to the east to the Kidron Valley. The next hill to the east is the Mount of Olives. We got off the bus on top of the Mount of Olives and walked down the east side of the mount into the Palestinian Arab village of At-Tur where Noor had rented a big, empty three-story house overlooking the Judean Desert. Closer at hand, we overlooked Beth Phage, the site where Jesus had mounted the donkey for his triumphal entry into Jerusalem. All the houses in this region are built of white, beige, or gold Jerusalem limestone.

There was no furniture. We lived on the floor. There was a stone staircase going up two stories and then farther up to a little cubicle with a door that opened out onto the flat roof. I laid my sleeping bag on the floor of that little space at the top of the stairs. That was my room, the hermit ledge.

"Your father is a banker," Noor said to me. "I want you to handle the money for the house."

I didn't really like taking on that role, but I could hardly refuse. Noor gave me a bunch of cash to take to the bank. Then he walked with me through the village to the bus for downtown Jerusalem. When we both got to the bank, the money was gone from my bag.

"You lost the money," Noor said. "You need to replace it with your money."

I definitely did not like this, but once again, I could hardly refuse. I took the money out of my account and put it in the house account. I've always wondered what happened to that money that was in my bag. Was this some kind of a Sufi test? Did Noor swipe it out of my bag? Could I really trust my teacher? Be that as it may, that was the start of nine years of handling money for the group and then for Lama Foundation and then twelve years working as an accountant in the business world.

Soon enough, the rest of the crew arrived: Quddus, BlancheFleur, Yahya, Ghalib, and Nooraissa (Frances was now Nooraissa, "the light of women"). Already used to living together and working as a group, we settled into our new routine: morning and evening zikr, study of esoteric papers, cooking and cleaning and shopping, and working on the Jerusalem book.

Our work involved going out into the neighborhood, into the Old City and the New City, taking pictures, conducting interviews, and gathering materials that would then be cooked into this new book. Quddus and I were the photographers, sometimes accompanying Nooraissa or Maryam to document interviews, often just roaming around and capturing images. I'm not clear what everyone else was doing. We amassed a great deal of material, but an actual book was never published.

I have a crude recording I made walking down the stone stairs in the house, drawing closer and closer to a spontaneous zikr outbreak in the kitchen, with wild beautiful chanting, the beating of pots and pans, heavy breathing, and Noor singing *"Ya Hadi"* (Oh Guide) over it all. Such was the love breaking out. Our Shabbas ceremonies were very wild as well. One Friday evening, Noor went around the circle giving each one the Shekinah's kiss, a mouthful of sweet wine from his mouth to your mouth.

A week after we arrived, Ramadan began, the month of fasting by day and feasting by night, locally called "the month of sweets." All the marketplace activities of the morning would fade away by afternoon as everyone went inside to be quiet. At night, we would go up on the roof and gaze out at all the other rooftops, which were strung with colored lights, and enjoy all the family gatherings on the rooftops, where people danced to loud music late into the night.

One day toward the end of Ramadan, I was sitting and singing at the top of the staircase, my guitar in open tuning, improvising melodies, singing zikrs and ragas, when two women came up the stairs and walked right by me out onto the roof. I paid them no attention, "absorbed in the solitude of my unity," as Noor would say.

A few minutes later Maryam came back inside and said to me, "Honey, your bride has come. Come and meet your bride."

She said her name was Ahava ("love") and her birth name was Varda ("wild rose"). She was a honey-blonde American of Ukrainian and Austrian ancestry, just my age—we were born three days apart—and beautiful to my eyes. She had been living with family in Israel while recovering from a nervous breakdown. Her family had been taking care of her and she had just gone out on her own. She was very intelligent though emotionally fragile. We became absorbed in conversation. She was very attracted to our group. I was very attracted to her.

She invited us all over for Shabbas at Ein Kerem, where she was staying with some friends. Ein Kerem is a quiet village in a terraced green valley west of Jerusalem. We stayed from sundown Friday through sundown Saturday. After the Shabbas meal Varda and I went to an upper room to make music together. This was something that really attracted me to her—she played deep sonorous violin, both folk music and ragas. I really wanted someone to play music with. We eagerly got tuned up and tried to make music together, but for some reason it just wasn't working. She kept stopping. Something was getting in the way. I could have paid attention to that.

Finally we gave up making music. She said, "How about some good old-fashioned loving?"

We went outside to her little red tent. We made love and slept together. The next morning she was very angry with me. I could have paid attention to that too. But I was in love—and soon enough started writing love poetry to her.

Meanwhile Noor and many in the group started visiting Sidi Sheikh Muhammad, who was the *qadi* (religious judge) living on the Mount of Olives. For some reason I was never invited or was never interested in going to these meetings. I must have been out and about all the time. What was happening, though I did not realize it at the time, was that Noor and Nooraissa and most of the others in the group were being converted to Islam. But I was in the dark about this.

At the end of November, there was a full moon eclipse just at sunset. We stood on the roof of the house watching a blood-red moon rising over the folds of the Judean desert in the east. It looked like an omen of bloodshed. Not long thereafter, Noor and Nooraissa left and the household dissolved. We had collected an enormous amount of material for this book we hoped would contribute to peace in the Middle East. I had no idea what would become of it.

Meanwhile, I kept romancing Varda and she kept pushing me away. I wanted to get us a place to live together, but she wouldn't hear of it. I stayed on for a while but then decided that this love was futile, and that it was time for me to go to India. I was more than halfway there, and I wanted to discover what so many of my friends had.

I called Varda and told her I was leaving for India.

At that last moment, she said, "I've changed my mind. Let's get a place together."

My soul has made decisions that have molded the course of my life. One could say that a soul makes decisions outside of time, postulates that enter into the time stream and create or uncreate realities over time. Soul decisions are more definite than intentions and deeper than desires. The conscious personality may not give much attention to or even be aware of the decisions the soul makes, but these decisions are effective, nonetheless.

In high school my best friend and I were imaginative, aesthetic rebels and beatnik wannabes. We were disgusted with the snobby, superficial, cream-cheese debutantes, the good girls who surrounded us. If they were normal, we wanted nothing to do with normal. If they thought we were crazy, we wanted to be crazier. We vowed to each other, "We'll never go out with any girls who aren't crazy!" That decision has come back to haunt me many times.

Seeing Veda Rama and saying to God, "I want to be with this woman," was a soul decision given to God. The soul says, "I want to experience this reality," and gives it to God in prayer. My ego had no expectation of any outcome at all, but my soul knew to give it to God.

I had been well provided for as a child, taken care of by generous and loving parents, but there were always strings attached to all the gifts I was given. It ended up feeling like nothing but strings of attachment and expectation. Now that I was experiencing the generosity of friends with no strings attached, the generosity of Ram Dass, of Maharaj-ji, of the dervishes, I began to sense that there was something missing in my wholeness.

I became aware of the inherent selfishness of my nature. All my life I had been given to and had not given back. Even in romantic love relationships my attention had been focused on my emotional turbulence and the poetry it engendered rather than on the other person. No matter how much love, attraction, and desire I might have felt, I had to admit to myself that I was objectively incapable of loving another human being.

It seemed to me that the way to begin was to be able to give something to someone rather than receiving all the time. I decided that I was ready and needed to take care of someone else, to provide for someone other than myself.

I made a definite decision: "I want to give something to somebody." It was subliminal, not entirely conscious. I didn't write it down. It wasn't a wish. It wasn't a prayer. It was a soul decision.

"I want to give some thing to some body."

## January 1975

Varda and I moved into the bottom floor of the house of Ahmad Khamies Kweiss on the Mount of Olives. Our communal house had been down under the hill, toward the bottom. Our new home was almost at the top of the mountain, just below the Russian Orthodox Convent and Church of the Ascension, the actual place from which Jesus ascended to heaven. To get to the house one walked down the street, downhill from the bus stop, and then up a narrow alley to the right, all the way to the end. Above us lived Ahmed, his wife Imm Fuad, and his son Fuad. We saw the most of Imm Fuad, a kindly woman who never left home except to visit family or go shopping.

We lived in two stone rooms with no heat, a mattress on the floor, a sink, and a Bunsen burner to cook with. Varda was incapable of taking care of herself, so I did all the shopping, all the cooking, all the cleaning, and all the laundry. I wasn't all that good at any of this, so gradually she began to pitch in. One evening she insisted on cooking the meal, so I lit the Bunsen burner for her and went into the other room to let her cook. After a while, hearing nothing happening, I went back into the kitchen to find her just staring at the flame.

Over time she became more grounded.

I actually did enjoy being the man of the house and taking care of someone else for once in my life. Ram Dass repeatedly asked Maharaj-ji how he could raise his kundalini, and Maharaj-ji repeatedly and consistently answered, "Feed people."

Varda and I spent every morning up on the roof of the house

View from the Mount of Olives, Jerusalem, Israel, fall 1974.

meditating, praying, reading, and writing. It was a sunny, bright, cold desert winter, not too hot to sit in the sun. We were close to the top of the crescent hillside village, looking out over the Judean desert. There were five or six mosques in the village. Five times a day the *adhan,* the call to prayer, would cascade in interweaving waves from the five or six mosques, passionate vocal calls to prayer, not the tinny recordings you hear in big cities. Over the tall wall above us were the ancient green pine trees in the Garden of the Ascension with black-robed nuns occasionally scurrying between the buildings and a huge bell tower crowning the mountain. When the choirs of birds were singing in the trees and the bells ringing and the muezzins calling out across the houses under the blue sky, not to mention the roosters crowing and the children laughing and me singing with my guitar, it was chaotic and messy and an absolutely glorious raising of praise to Allah.

When I walked on the streets of At-Tur, everyone would look at me curiously, greeting me with their eyes and hearts. Children would run after me, demanding my attention. This was a world away from walking the big city streets, keeping my gaze tucked away, not looking at people. Here, everyone was out in the open with each other. Life was peaceful and calm in this Arab village. Slowly, slowly, healing came over the four months we lived there.

I wrote Varda a long invocatory poem, resonant with tantric hymns to the Goddess, inscribed it on a long sheet of paper with multi-colored felt pens, tied a ribbon around it, and presented it to her. I thought this was the deepest, most beautiful, and certainly the longest poem I had ever written. She opened the scroll, began reading the poem, and got very angry.

"What is this shit?" she said. "This isn't me!"

I could have listened to her, but no. . . .

> Oh Mother mutter in the mud
> more hidden than mating chromosomes
> or gardens before the flood
> Summer substance of all our dreams
> you weave and unweave every day

*your ancient remembrance*
*some old story about a path a way*
*some music you play to hold your suitors at bay*
*whirlpools of ten thousand worlds*
*born and destroyed on the whim of your sway*
*deep green song of your cycling*
*endless multiplication consuming itself*
*filmy green mirror mantling us*

She was right. It wasn't about her at all. . . .

Maryam was living down the mountain in the *zawiya* (Sufi school) under the home of Sheikh Sidi Muhammad. We would visit her there and meet with Sidi, a fair-skinned, red-haired luminous man with a neatly trimmed beard. He ate very little, slept very little, and walked everywhere, looking after his people. He was always talking, always teaching. Then he would stop and listen—and say, "The message is coming from The God"—and resume talking.

In Palestinian English, Allah (Al-illah) is not God but The God.

Maryam was on fire with love. She would stop people on the streets to tell them of the glory of God and the Sufi path. He gently corrected her. "Sidi Maryam," he said, "the truth does not go out." (The mystic is not an evangelist.)

One day, I was walking down the road on top of the Mount of Olives with our friend Hasan al-Sharif from Hebron. Out of the blue he said to me, "Ahad, give me everything in your pockets. If you are my brother, you will give me everything in your pockets."

I was dumbfounded, yet intrigued. This went against all my conditioning. No one would ever . . . but what if? Was this some kind of Sufi test? Well, it was definitely an opportunity to give something to somebody. I gave Hasan everything in my pockets, which he put in his pockets, and we kept on walking and talking. Before we parted, he gave it all back to me and said, "Now I know we are truly brothers, damaged together in the Name."

(In one form of group zikr practice you interlace fingers with the person on either side of you. In Palestinian English, you are now damaged together in the Name.)

As the days grew warmer, Varda and I started to travel around Israel. We went to Jericho to visit a messianic teacher and his companion, who were tucked away in a shady house, waiting for the end times. We hiked into Wadi Qelt to see the ancient St. George's Monastery built into the wall of a desert canyon. We visited Nazareth, Mount Tabor, the Mount of Beatitudes, and Capernaum. It was glorious to walk where Jesus walked on the green hills above the Sea of Galilee. We stayed with friends in Rosh Pina, an artist colony in a partially bombed-out mountain town near the Lebanese border. We visited Safad, Kibbutz Gan Shmuel, Be'erSheva, and Hebron. Varda had family and friends all over Israel.

The practice of perpetual prayer, such a strong concentration at first, merged into the fabric of my life. Prayer was always with me, like dolphins swimming alongside a ship, occasionally breaking surface, sometimes becoming invisible, but always there. It was more spiritual practice than prayer, a way of remembering and staying connected to essence in the midst of everyday life. Spiritual practice was a psychological necessity, a refuge from my agitated and anxious mind, a way of finding my place in the greater whole of which I am a part.

I would walk down the streets of Jerusalem with peace on my breath, breathing in Salaam, breathing out Shalom. Right foot, left foot, Salaam, Shalom. . . . I would walk through crowds of people speaking languages of which I was blissfully ignorant. All the hubbub could not distract from breathing in Allah, breathing out Hu. I would ride in sheruts or sit in cafes listening to Arabic music on the radio, and every singer in every song was singing *"La ilaha il Allah Hu."* I forgot to pray a lot. My everyday was always better when I remembered.

My indulgence in the thick harsh smoke of Lebanese hashish cast a shadow over my time in Jerusalem. One Shabbas evening, I was so ungrounded that I left my passport and all my money on the back seat of an Arab sherut. I had to go to the American Embassy to recover my identity.

One bright day, Varda and I went to the Temple Mount and went into Al-Aqsa Mosque to pray. On the way out, a young Israeli soldier stopped us and searched us, finding a matchbook of hash on me. He told me to be more careful.

Jerusalem itself was, and is, an enigma to me. An ancient city of gleaming white limestone, there is a very high, light spiritual presence here, undeniably at the center of interminable violence. This city is so holy that everybody will kill everybody else to possess it. It's hard for me to see any resolution for the Israeli-Palestinian conflict that has raged since the time of Joshua. I know I've been here before. I don't think I want to be here again.

Years later at Lama Foundation I was sitting in the window seat of the library reading *Newsweek* about the Israeli invasion of Lebanon, reading about how the Israelis had surrounded Sidon and were bombing Tyre, and so on. I had a feeling of déjà vu all over again. Where had I read these words before? I pulled out a Bible, turned to the Old Testament, and there it was—same actions, same players, three thousand years ago.

Image courtesy of Ovidio Salazar.

One day early in May, Sidi Sheikh Muhammad told us that war was coming, and we had to leave Israel immediately. The Palestinian insurgency in South Lebanon was just beginning. Israel would invade Lebanon seven years later.

The message was coming from The God, so we hastily packed up and took a sherut to the airport. Israeli security stopped us—Maryam and Varda were in their Arab dresses—and searched us so extensively, even ripping the film out of my camera, that they had to halt the plane taxiing down the runway and pull out the stairs for us to board the plane.

When I look at a map of Israel today, the general area of At-Tur is marked as an "Arab Enclave," surrounded by illegal Israeli settlements. In 1975 there were ten thousand Jews living in East Jerusalem. Today over two hundred thousand Jews live in East Jerusalem. When I pull up the view east from the Mount of Olives, I see wave upon wave of high-rise apartment buildings, looking like white, grilled Darth Vader masks, marching toward the Dead Sea.

∽∽

## May 1975

Maryam, Varda, and I got off the plane in Istanbul and asked the taxi driver to take us to a good hotel, which turned out to be a whorehouse and party venue, which kept us awake all night. After five days in Istanbul, we boarded the Orient Express, which took four days to get us to Paris, from where we went on to London.

We were stopped at British customs. We didn't have enough money to get into the country nor did we have tickets home out of England. We looked like deadbeat hippies, so they weren't going to let us into the country without money. No problem, I said, let me call my parents, they will send some money. Ten years before, I had inherited some DuPont stock from my grandfather. My parents could sell off some of my stock for me and send me some of my money. Imagine my surprise when they refused.

My father disapproved of my hippie lifestyle and life choices. He still was not speaking to me, ever since I shamed my parents and disgraced myself by going home with Wendy. And now I was coming back from Israel with this "Jewish hussy" they wanted nothing to do with. It was only when the British official told them that I would be sent back to France and end up in jail on vagrancy charges, and I reminded them that it was my own money after all, that they relented.

We stayed with friends in London, with Quddus and Latif and Ghalib, for eighteen days. There were always friends to stay with and friends to travel with at this time in my life. We didn't have much money, but we were full of life and art and Allah. It was cold and rainy and the flat had no heat. Varda and I caught cold, got sick, and stayed in bed together for several days. We both became acutely aware of a spirit presence hovering in the space above our bed. Later on, we would agree that this was the soul presence of the child waiting to be born through us.

In June we flew back to the States. Walking around in lower Manhattan in the sweltering heat, immersed in all the clamor, with jostling, barely clothed, sweaty bodies and noisy traffic, was quite a culture shock after living for eight months on the Mount of Olives, where modesty of dress, gentleness of voice, and slowness of pace were the norm. We were home, but it didn't feel like home.

Predictably, my parents refused to let me bring Varda home to meet them. We spent a month on the east coast before driving for six days cross-country to Lama.

# 5 HOLY WAR, 1975–1977

I returned to Lama with Varda in July 1975 to join the first program in the yet-to-be completed Intensive Studies Center (ISC).

In Steve Durkee's original vision, Lama Foundation operated a Center for Basic Studies with families living on the land, a community that sheltered and nurtured a retreat center within the retreat center, the Intensive Studies Center, where people could engage in prolonged spiritual retreats under the guidance of a teacher, such as a traditional three-year Buddhist retreat under a lama's guidance. The site plan was a circle of twelve cells surrounding a central dome. On the back of the dome were a large kitchen, a dining room, and a work/study area.

The image was that of an alchemical retort. The twelve cells formed the bowl of the retort and the dome formed the stopper and the plug of the retort—all surrounded by fire and cooking intensely. The ISC did indeed prove to be a place of intense transformation.

Work on the ISC had begun during the summer of 1971. The foundations had been laid and the adobe walls rose rapidly. However, since Steve had left the land, construction had slowed down dramatically and stopped altogether at the ISC. Now, four years later, the ISC was incomplete, with only foundations and walls, no floors, no windows, no roofs.

Now Steve returned to Lama as Nooradeen ("Light of the Faith") and contracted to complete the construction of the ISC while simultaneously running the first intensive program of Islamic studies at the

ISC. Nooradeen would raise all the money needed. The project and the program would be completely self-funded and autonomous from Lama Foundation. The ISC would not participate in Lama, and Lama would not participate in the ISC, although presumably relations would be cordial between the two communities. Nooradeen's former brother-in-law, Siddiq (formerly Hans), was now Coordinator of Lama Foundation. Nooradeen was now married to Nooraissa, Siddiq's former wife.

Most of the group from Jerusalem was there—Nooradeen, Nooraissa, Quddus, Yahya, and Maryam—all recently converted to Islam, except for me. I was prepared to trust the process and learn from the experience of living and praying in a Muslim community as the next stage on my spiritual journey. I was part of this group, after all. But first, as soon as we got there, we had to leave the land.

Nooradeen chose to vacate the premises because his former friend, Ram Dass, was coming to host one of his big love-fest retreats at Lama and Nooradeen wanted nothing to do with him. In fact, one of the first symptoms of this Islamic conversion was antipathy if not animosity toward Ram Dass, Pir Vilayat, Murshid Sam, and Hazrat Inayat Khan, all "pseudo-Sufis," and all sorts of deluded New Age "Hinjews, Bujews, and Sujews," led, of course, by "Rammed Ass."

Recent converts to a faith are often the most fanatical and intolerant true believers. It was dismaying and confusing to hear my beloved teachers and friends bad-mouthed and vilified. This tarnished the light of Islam in my heart from the beginning.

We camped out around northern New Mexico for the next two weeks, in El Rito, by the Chama River, in Shiprock, in Jemez Springs, until it was safe to return to Lama.

That summer was a work intensive to get floors down and windows in and roofs over our heads before winter came. I remember cutting and laying vigas, cutting and laying *latillas* (the wood laid between the vigas), putting on insulation and roofing, putting foam insulation on adobe walls, and then mudding the insulation on the walls—and stopping five times a day for *salat,* the ritual prayer, in the empty prayer dome under the blue sky. The silent intensity of concentration was a lot like early Lama, with salat five times a day instead of meditation

Unfinished Prayer Dome, Intensive Studies Center, Lama Foundation, fall 1975.

three times a day. This was intensified further in September when we observed the month of Ramadan, fasting from sunrise to sunset.

Nooradeen would engage us in Islamic studies in the evening, immersing us in the language and lore of Islamic Sufism. He was beginning to produce transliterations of certain verses of the Holy Qur'an—the Ayat an-Nur, the Verse of Light, for example—that would help us recite the Arabic without having to learn the script. Eventually he would transliterate the entire Qur'an.

Sufism, we learned, was a worldwide phenomenon of initiated brotherhoods that included the esoteric teachings and practices of Islam. All Sufis were Muslims, observing the outer forms of Islam as well as the inner disciplines of Sufism. Hazrat Inayat Khan and his followers were pseudo-Sufis, we learned, because they did not practice Islam.

Our powerful, if somewhat more sober, group zikr practice continued, particularly on Thursday night, as is customary. One Thursday evening, I was warming up for zikr singing "Om Namo Shivaya" in my room when Nooradeen came rushing down the pathway and burst into my room, shouting, "Haram! (Forbidden!) Haram! No Shiva here! Shiva is not welcome here! La ilaha il Allah!" That stopped my heart dead in its tracks.

Hazrat Inayat Khan's prayers, such as Salat, had taught me to recognize God in all the names and forms God comes in:

> *Thy Light is in all forms, Thy Love in all beings:*
> *in a loving mother, in a kind father, in an innocent child,*
> *in a helpful friend, in an inspiring teacher.*
> *Allow us to recognize Thee in All Thy holy names and forms:*
> *as Rama, as Krishna, as Shiva, as Buddha.*
> *Let us know Thee as Abraham, as Solomon, as Zarathustra,*
> *as Moses, as Jesus, as Mohammed,*
> *and in many other names and forms, known and*
> *unknown to the world.*

Now it seemed that Allah, the One True God, or at least the newly converted, the newly surrendered to Allah, the ISC Muslims, were at war with all the other names and forms in which the One True God has revealed Him/Herself to humanity. I couldn't go along with this. The Holy Qur'an says, "There is no compulsion in religions," but we hadn't gotten there yet.

I could have left, but I didn't. Not yet.

That winter I sank into a deep depression, overwhelmed by my own impotence, my own inability to be authentic, and all the repressed anger I was carrying from my youth. Try as I might to pretend to be a Muslim, Islam was not my religion, and I could not forget that I was just pretending. One thing all Muslims agree about is that the Holy Qur'an is the Word of God. Try as I might, I just could not get my head around it. I loved learning to chant sections of the *suras* (chapters in the Qur'an) in Arabic transliteration. The passages were poignant and poetic, the language sonorous and resonant—they were another dimension of consciousness. I would be inspired by many sublime, mystic invocations in English translation as well, but a large portion of the translated text consisted of dire warnings and threats of the consequences of not heeding and obeying the Word of God. This impacted me like the word of the punishing father rather than the "Perfection of Love, Harmony, and Beauty" invoked by Hazrat Inayat Khan or by Murshid Sam, who said, "God is your lover, not your jailer." For all my love of the sublime, mystic invocations, try as I might, the Holy Qur'an seemed chaotic, confusing, and threatening.

Likewise, the practice of salat, the five-times-a-day ritual prayer, seemed dry and rote to me, conformity to social uniformity rather than surrender to the Will of Allah. I did believe the friends who told me of their mystical experiences during salat. My friend Karima told me, "Every time I put my head on the carpet I fall into vast space among all the stars and all the galaxies."

Surely standing surrendered to the Will of Allah can be direct communion with God. But try as I might it eluded me.

My name was now, in proper Islamic form, Abd'al Ahad, Slave of the One. Names such as Ahad, Quddus, and Latif may be given in

Turkish or Indian cultures, but in Arabic culture it is not permitted to give a human a divine name, hence Nooradeen instead of Noor, Abd'al Ahad, Abd'al Quddus, Abd'al Latif, and so forth. We all underwent a name change. I accepted Abd'al Ahad for ten years, until I was working in the business world and it just didn't work.

Nooradeen had gone from being the recipient of all my good father projections to being the target of all my bad father projections. I felt I had gone from living in the house of one despotic, intolerant, authoritarian, fanatic, controlling son of a bitch to living in the house of another. I was dominated and manipulated by the same outbursts of anger, irrational fiats, demeaning criticism, and sarcasm from someone I thought I loved and respected. And my response was identical: withdrawal into my shell, mute submission, lethargic cooperation, and sullen rebellion. I had not learned how to own my own emotions and take charge of my own life. It was going to be a very long and painful lesson.

I was living in a tiny room with a woman I thought I was in love with who was definitely not in love with me, but was powerless in her own way to escape this situation, try as she might. It's not hard to fall in love with someone who's not in love with you—just listen to the radio. It must be more difficult to be loved by someone you're not really in love with. She did love me in her own way, but neither of us really knew how to love each other.

## December 1975

We all lived in a semi-circle, a horseshoe of twelve adobe cells, maybe a hundred feet across, around a central courtyard. The walls between the cells were one brick thick. We were very sensitive to each other and kept it very quiet. The ISC was like a twelve-cell battery continually charging, like an alchemical retort building up internal pressure. Then something awful happened.

Something had happened to Yahya, who was lying immobile in Room 8. We were forbidden to ask about it or to visit him or, above all, tell anyone about it. We were told that Nooraissa, who had healing gifts, was looking after him. A cloud of unknowing and mute anxiety shrouded the horseshoe of cells at the ISC. We couldn't know what was happening so we couldn't be involved in it, and above all, we couldn't tell anybody about it.

Finally, after two nights, Quddus broke the wall of silence, walked two miles down the road, and used a neighbor's phone (we still had no phone at Lama) to call an ambulance, which came and took Yahya to St. Joseph's Hospital in Albuquerque. He was put into intensive care and diagnosed with a spinal injury, paralyzed below the neck.

Now we were told a story. Yahya, John Daniel Evans, a bright young Welshman, had brought his girlfriend, Zuleikha, an exotic Dutch Surinamese woman, to live with us. They lived in adjoining cells at the ISC. Apparently, Zuleikha had been growing distant in her affections and Yahya was disturbed by this. Just before the incident she had been cutting another man's hair, which aroused an intense jealousy in Yahya. He came barreling down to her room, seething with jealous rage, and burst through her door, coming at her physically. But, being a gentle man, he could not strike a lady. Rushing at her in the tiny space of the room, he checked his violent impulse the only way he could. He tucked his head under and put his forward momentum into flipping his body heels over head, landing on his neck and causing the dislocation of two cervical vertebrae. The dislocated vertebrae had pinched off the flow of spinal fluid, resulting in the atrophy of the spinal cord and paralysis below the neck.

This was the story we were told. I have no reason to doubt it and no way to confirm it. What is heartbreaking is that we allowed ourselves to be kept in the dark for two days and that it had to take great courage for Quddus to defy the powers that be and do the obvious: call an ambulance. Yahya's outcome might have been better if he had not been kept immobile for two days with his spinal cord withering away. Or it might have made no difference whatsoever. I have no way of knowing the truth of the situation. To this day, I feel great shame and pain at my inaction and submission to authority.

We all went down and camped out at St. Joseph's Hospital in Albuquerque for the better part of a week to give Yahya what support we could. Zuleikha never left his side until after his operation. But the group started to disintegrate after this. Quddus left. Maryam left. Others left. But others would come to take their places.

They operated on Yahya a month later. With physical therapy he regained partial use of his hands, although his lower body remained paralyzed. What amazed me was that through all of this Yahya never stopped performing salat five times a day, bowing and prostrating mentally if not physically. Or so I am told.

There was a barbed wire fence with one small gate between the ISC and Lama Central. It was not a boundary fence but a large enclosure within the boundaries to keep out the cows that were allowed to graze in the forest when we first came to the land. Now there were no longer cows grazing in the forest and the fence no longer had a function. The fence became symbolic of the increasing rift between the (no longer Intensive, but rather) Islamic Studies Center and the Lama community. Politically, Nooradeen and Nooraissa were still continuing (meaning lifetime) members of Lama Foundation, although they refused to participate in the political process. Siddiq and Asha, formerly Barbara, were also continuing members. At that time continuing members were members for life. They could not be voted out, and they could intervene at any time they chose.

As time went on Nooradeen expressed increasing antipathy and antagonism toward the unbelievers, the *kafirs,* those who cover up the truth, in the Lama community. He felt they should all leave the land and that Islam, the one true faith, should rule the behavior of anyone living on the land. Submit to Islam or leave.

Nooradeen was the visionary genius and taskmaster who, together with his now-divorced wife, whose name was now Asha, had begun the creation of Lama Foundation from the ground up only seven years ago. It is understandable that he felt a strong personal investment in Lama's future. For Nooradeen, the Lama experiment had failed and Islam had triumphed. For others, however, the Lama experiment was still vibrant and valid. These were the seeds of the Holy War at Lama Foundation.

Marijuana use was still a daily practice. Getting high fueled the fire of Islamic studies. Our supply was constantly running out. Nooradeen directed me to grow ganga in the forest so that we could have our own supply. I cleared and planted seven small plots on the south ridge above the ISC, the same place I used to escape to, to meditate. This was a time when growing marijuana in the National Forest was prevalent and highly illegal. I was aware that random helicopter overflights scouted for pot plantations. So, I created small plots in shady spots and fenced them in with chicken wire spray painted a light green to blend in with the landscape. My friend Emily helped me carry up five-gallon tins on backpacks to water the gangitoes.

I was increasingly depressed, dissociated, and suicidal, trapped in my own inability to speak my truth, to act from my truth, and to free myself from this intolerable situation. "Good father" had morphed into "bad father" and I was trapped "at home" again. Suicidal imagery was rampant and insistent. I saw a hand bring up a gun pointed at my head and pull the trigger, I saw a hand bring up a gun pointed at my head and pull the trigger. . . . Where was this shit coming from? I wasn't about to act on it, but it was disturbing and distressing that such movies were playing in my head. Sometimes, I could not get back into my body to get up in the morning, even with Nooradeen standing over me and yelling at me.

Then came the final kicker. We were building an adobe utility shed to house a generator below the ISC, digging out the site, pouring concrete foundations, putting up the walls—days of hot, sweaty group work. Nooradeen, who had always worked right along with everybody, who had always worked harder than anybody, had a new profile. Now he sat on a log, dressed in robes, puffing a pipe, talking to a crony, and watching us as we labored in silence. This was really pissing me off. When I had had enough, I laid down my shovel and walked away. Nooradeen leaped up, ran after me, shoved me to the ground, and started kicking me, cursing me, and demanding that the devil leave my body. Everybody else just stood around and watched in silence until, devil cast out, I got up and went back to work.

I never fought back against Nooradeen, just as I never fought back against my father. Having been raised in an authoritarian family, I adapted well to an authoritarian cult led by another authoritarian individual, Noradeen. I grew up in a home that felt like a military prison camp. Now I felt like I lived in an Islamic internment center, trapped by my own submission-to-authority complex.

In April, Sufi dancing began again in the Lama Dome, much to my delight. Nooraissa, a dance leader herself, joined the circle. But when the chant became *"Hare Krishna Hare Rama,"* she fled out of the Dome shouting, "Not two gods! Only One God! Only One God!"

Varda was getting restless and finally left me and Lama. First she went to New York for a month. Then she left for California, indefinitely. But we stayed in touch.

There was a Sufi dance camp at Lama in June. I had to leave the ISC and move to Lama for the week to participate in this wonderful gathering of musicians and dance leaders from the Bay Area.

I was living back at the ISC when, at Annual Meeting, I was given consensus to be a continuing (lifetime) member of Lama Foundation and was elected by the Board of Trustees to be the Lama Treasurer for the coming year. This was something Nooradeen had set up so that he could have an inside man among the officers of the Foundation. But it didn't work out that way. I had had enough.

I promised Siddiq, the Coordinator, that I would be back in the fall to take on the bookkeeping. Within a week I packed up my VW van and left my room at the ISC. Nooradeen refused to speak to me. Nobody waved goodbye. I drove out to California in search of my beloved Varda.

## July 1976

I was driving to San Francisco when my van burned out in Bakersfield. This happened a lot with the old VW air-cooled engines, especially while driving across places like the Mojave Desert, even more so when driven by unmechanical, ungrounded types like me. I left my bus to have its engine rebuilt in Bakersfield and took the bus to San Francisco, Marin County, and the Garden of Allah, where they let me crash for a few days until I could move into Karima's house on Dominga, in Fairfax. Her house was a godsend, a shady little cottage whose main room was a wooden-floored dance space with an upright piano. The deal was that I was housesitting so that Karima could remain at Lama for a few months.

Ahad Cobb, Fairfax,
California, fall 1976.

Transiting Sun was conjunct transiting Saturn and this was the exact time of my first Saturn return. I was totally stuck and my life absolutely had to change, whether I knew it or not. As lord of the ninth house of father in my horoscope, Saturn represents the father and, more specifically at this time, the failure of the father to provide a workable model of how to deal with reality, or more truthfully, my failure to have a workable model of how to deal with reality. This was not the fault of my blood father nor my other father figures. This was the archetype I was dealing with at this time.

Saturn is conjunct Pluto in my chart. Personal, paternal parental authority, my own ability to have a grounded, stable life maintained by hard work, self-discipline, and healthy boundaries (Saturn) is undermined by the transpersonal collective necessity of evolution as embodied in mass movements, spiritual and communal in my case, and accompanied by the unleashing of the collective shadow in drugs, sex, and rock and roll (Pluto).

Saturn is right at the bottom of my chart in the life arena of family, home, and motor vehicles, among other things. My VW bus with the mattress in the back was my home, home on the road, my nomadic home to carry me through all life's changes without ever having to pay to stay anywhere. And now I was without a car.

In two weeks' time, I went back to Bakersfield to pick up my bus, but on the way home, the oil cap blew off the engine and I limped into Marin with another burnt-out motor—and this time it took two months for my engine to get rebuilt again. I didn't have a car the whole time I was in Fairfax. My car karma was an image of my life. I didn't know how to take care of myself. I kept overheating, running out of oil, and blowing my gaskets. I was massively depressed, withdrawn, isolated, intoxicated, and *incommunicado* the whole time.

As soon as I moved into the little house in Fairfax, Varda came to join me. It was her Saturn return, too, and she was undoubtedly equally disoriented. But we did our best to love each other and have a home together. We had several pregnancy scares, but nothing ever came of it.

At that time I became more acutely aware that I still did not know how to love another person. Mr. Gurdjieff suggests that ordinary man is incapable of love; if he wants to learn how to love another, he should start by loving an animal. So, I decided to try loving the shy white cat that passed through our backyard. I left milk out for her. After a while she was coming for milk every night. After a while she came into the house for food. After a while she jumped up onto my lap to be stroked and adored. After a while she moved in. Loving the cat was successful.

> *Let everyone ask himself simply and openly whether he can love all men. If he has had a cup of coffee, he loves; if not, he does not love. How can this be called Christianity?*
> GEORGE GURDJIEFF

Bizarrely enough I was still practicing Islam. What else was there to do? I observed Ramadan all alone, fasting from sunrise to sunset in the heat of late August. I found that I love fasting but that not drinking any water all day is very hard on the body. Between fasting all day, then smoking dope and making music at night, I was pretty blitzed.

One afternoon I went to visit Frida Waterhouse in San Francisco. Frida was the almost blind, wise old woman of the Sufi community. I went to visit Frida just to hang out and help her with shopping, or so I told myself.

"Now what's the real reason for your visit, dearie?" she said. "If you're thinking about killing yourself. . . ."

(What? I hadn't said a word about anything like that.)

"If you're thinking about killing yourself, you can just forget it right now. If you were to get rid of your body, nothing would change. You'd still be here with all your problems. Everything would be exactly the same—except you wouldn't have a body in which to work out your problems."

Wow! Frida set me straight once and for all.

໑໑

All too soon our romantic idyll was over. In October it was time for me to leave Varda and drive back to Lama to assume my duties as Treasurer. Along with breaking down my ego, my car, and everything else, Saturn was giving me a certain recognition and responsibility, a job to do in the community, a chance to do something real with my life—and stop being a pseudo-Muslim serving the wrong master.

The main function of the Treasurer was writing checks, making deposits, keeping the books, and bringing all financial decisions to the community. Siddiq was my accounting mentor. Back in the day before computers, before Quicken, before there was even any electricity at Lama, bookkeeping was done the good old-fashioned way, with pencil and eraser and an adding machine on which you punched in the numbers and pulled the lever and clank-clank-clank got a printout on a roll of paper. Every sum had to be done twice to double check it. Transactions were entered into a journal, and each journal entry was categorized in a general ledger. It was a long, tedious, detail-oriented process certain to keep me grounded.

There was a good solid community at Lama that winter: Siddiq, Jamil and Arielle, Micha, Peter and Polly, Emily and Peter, Kate and Leroy, Shirin, and Joe Jackson. Varda came to join me at the end of January. We lived across from the kitchen in the Dewdrop Inn, a single room with a great view built on top of the larder.

The rift with the ISC was growing deeper. Nooradeen was growing more bellicose in his demand that everyone who was not Muslim leave the land, although he did relent and said that he would allow "People of the Book," observant Jews and Christians, to stay as well. As someone who had been practicing Islam and was no longer practicing Islam, I was worse than a kafir, an unbeliever, in their eyes. I was a *murtad,* an apostate. I was shunned. My former so-called friends at the ISC refused to speak to me, refused even to meet my eyes. Given that the traditional punishment of *irtidad,* apostasy, is imprisonment or execution, I was lucky just to get the cold shoulder.

Lama Foundation held consensus meetings in the fall and in the spring, when continuing (lifetime) members would give consensus (or not) to each participating member to continue for the next six months. Everyone's residence and membership had to be renewed every six months. Although he had not participated in Lama politics for the last six years, Nooradeen was a continuing member with permanent voting status. He announced that he was going to come to the spring meeting and deny consensus to everyone who did not obey the law of the Torah, the Holy Bible, or the Holy Qur'an. This is the fatal flaw of governance by consensus: one ego can block everything. This was the start of the Holy War at Lama.

This was shaping up to be a *mano a mano* confrontation between Coordinator Siddiq and his ex-brother-in-law Nooradeen, who stole his wife and now wanted to steal back possession of the land. Before calling the formal spring meeting, Siddiq asked for an informal pre-meeting between the two sides to see if our differences could be ironed out.

The day of this pre-meeting I got word that Nooradeen wanted to talk to me at the ISC. This aroused my curiosity. He had not spoken to me or me to him for eight months now. I went through the gate in the fence and into the ISC. No one spoke to me or looked me in the eye, but I was shown a place to sit down by the wood stove. It was creepy. After a while Nooradeen came over, sat down, and started talking at me, not looking at me, just talking, setting forth all his well-known arguments, trying to persuade or influence me. As he was talking with me I became aware of a warm delicious energy flowing into my belly and filling my whole body. I was astounded. I was witnessing a warm blissful energy that presumably flowed from his belly into my belly and filled every cell of my body with a golden glow. He was definitely influencing me. Was he doing this intentionally or was this happening unconsciously? Had I been energetically influenced, mesmerized, all along and could only recognize it after going cold turkey from him for eight months?

I'll never know the answers to these questions. What I do know is that I sat mute through the whole meeting that day, never saying a word, my body glowing with a warm blissful buzz. I felt like I had just been laid. My body was in love. Nooradeen was, of course, intransigent and unyielding in his demands to refuse consensus to everyone, to act as the religious judge of people's behavior. Siddiq, very wisely, not to mention cleverly, asserted his authority as Coordinator and refused to call the spring meeting at all—so that the status quo of membership and residence would, by default, extend to the Annual Meeting in June, at which time all concerned with Lama could gather.

∞∞∞

## May 1977

My mother came to visit me and Varda, consciously or unconsciously giving our union her blessing, which had been withheld for two years. (My father still refused to speak to me.) Mom had us all stay at La Fonda in Santa Fe.

In my imagination it was on the big colonial bed surrounded by adobe walls painted with colorful New Mexican folk scenes that we conceived Abe. In Varda's recollection it was in the Muffin House the night before my mom came. "You looked like a prince, golden. I had never seen you like this before."

Varda saw Abe's spirit very clearly: "a handsome blonde boy full of joy and enthusiasm for life," which is exactly the way he was as a child. I have to accept her recollection, because women have a way of knowing these things, and I know I was totally in the dark at this time.

Two weeks later, a big drama ensued. I needed a retreat to prepare for a program I was going to offer with Jamil that summer: Astrology and The Night Sky. I was Astrology. Jamil was The Night Sky. I needed to get away from Lama so that I could concentrate and generate a lot of teaching material or at least talking points. I had found a place to stay in Santa Fe for the weekend. And of course, Varda had to come. She wouldn't let me go away to be alone. She swore she wouldn't bother me. She wouldn't say a word. But just having her there made it difficult for me to concentrate. And of course, she did say a word. I didn't start writing until Sunday morning.

Her anxiety drama centered on whether to go to Tucson and study with the so-called Sufi teacher E. J. Gold. Back and forth she went in a maelstrom of indecision. I was frustrated and angry that she was intruding on my work space. Finally, on the way back to Lama, I put her out of the car on the side of the road and drove away—and then came back to get her. The next morning she left for Tucson, leaving me wasted from all this drama.

I was disgusted with myself for putting up with all of this. I came to a firm, unshakeable decision that I was going to separate from Varda once and for all. I would never sleep with her again. This was just too crazy-making for me. Never again. That's when she came back from Tucson, two weeks later, and said, "Guess what, honey—I'm pregnant!"

Tremendous joy and life flooded my body. We were going to have a child! I was going to be a father! Both of us were blissfully happy. Something soulful and hormonal momentarily overrode all our personality difficulties. This was bigger than both of us. We had to get married right away!

The last two times we thought we were pregnant there had been no doubt in our minds. There was no way we were going to have a child. We would do anything to prevent it except, of course, use birth control. But once we were actually pregnant and full of new life, there was no doubt or question for either of us. We were blessed with new life to cherish.

## June 29, 1977

All dressed in white, Varda and I were married in the Lama Dome under the *chuppah,* the Jewish wedding canopy. Shirin graciously presided. She told us to write our own vows. Varda pledged some incredibly idealistic, romantic vows that would be impossible to fulfill. I realistically pledged to do all I could to resolve the differences between us, which also proved to be impossible to fulfill. It was a beautiful wedding celebration, full of sparkly love and tears, music, and dancing in the Dome. Even the Muslim brothers and sisters came, although when we were doing a blessing dance that asked you to touch the tips of your fingers to your partner's heart, they all muttered, "Haram! Haram!" and fled out of the Dome. If I had known they were going to leave like that, I would have had wine rather than grape juice at my wedding.

Varda and I were given the Muffin House to live in, a three-room adobe house, with two bedrooms off a central round room, in a clearing in the forest way down the hill in the southwest corner of the property. Surya had built this house for his wife, Tenney, when they had a little muffin in the oven. Now we could nest.

☙❧

Simultaneously, the Holy War was in full swing: anxiety and insecurity, suspicion and paranoia, wars and rumors of war, fear and loathing at Lama Foundation. Things got very weird very fast. I can only remember a few exemplary incidents.

Leroy told me that he had been a tracker in the army in Vietnam and that he had spent an entire afternoon tracking Nooradeen, who had been skulking around the forest spying on people's houses. "Oh, that's what he was doing," I told him. "I saw him sneaking away through the scrub oak from the window of my house one afternoon."

At the ISC the Muslims said that they had tethered a lamb outside to be slaughtered for one of their feast days, but when they came outside the next morning the lamb was gone, stolen away by the kafirs. None of us at Lama heard anything about this at the time, but then again why would we? At any rate, the purloined lamb is part of the mythology.

Shirin, however, was not worried. She said she saw a positive outcome of this.

"How can you possibly see a positive outcome of all of this?" I asked her.

"I see the back of Nooradeen and Nooraissa's heads driving down the road off the mountain," she said. "I see them going forward to fulfill their vision of founding an Islamic community."

And that is exactly what eventually happened.

## June 21, 1977

At Annual Meeting, Nooradeen brought in Muslim scholars to expound on the superiority of Islam. They sat on one side of the circle in gleaming white robes, with neatly trimmed black beards and turbans. Their arguments were very convincing but no one was convinced. They spoke over our heads but never touched our hearts.

Lama Dome interior.

On the other side of the circle in the Dome many longtime friends of Lama came to listen and support the residents—Ram Dass, Cynthia West, Henry and Suzy Gomez, John Kimmey, Saul Baradofsky, Wali Ali Meyer, and Joshua Zim. Many of them made statements testifying to the vitality and validity of the Lama experiment, as did resident community members Siddiq, Jamil and Arielle, Micha, Peter and Polly, Leroy and Kate, Shirin and Joe.

It was the myth of Kronos, the Saturn father, trying to devour his children. All of the people participating in the Lama experiment were the embodiment of values, structures, and intentions that Steve Durkee had originally set forth. Now Nooradeen wanted to deconstruct Lama and recast it in the mold of Islam, not with warmth and generosity, but with the harsh fanaticism of the newly converted. The people participating in the Lama experiment stood their ground. The children would not allow the father to devour them.

I was determined to play my part in this fray. I had to give the Treasurer's report, usually a boring non-controversial topic. I wanted to challenge the ISC's claim to be economically self-sufficient. I knew for a fact that they were taking generous quantities of fruits and vegetables from the Lama larder and giving us a mere pittance in compensation. I presented a detailed six-month study of exactly what foodstuffs the ISC took from the Lama larder as compared with the measly compensation they rendered, demonstrating that in fact the ISC was sucking money out of Lama despite claims to the contrary.

Nooradeen leaped to his feet, glared at me, and growled, "You cur!" as he stormed out of the Dome.

That was the last I saw him or spoke to him in this life. That was my thirtieth birthday.

The final resolution was reached by the Board of Trustees, on whom the final responsibility for Lama Foundation rests, at a separate meeting off the land. They decided that all the founding members of Lama should leave the land and entrust the Foundation to the care of the younger generation of residents, releasing the Foundation from the original family constellation, which had been torn apart by infidelity and religious divisiveness. It is likely that some kind of payoff was given to Nooradeen on his way out.

Jamil was elected Coordinator, Arielle became Secretary, and I stayed on as Treasurer.

Micha, Abd'al Hayy, took over the Islamic studies program at the ISC in a kinder, gentler mode. Eventually the fence came down. There were no longer two separate communities. Eventually the prayer dome on the ISC was completed. The ISC became a study center within Lama Foundation. Islamic studies continued for several years. Then Ron and Bonnie Reese led two years of Christian studies there, the last major resident study program at the ISC. Some summer retreats were held at the ISC, but gradually it became used for guest housing in the summer and overflow housing in the winter. Over time it lost the focus of its original purpose.

The so-called Holy War at Lama was a subtle foreshadowing of the global conflict between fundamentalist Islam and modern culture. The Lama community was firmly in the tradition of idealist spiritual communities going back through the Shakers all the way to the Essenes. The community of newborn Muslims reflected some of the paradoxes inherent in Islam: tolerance and yet intolerance, peacefulness and yet wrathfulness, surrender yet struggle. Although I had experienced the deep peace and beauty of Islamic culture in Turkey and on the Mount of Olives, my experience at the ISC was that of demand for uniformity and conformity under threat of punishment, spiritual and otherwise. In this situation my challenge was to reclaim the truth I knew in my being and take back the power I had ceded to Nooradeen. I didn't have a prophetic message for the community or the world, but I knew the love in my heart and the authority in my voice were welcomed by the brothers and sisters at Lama.

That fall I received a letter from the Sufi Order. Pir Vilayat was asking all his mureeds to pledge to not use marijuana. If they could not make this commitment, he asked them to resign from the Sufi Order.

I took inventory. I was using marijuana at the time. I did not foresee stopping any time soon. I had been initiated into the seventh level of the Sufi Order with the requirement that I smoke copious amounts of ganga at an ungodly hour, initiated by a man who had now rejected the Sufi Order. My original initiator, Pir Vilayat, was remote and distant. I sent in my letter of resignation. I was decommissioned from the ranks of the spiritual hierarchy.

# 6 LIVING LAMA, 1977–1983

After the founders left Lama, the next generation was young yet matured by the fire of the Holy War, chastened and strengthened by the threat to our very survival as a group on the land. Community meditation practice continued morning and evening in the silence of the prayer room. Core community values seemed to be living love, selfless service, and welcoming the guest. Travelers from all spiritual traditions and no traditions at all were welcome. The primary streams of blessing came from Murshid Sam, who was buried on the mountain, and Maharaj-ji (Neem Karoli Baba), whose ashram was being built in Taos.

Asha later observed that in the coming and going of generations of Lama beans (beings), certain groups would fall in love with each other and flourish in harmony for a while before everything and everyone moved on, as they always do, and there would be less cohesion for a while. The next four years under Jamil and Arielle as Coordinators were one of those times we fell in love with each other and with God in one another.

At the very beginning Lama was a closed community with a strong gate. We discouraged visitors and were very selective about who was allowed to stay.

> *When the oak is small you keep a fence around it to keep the cows from trampling it. When the oak is full grown its shade can shelter many cows.*
>
> HARI DAS BABA

Lama Foundation Dome.

Now we welcomed the guest, albeit in measured doses. Every Sunday in the summer was visitors' day. We would have a land tour, feed everybody, answer questions, and have a large circle in the Dome for the Dances of Universal Peace. Visitors were welcomed warmly. But we weren't a campground or a crash pad. If people were interested in joining us, they were invited to come back and ask for consensus at our next business meeting. One would get consensus for a week or two at a time, coming back up for consensus, then a month or two at a time, leading up to forming the winter community at the Fall Meeting.

Maharaj-ji told us to love everyone, serve everyone, and remember God always and everywhere. Murshid Sam's program for peace on Earth was to eat, dance, and pray together.

The ideal of seva, or selfless service, is an antidote to the inherent selfishness and competitiveness that is society's norm. Most of us are conditioned to act from self-interest. Karma yoga offers service to others as a path to God. We habitually walk through the world seeing all the things that need to be done, that should be done—by someone else. "Someone should. . . ." "They should really. . . ." "You really need to. . . ." Lama's watchword was, "A being sees it, a being does it." Don't stop to think that someone else should do something that needs to be done. Just do it. Wash the dishes. Sweep the floor. Clean the outhouse.

Find joy in selfless service. Polish the mirror of the heart with the cloth of service.

A being sees it, a being does it.

Of course, if just a few people do this, then they are the servants of everyone else. But if everyone agrees to this ideal then we all serve each other and great harmony prevails. I have no complaints whatsoever. Thank you very much.

This was and continues to be a great antidote for my inherent self-absorption, laziness, and inattentiveness, no doubt a by-product of my mother doing everything for me when I was young. When in doubt, serve somebody.

There was great heart openness in the Lama community. We were glad to see each other every morning and enjoyed an ease of intimacy at all hours of the day. We all had our tasks, but what was going on in one another's souls was of primary importance. At the morning tuning circle, before getting to the business of the day, we would do a brief practice and then go around the circle for a brief check-in from each and every person. How are you today? No hiding. Our personal lives were part and parcel of our public lives. There were secrets kept at Lama, but not that many. There was an atmosphere of instant intimacy, even with strangers who came up the road, who were probably long-lost friends. It was a caravanserai where souls were curious and loved to get to know each other, to know one's self in another.

Friendship at Lama was deep and tribal. We had left our homes behind and now were home to each other. We were living on the land together, most of us for the first time, caring for and being nurtured by the mother. We maintained daily, weekly, and seasonal cycles of sacred ritual and prayer. We had fought a war together and prevailed. We had no charismatic leader. We held everything in common and did everything together. Submission of personal wishes to the needs of the collective, sitting together to find the will of the collective, was a daily activity. We were seeking unity of heart, not uniformity of behavior, respecting, honoring, and even admiring the uniqueness of each person's spiritual path. We came together for community work and practice, but that did not define us as individuals.

*The democracy of the ego and the aristocracy of the soul. . . .*

PIR VILAYAT KHAN

Hanging out was a major spiritual practice. Later on, my analyst told me that at Lama I experienced the peer group bonding I had missed out on in high school. Then I was always seething and curdling on the fringes of adolescent agony. Now I was bathing in the warmth of a big group hug.

*If you love not one another*
*in daily communion,*
*how can you love God*
*whom you have never seen?*

SHAKER SONG

We had no telephone, no TV, no radio—just one funky cassette player and a few chanting tapes in the kitchen. We didn't read the news or go to movies. We had each other (and the Lama library) for inspiration, information, and entertainment. We had each other's songs and stories and dreams and dramas, and never-ending maintenance, construction projects, gatherings, and meetings, meetings, meetings. . . .

Each morning the work for the day would be allocated at the tuning meeting. Lama was a volunteer organization. Everyone volunteered to work and nobody got paid. I was somewhere in between the full-service beans who would volunteer for every and any thing and the slacker beans who got assigned because they never raised their hands. I knew I had to do something for the community every day, so I found the jobs that fit me best and volunteered for them. For instance, I didn't like to cook, so I learned that I loved to clean.

Aside from the work wheel (cooking, cleaning, etc.) and the ongoing projects, there were a number of "masterships" or semi-permanent roles of responsibility for certain areas, such as kitchen master, dome master (housekeeping), garden master, hermit master (hermitages), outhouse master, and trash master, to name a few. My favored roles were trash and cash.

The most important function that rotated among us was the watch, changing every new moon. The watch was the time-keeper and overseer of the community. The watch would ring the wake-up bells and lead the sit in the prayer room. The watch would lead the morning tuning meetings, starting off with simple practices and prayers. The watch conducted the weekly business meetings. The watch greeted all visitors to the land and kept an awareness of the comings and goings of residents. Anyone coming to the land had to check in with the watch. The overall function of the watch was to be the one to hold the whole community in one's heart and mind for a full lunar cycle.

The most eternal and ever-changing aspect of Lama mountain is the vista, the west view from anywhere on the land. The mountainside sweeps down fifteen hundred feet to the flat ancient seabed of the Taos Mesa, which is split open north-south by the rift of the Rio Grande Gorge, as if hands had reached into the earth and torn it apart. The mesa stretches west to Ute Mountain and Antonito Peak, gently sloping like flattened footballs, and what look like small volcanic cones. In the early days there was a perpetual white plume coming up from a perlite mine in one of the cones. In the far distance the snowy peaks of southern Colorado are just visible, and to the southwest the tabletop of Abiquiu's Pedernal.

West view from Lama Foundation.

You can always see the weather coming in from the west, clouds sailing over this vast serene space, high wispy clouds, white puffy clouds, towering cumulus clouds, dark and stormy clouds, a never-ending invitation to open your mind and let the clouds drift through. You can always see a rainstorm coming from far away, although in the summer monsoons, thunder clouds tend to build over the mountains to the east and then suddenly come down with intense rain. On winter days, the whole sky can be overcast and gloomy, promising snow, sometimes with mysterious lenticular clouds embedded in the gray curtain. Most enchanting is the walking rain. Groups of clouds trailing veils of rain move across the distant landscape. Shafts of sunlight weave through the walking rain. All sorts of fantastical creatures, especially birds and sky dragons, appear in the clouds at all times of the year.

I was in love with the clouds and spent many years capturing cloud language on film at the Lama Mountain Cloud Observatory.

*Stunned dry in the sun*
*we see the sky armada come*
*over two hundred miles of whaleback mountains*
*sagebrush and seco plateau*
*endless clouds*
*trailing bridal veils of rain*
*the Tewa call "the sky loom"*
*high white wandering shrouds*
*soon gray clouds bleeding over us*

*The crickets rouse*
*The birds hush*

*After the shower*
*when the rain shakes down from the trees*
*we find turkey feathers in the forest*
*and new grass in the dust*

What I valued most highly in this time at Lama was the ordinary, everyday communion of souls in relaxed and open communication in a spacious, non-pressured environment. Waking up together was an unpretentious ongoing conversation—the big quack, as Arielle would say. One could pretty much say anything to anybody or hear anything from anybody—with soul resonance and without judgment. Some of my best conversations took place while mudding adobe walls or mixing mud for the mudders. I made friends with all sorts of people who were definitely not "my type." My humanity deepened as my heart opened. The circle and the mountain itself seemed to polish our auras and allow bright shiny beings to show through the clouds of personality.

One did not come to Lama if one was pursuing sex or money or power. Imagine an environment where you're not constantly digging into your pocket for money to make your way through the world. Imagine not being in constant competition with others to get a little money or status or power. Imagine a cooperative society based on mutual service with no material rewards to take away. Lama was and is a caravanserai for souls on the inner journey—Hindus, Sufis, Buddhists, Jews, Christians, Yogis, lost souls, found treasures, basket cases, and nascent geniuses.

Personally I liked adobe work. Shovel the dirt and sand into a tin-lined trough, add water and a splash of asphaltum, get your hoes, and start mixing. Adobe mud is funky, messy, and very forgiving. Put the mud into buckets and carry it over to the wall. Grab handfuls of mud and put it up on the wall. It is very hard to do it wrong, although there is an art to it, as you discover. Mudding is such a no-brainer, it allows the mind to wander, to open up to speculation, to conversation, to song. . . .

*If you love one another*
*and God is within you,*
*then you are made pure*
*to live in the light.*

SHAKER SONG

Most of the Santa Fe–style houses you see are not adobe; they are concrete block and brown stucco, much easier to maintain. Adobe, they say at Taos Pueblo, washes down off the walls every winter and every spring you scrape it up and put it back up on the walls.

Most of the pilgrims who came to Lama were hippies, but there were some notable exceptions. Lomax Littlejohn had been a wealthy stock-broker with a wife and children, a big house on Long Island, a yacht, and a private airplane, so the story goes, until he took LSD, dropped out, and went to India. At Lama this big handsome man was a blissful soul who tended the chicken coop with great affection for his hens. He plastered the walls of the chicken coop with pictures of Maharaj-ji, Jesus, and himself—guru pictures for the egg-layers. He moved on to become Mr. Hotsie-Totsie, the cheerful hot-dog vendor on Taos Plaza.

Peter and Polly Adams were successful businesspeople who left Philadelphia and came to Lama with their three children. Polly had a normal Christian background. One day she spoke up and said, "I have found all this mantra practice very difficult to relate to, but I want you all to know that I have searched and I have found my mantra. My mantra is "Thank You."

She inspired me to make gratitude a perpetual practice.

In the fall of 1977 Peter Adams was replacing the insulation in the Tower House so that his family of five could spend the winter there. (This was the house that Steve built on the ridge over the garden next to a tree that had been struck by lightning to replace his first house that had gone up in flames.) One cold November morning I was woken up by the fire bell ringing and came down to see the Tower House totally engulfed in a pillar of flame. Fortunately, there was no wind that morning or the fire would have leapt into the forest. With bucket brigades and hoses we managed to extinguish the fire. We realized that it was a blessing that no one was living in the house at that time. Our best guess was that the gas heater in the house had caused the fire.

We were all standing around this huge mound of smoldering black timber in the pale dawn light when Peter, a Libra, said, "Anything that brings us all together can't be all that bad!"

## February 7, 1978

In the early morning hours, Varda went into labor in the Muffin House. We called the midwife, Trish Denim, to come up the mountain, which was deep in snow and very cold. We were going to deliver the baby at home. But, when Trish came, she found the baby was presenting posterior and she didn't have the forceps needed. We were going to have to go to the hospital. I loaded Trish and Varda on the bed in the back of my van and drove down the snowy road to Taos. By the time we got to the highway, Varda was screaming her head off, terrifying me. I kept looking back at her and swerving all over the road.

The sun was coming over the mountain by the time we pulled into Taos. Smoke was pouring out of the rear wheel wells of my bus. My brake pads had burned up and I hardly had any brakes. Somehow I maneuvered through morning traffic with minimal brakes and got us to Holy Cross Hospital on the other side of town—just in time.

Within the hour, Varda delivered a healthy baby boy. He was tiny and quiet and alert, looking around with bright little eyes. The only time he cried was when they put silver nitrate drops in his eyes. I held my baby boy while Varda was being sewn up from the episiotomy they had to perform. He was a fully present, fully conscious being. I spoke to him this way: "Welcome to Planet Earth. My name is Ahad. I am your earthly father. This is Varda. She is your earthly mother. We will love you and provide for you and guide you until you are fully grown. . . ." We both were fully aware of each other.

When Varda was ready I gave the baby back to her. Micha and Karima were present at Abe's birth. Micha took pictures for us, including the crowning moment. We all went to a quiet room where

Karima led us in singing angelic greetings of peace. Varda never let go of her baby. She stayed two nights in the hospital while I stayed with my friend Tui and got my brake pads replaced.

Varda wanted to name him Abraham. I wanted to name him Gabriel. We named him Abraham Gabriel Cedar Cobb. We called him Gabe or Abe Gabe when he was young, until he was six years old and began calling himself Abe and Abraham.

On the third day, a gentle snow started falling just as we drove up the mountain, which the Tibetans say is a good omen. We settled into our little nest at the Muffin House. Gabe spent the first days of his life in his mother's arms and at his mother's breast. But on the fourth night he was crying so much that Varda finally lost patience with him, put him down, and said to me, "I can't deal with this anymore. You deal with him."

So, I went in and held my son and loved him, to no avail. I smiled and cooed and talked to him. He was howling and screaming. I sang little songs to him just as my grandmother had to me. More howling and screaming. Nothing I did had any effect on his unhappiness. Finally, something inside me snapped, and a brutal surge of raw anger filled my whole body. I shook my baby—just once. Immediately, I heard my own voice saying inside me, "I'll never do this to anyone. I'll never do this to anyone."

When I was a child I would be shut away in my room when I was "out of control." I must have had a lot of energy, too much energy for my parents to deal with. I would be talked to, shouted at, not talked with nor listened to. And when that didn't work, I would be shut away in my room until I could calm down. My energy would turn into anger and go global as unrestrained howling and screaming until finally I exhausted myself.

I was outraged that my father would so disrespect and suppress me that he would lock me in my room until I could calm down and shut up. I cried and howled and screamed and told myself over and over again, "I'll never do this to anyone. I'll never do this to anyone."

As a small child I felt that I was unfairly treated, not listened to, not respected, not held, not loved, and I vowed that I would never do this to anyone. I had forgotten all about this, never thought of it, but the minute I lost my temper with Gabe, my decision spoke to me clearly and forcefully across twenty-five years. "I'll never do this to anyone."

I recognized that this awesome anger arising in me was not my own creation. It was my father's anger expressed on me that I had stored in my body . . . which in turn was his father's anger that had been expressed on him and stored in his body . . . which in turn was his father's anger . . . and so on back to the caveman. Did my father shake me when I was a baby to get me to shut up? My mind doesn't know, but my body remembers.

I was grateful for that decision, a truly healthy decision that I had made as a child, and amazed again at the power of a decision, which, once made, is imprinted on the soul, though it may sleep for centuries. I never again used any physical force on my son.

Abe Gabe was a total delight. The luminous presence of the newborn grew into a sturdy blonde toddler who explored the wonders of nature and all the big friendly people in the community. Gabe was not a fussy or whiny baby. He was calm, curious, joyful, and playful. He had plenty of little friends to play with and no need of direct supervision since there were always adults nearby.

The first time we took him to a restaurant he would not sit still. He had to go around to all the tables and see what everyone was eating. The first time we took him to a movie, *The Last Waltz,* he could not stay still. He went up and down the aisle offering our bag of popcorn to everyone.

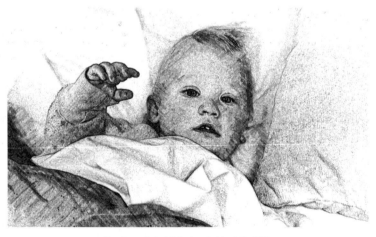

Abraham Gabriel Cedar Cobb, fall 1978.

Parental love was unlike anything I had ever experienced: deep, unshakeable, grounded, protective, nurturing. Someone to give everything to. This new station of fatherhood altered my relation with everyone around me. I began seeing the world from a parental, paternal perspective. I was walking by the garage one day and noticed someone doing something potentially dangerous with a chain saw. I walked right over and corrected him. Before, I would not even have noticed and just walked right by.

When Gabe was seven days old, he was ritually circumcised by a Jewish doctor who put on a little yarmulke, said a few Hebrew prayers, put Gabe's penis in a cutting machine, and *whack!* I fainted dead away.

Varda was very happy as a mother. She loved nothing more than to be with her baby. But she was very pissed off and unhappy with me. "I've never been treated more horribly in my life than the way you treated me when I was pregnant." We both loved Gabe equally, but we slept separately from each other. We tried to make it work, but it just wasn't working. Varda was too angry and contemptuous and I was too . . . creepy, arrogant . . . a total bastard? I don't know. You'd have to ask her. At any rate, by the time Gabe was six months old, I had moved out of the Muffin House into my blue tent.

I had a newborn child and I was broke. I took the last of my money out of the bank the day Gabe was born. I knew I had to make some money to support my child.

I went on a two-week tree-planting contract in the mountains, ten thousand feet above Dolores, Colorado. It was miserable, back-breaking work in the rain, hail, and snow on steep, ugly, clear-cut slopes. These hippies were very competitive, and all they could talk about was money. The crew bosses had figured out a complex and highly inequitable compensation scheme enabling them to keep most of the money. I worked for two weeks, planted two thousand seedlings, and came away with just enough money to cover my gas and food for the trip. This was not the way to go.

I put the last of my money into printing up my Cloud Cards, a packet of eleven stunning black-and-white cloudscapes for $1.11. This was back in the days of offset printing, back when you had to do a large enough run just to cover the setup costs. I ended up with a huge inventory of Cloud Cards only to discover that I had no gift for self-promotion and could barely market my own product. This was not the way to go.

Although we spent another winter in the Muffin House, Varda took Gabe and moved out for good in the summer of 1979. We lived in separate houses the next winter. We divorced in the spring of 1980 when Gabe was two years old. We agreed to joint custody and honored that in the years to come. At the end of August, Varda took Gabe and moved to Santa Fe.

This was a heartbreaking and perilous decision. Gabe was two and a half years old. Varda had no car, no money, and minimal job skills. But she was very resourceful and soon found public assistance to support her while she developed job skills.

At the time I had to ask myself, "Would you rather be married to this woman or be alone for the rest of your life?" The answer was clear.

I was in a paradoxical position. I was finally comfortable and happy at Lama, taking responsibility and getting respect in the community, and my young family had been torn apart. It would take me time to realize that I needed to leave and be with Gabe.

Fall Meeting was the pivotal time every year at Lama. Everything stopped. We would have all-day meetings every day for as much time as it took to find consensus for membership in the winter community, generally a two-week process. It was a combination of job interview, soul sharing, life coaching, peer counseling, and relationship workshop, in which we really got to know each other. The group got to know each individual, and each individual got to know the group. The open-hearted part was easy. We all mostly loved each other, and there was a lot of space to become intimate with each person's personal reality. The hard part was setting the work agenda, responsibilities, and commitments for the next six months. Who would take on kitchen master, outhouse master, summer program planning, and so on? Commitment to community work and community spiritual practice was the area where the conversation often got stuck in negotiations.

Meeting in Lama Dome, image courtesy of the Lama Foundation.

As an example, I had great fondness for Gurnie Dobbs. He was a charming, elusive, enigmatic singer-songwriter who had a great fan base among the women. He thought he could get away with not committing to anything at all. Don't we all? Personally, I was in total agreement with him, but as a community member in the Fall Meeting, I had to let him know that if he could not commit to some specific forms of community work and practice, I could not give him consensus for the winter. I was speaking for the group, not for myself. I would have loved no commitment myself, but that's not the way a functional society works. I drew a hard line. He said he would think about it overnight, and he thought about it overnight, and the next day he said that, well, yes, he could commit to something.

Consensus process applied not only to membership, but to all decisions at weekly business meetings or any other meetings. We were told that consensus was the mode of governance in Native American tribes where a council of elders was responsible for the community. If we all came to agreement about something, we were all behind it. There could be no subsequent questioning or undermining of our decision, for we had all agreed. This involved a good deal of expressing individual opinions (everybody's got one) and then surrendering personal biases to the good of the greater whole. Since almost everyone had an opinion to air, the consensus process developed the compassion to listen to almost everyone's opinion almost all of the time. At Lama Foundation, we would say, process is our most important product.

> *In any organization there is a balance between efficiency and compassion. The more efficient, the less compassionate the organization is, and vice versa. Lama is a very compassionate organization.*
>
> RAM DASS

Consensus is a profoundly conservative method of governance. Nothing changes unless everyone agrees to it. It is difficult to budge the status quo from its default setting. Old way, good way. And the fatal flaw in consensus governance is that one person can block the will of the whole group, no matter how irrational or emotional the motivation (like a two-year-old shouting "No!"), and nothing can be done about it. Over the years, Lama has evolved ways to expand voting classes of membership and ways to dilute the tyranny of the veto. In some cases "an 80 percent majority vote shall suffice to make a decision, although the spirit of consensus is still to be sought" (Lama Foundation Bylaws). Or the lone dissenting person can choose to stand aside and not vote.

When you sit in a circle, there will always be someone sitting opposite you. Micha and I often found ourselves on opposite sides of the circle when it came to admitting short-term residents in the summer. Micha would ask tough questions and be very resistant to admitting certain people. I was generally willing to let anyone in.

Then one weekend, a very unique individual arrived. He had a bald head, big mustache, and hypnotic eyes. Within a day he had charmed all the ladies and most of the men. But not me. He rubbed me the wrong way. I thought he was the devil, not a typical thought for me. He came to the Monday business meeting and asked to stay for a while. Everybody was gushing over what an amazing being this was, even Micha. I looked him in the eyes and said no. I refused to let him stay, and I refused to explain myself. Everybody thought I was nuts, but it

Lama Dome window.

was my right to say no, with or without explanation, and we had lots of other business to take care of, so there was no discussion.

After the meeting, on the way out, this man came up to me and said, "You're the only one who recognized me for who I really am." He walked away, never to be seen again.

When I first came to Lama, I had to sit silently, mind churning with things to say, and watch others make the decisions. From having no voice in the circle at the beginning, I went to having a voice in the circle and then having a big voice in the circle. I just loved to hear myself pontificate, and so did everyone else, because they all got their turns as well. I discovered that I had a gift for listening, for synthesizing, and for presenting a clarifying overview of the topics under discussion. This ability sometimes served to give a unifying perspective on the diversity of the voices. For a while, I imagined that my voice was crucial to Lama's functioning.

As the years went by, I got tired of the sound of my own voice and my endless opinions about everything. I became more and more quiet, more and more trusting in the ability of the group mind to find its way without me straining at the bit to lead the way. I began to sit back and watch other people process the issues and realized that Lama could function just as well without my voice. All I needed to do was love, bless, and support the process.

☙❧

One cold full-moon November night in 1978, I was wandering around the forest paths near the ISC. The belligerent Muslims, under the leadership of Noradeen, were all gone. The ISC seemed like an empty shell in the bright moonlight, which flooded the meadow and penetrated into the forest. It was a beautiful night, yet I was restless, aimless, wracked with strange feelings of grief, devastation, and confusion. I could not understand where these feelings were coming from.

Several days later we heard that, on that very night, nine hundred people had been murdered and committed suicide in a religious cult community in Jonestown, Guyana. This cast a deep shadow on all spiritual communities, including us at Lama, and demonstrated the danger

of blind faith in charismatic cult leaders. This was what I had been picking up on, the source of my strange feelings that moonlit night.

*Communes gather at the edge of the desert like wagon trains making camp for the night. They dig in for winter along the mountain spine of the continent, big families holding hands around the hearth before meals, slowly learning the old ways, how to bless, how to pray. Taos Pueblo is quiet for weeks around the solstice, to let the Earth rest and watch the sun turn round. . . .*

*The horses shiver in their cold sleep. The eagles spend the long winter dreaming dazzled flight patterns, absorbed in the tongues of the Sun Heart dying in the south. Reading each other's minds, dreams, they finally awake with the same scream . . .*

*The tribes move like clouds over and live like birds in the mountains. Gypsy hermits hitchhike from forest to forest, steal away to hidden caves and canyons, eat brown rice, silence and light. The tribes find out who they are by what they eat and what they do when they do it all together. Old Tewa movies flicker at the empty drive-in. The drumming goes on until dawn . . .*

Lama closed down to a small resident circle during the winter snows and then opened up and blossomed during the late spring and summer. We would begin with a spring work camp in May, inviting people to come join us on staff for the summer. Typically people would pay for their room and board for six months before either becoming self-supporting resident staff or moving on. Ram Dass suggested to us that we have a refugee status, that we allow space for one or two people who couldn't pay for themselves, who couldn't take care of themselves, who just needed refuge.

Lama was the place in my life where I experienced essence, essential presence, in a sustained, normal, everyday sort of way—not as a numinous experience set apart from daily experience, as a radiant spiritual high generated by retreat, meditation, fasting, prayer, or chanting, but as simple all-pervading presence, so subtle that it is barely noticeable except as a lightness of being.

There were some days when harmony seemed to pervade the land, when there was such harmony between people simply living everyday lives, doing everyday tasks, nothing new, nothing special, when there was such deep harmony and love that it was like a little bit of heaven on Earth.

I am walking down the path in the sunny forest on my way to my job making mud. There is a gentle breeze, birdsong in the trees. I feel at ease with everyone. Everyone has their place, their job to do, their someone to love. There are no major dramas right now. We are making a life together on the land. Life is good. People are beautiful. We are truly blessed. Every now and then my heart lifts, and I feel harmony pervade the land.

Dream . . .

I am driving across the New Mexico desert in the moonlight in the backseat of an old Buick convertible with two ladies, getting very high and ecstatic . . .

We float straight up out of the moving car into the night . . .

momentary twinges of panic . . .

but we keep cool, keep gliding along, and after a while float gently back into the backseat in each other's arms, laughing . . .

Communal living was, for me, the perfect laboratory for astrological study. Not only were most people interested in knowing about their birth charts, but more importantly I could live with people for months and years, unobtrusively observing the ways in which they manifested (or not) the qualities of the planetary archetypes represented in their natal horoscopes. The apparent effects of the planets (Jupiter rising) and their locations (Saturn in the twelfth house) and their relationships (Mars square Venus) became gloriously and sometimes painfully obvious. I was learning astrology from life.

Although I did do a lot of readings, what mostly interested me was the astrology of everyday life. Where is the Moon today? What sign is it in? What aspects does it make to the other planets? What aspects do the planets make to each other? How do I experience this, if at all? What could be the effect on other people? Does Moon with Jupiter or Venus bring rain? Does Moon with Saturn bring windy, dry, and cold weather? Does the Moon changing signs reflect our ever-changing moods? Over time, I experienced the validity of astrological correspondences.

My two greatest guides in astrological study were the calendar and the ephemeris. A good astrological calendar shows lunar phases, lunar transits of signs, lunar aspects to planets, and all the planetary aspects. It is like reading an astral newspaper and staying alert to synchronicities and correspondences. Since the Moon is by far the most rapidly moving light in the sky, attention to the Moon yields the greatest wealth of day-to-day significances. Reading the ephemeris gives a broader long-term overview of past, present, and future planetary rhythms, more on a month-by-month basis.

When we are learning astrology, we tend to learn keywords, meanings, and rules of interpretation. We tend to say this planet means this or does that or causes this to happen, which, though inaccurate, is forgivable as a learning methodology. We could learn such dictums as, "If Saturn is in Leo in the eighth house, the person will be killed by lions in the desert." Symbolically, it is suggestive and memorable, but don't take it literally.

In reality, it is not planetary causation that is happening, though sometimes it seems as if it is, and sometimes very acutely. It is the correspondence, the resonance, the reflection of my tiny individuality in the greater whole of which I am an infinitesimal part that I am seeking when I gaze into the cosmos. I am looking for a greater frame of reference—not to understand how the greater picture fits into me but to understand how I fit into the greater picture.

Back in the day I did all my astrological calculations by hand, using an ephemeris, a slide rule for algorithms, and a table of houses. I drew up my charts by hand with colored pens on a circular template. It would take at least half an hour to erect a chart, not counting detours and errors. It was a tedious labor of love that rewarded me with a certain intimacy with the chart and often some unexpected surprises. Sometimes divinations emerged directly from calculations.

Of supreme interest to every young person is the perspective that astrology offers on love relationships. How does my chart match up with his? Is she the perfect match for me? Blind hormonal impulses do not always yield a stable or even workable relationship. In the Lama living laboratory I got to witness many dramatic couplings and un-couplings from an astrological perspective and discern the compatibility (the glue) and the challenges (the friction) between two charts. Her Moon conjunct his Sun means she loves him, all other things being equal. My Jupiter conjunct your Sun means I am big on you, all other things being equal. Your Saturn conjunct my Moon is a heavy, deep connection. And this one's Mars conjunct that one's Saturn is trouble waiting to happen.

True love does not always play by the rules. Some of the deepest love matches are not always the easiest or most comfortable, perhaps particularly for spiritually evolving people. But there does need to be some fundamental strength, some good glue, for a relationship to survive and thrive.

I was really challenged when Wendy fell in love with me and loved me—and I loved her—because our charts seemed to be totally incompatible. Everything was squared everything else. I tried to run away from her, using this as my excuse, but she came after me, and I surrendered. Who can say no to love? So, we had our journey in love until nine months later, it all fell apart and we separated. Only years later did I discover that our incompatible charts came perfectly together by mutual secondary progressions for just those nine months!

As much as I was enthusiastic about reading other peoples' charts, I was reluctant, in fact resistant, to having anyone else read my chart. I did make an exception for Genoa Bliven, who was a magnetic esotericist living with his family in nearby Sunshine Valley, north of Questa. He drew up my chart in an anthroposophic style: the planets were luminous orbs of pastel light floating above the chart circle. He presented me with this beautiful chart and proceeded to give me a very elevated reading without once looking at the chart or even referring to the planetary positions. He mostly seemed to be gazing at the space above my head. I'm not sure just what he was reading, but there was a lot of light in the room.

I was very impressed with Genoa's knowledge and enthusiasm. In fact, we went on to do some teaching together at Lama. Surrounded by glowing candles, he gave a very beautiful evocation of the death chart of St. Francis of Assisi. But I was dissatisfied with his reading for me, which seemed replete with generalities and platitudes that could apply to almost anyone on a soul level. I wanted to know what the stars had to say about the pickle I was in! What is my human drama? When will my suffering end? But I would have to wait for that.

The night sky is one of the joys of living in a high mountain meadow far from any light pollution, standing under infinite black space sprinkled with crystalline sparkles of light on which mind projects mythic patterns. Until very recently our ancestors sat under the eternal dome of the stars every night and told stories around campfires, recounted the legends written in the stars, the loves and battles and origin myths encoded in the sky, the stories the stars tell us. Awesome is the summer sky with the overarching Milky Way flowing down between the two giant southern constellations of Sagittarius and Scorpio.

> *The heavens are telling of the glory of God, and their expanse is declaring the work of His hands. Day to day pours forth speech, and night to night reveals knowledge.*
> PSALM 19:1–2

One Shabbas evening not long after sunset, red-haired Annie from down the hill said to me, "Ahad! Astrology is a lie! The calendar says

Image courtesy of Genoa Bliven.

the Moon is in Sagittarius and look! It's right in the middle of Scorpio!"

She was right. I could see the waxing crescent Moon smack dab in the ruddy heart of the heavenly scorpion! Fortunately, I knew it all already and had all the answers on the tip of my tongue.

Western astrology uses the tropical zodiac, I pontificated, which is based on the position of the Sun at the vernal equinox, the synthetic vernal point or SVP. Zero degrees of Aries in the tropical zodiac is defined by the ecliptic position of the Sun on that day in the spring when day and night are equal. Around the time of Christ this SVP was actually at zero degrees of Aries both in the tropical zodiac and the sidereal zodiac, the latter being the portions of the actual constellations in the sky. However, due to a long-term phenomenon known as the precession of the equinoxes, the SVP is seen to move backward against the stars over a cycle of—take a deep breath—twenty-six thousand years. Since that time two thousand years ago, the SVP has moved backward through the sky so that now the SVP, the Sun at the vernal equinox, is located at about six and a half degrees of the constellation of Pisces. This is zero degrees of Aries in the tropical zodiac. Whew!

All astrology was originally based on direct observation of the planets moving through the sidereal zodiacal constellations. But for some reason unknown to me, when astrology was rediscovered after it was lost during the Dark Ages, European astronomers and astrologers began using the tropical zodiac. It is probably more convenient to calculate. And all the significations the ancients assigned to the sidereal constellations gradually shifted into the displaced tropical signs. So, you see, I grandly concluded, that Moon you see in the heart of the heavenly scorpion is actually located at fifteen degrees of Sagittarius!

Little did I know that Annie had correctly discerned exactly what originally disturbed me about my natal horoscope. The tropical zodiac would prove to be a deceptive veil over the luminous truth of the sidereal constellations.

∞∞

We didn't walk around with money in our pockets. We didn't relate to each other through money. All our finances were communal. No one was required to give up all they owned. When one first arrived, one was asked to pay a daily fee for room and board for six months or so, but nothing thereafter when one was fully integrated into community work. No one was ever paid any money. All was held in common and each one had his or her own money as well.

I was a refugee from a wealthy family, to quote Joni Mitchell, although most of the boys I went to school with were from older, richer families. I experienced the wealth I grew up in as cold, isolating, and controlling. I did not appreciate all that I was given. Where was the love? Living on the land with hard-working people, some of whom were visionary artists, musicians, and mystics, allowed me to come into the warmth of humanity. Our lives depended on each other, not on credit cards or money in the bank.

Spiritual traditions place a high value on voluntary poverty or simplicity, choosing to have little or nothing and relying on God alone for everything. I had grown up isolated and independent, defiant and unhappy. I needed to experience the truth of interdependence with humanity and dependence on God.

I came to Lama in an old VW bus that was always breaking down or stalling out, that constantly needed to be jump-started or push-started. One summer I took my young son, three years old, camping in the wilderness north of Questa. Unwisely, I drove us up a steep rutted dirt road into the forest going toward Latir Lakes. An hour in, I foolishly drove straight into a big pool in the middle of the road and got stuck in the mud. The sky darkened as an afternoon thunderstorm drew near. Panic began to build. Here I was stuck in the middle of nowhere with my child with no help. God let me feel my helplessness before appearing in the form of two fisherman in a dirty rugged pickup truck, who threw a chain on my bumper and yanked me out of the muck. I was ashamed of my folly and grateful that there was help for my helplessness.

I continued to handle money for the group. I was Treasurer for four years and Assistant Treasurer for two years. I discovered that people's attitudes toward money were as varied and individualistic as their attitudes toward sex. I saw how certain people who had money never made a show of it but quietly gave support to certain other people who were in need. Lama did not support anyone financially, but as time went on, certain funds for discretionary expenses were created: an emergency medical fund, a tuition fund, an escape fund to help long-term residents make the transition back into the world. Certain people were permitted to stay without initially paying room and board, incurring instead a "karmic debt" to pay sometime in the future.

Income fluctuated seasonally and money was always fairly tight. We were often dancing on the edge of poverty mentality, wrangling over belt-tightening decisions such as whether to save money by buying margarine instead of butter. Our prayer flag cottage industry, Flag Mountain, provided some earned income but remained stagnant as a business enterprise due to constantly changing management. As Treasurer, I was constantly encouraging charitable giving, grants, and donations when opportunities arose, although it took some time for me to personally embrace tithing. There were no material rewards and no financial gain for service at Lama Foundation. The reward for time contributed at Lama was spiritual, not material.

One winter day, I was closing the books for the year, working at home in the Muffin House, transferring numbers from the journal to the ledger, a mind-numbing task, when a friend came over and talked with me while I was working. It was a welcome distraction, but when she left, I found that I was off by one cent for the whole year. I spent five weeks looking for that one cent. Later on, I found out that the first generally accepted accounting principle was materiality, materially relevant accuracy. In a $125,000 budget you don't sweat tracking down one red cent. It's materially irrelevant. It's simply not worth your time.

Our spiritual teachers were the stars in our galaxy, our movie stars and rock stars, living exemplars and guides on the spiritual path, whether they taught at summer retreats, came during our winter intensives, or just happened to come visit for a day or two. We didn't read newspapers. We had little awareness of politics. Our hearts and minds were always with our teachers and elders, whether near or far.

Meditation in Lama Dome.

We would host Vipassana retreats when the whole land went on silence, women's retreats with Asha when all the men would leave the land, men's retreats with Robert Bly, Christian meditation retreats, music retreats with Paul Winter, Sufi dance camps, Sufi music camps. . . . I offered several astrology weekends in which the highlight was always the Astrological Walks and Breaths of Murshid Samuel Lewis. Wali Ali would come in the quiet time and lead us in Walks and Dances in the Dome.

Reb Zalman Schachter-Shalomi was doing a retreat at one of the hermitages one summer. He spent his morning alone, every afternoon he would teach a class at the maqbara, every evening he would hang out with us after dinner, and of course, he led us in Shabbat. I read his horoscope for him while we sat in a shady oak glade. That is how he retreated at Lama.

Reb Zalman was also a Sufi. One afternoon I was coming down the ridge above the High Hermitage. Storm clouds were blowing in from the west, stitched with lightning and thunder. Below me I could see Reb Zalman standing on the crest of the hill, wind whipping his cloak and long gray hair, facing the storm, hands to his ears, calling out, "Allah Ho Akbar, Allah Ho Akbar. . . ."

Pierre and Vivien Elliot came to be with us in the depth of winter. They had a Third Way school community in Claymont, West Virginia. He taught us Gurdjieff movements in the cold bright Dome while his wife played the de Hartmann music on our battered piano. The movements demand superhuman attention. Imagine patting your head with your right hand while rubbing your belly with your left hand while hopping back and forth from foot to foot in three-quarter time while counting out loud backward from ninety-nine while imagining smelling roast duck. This would be something like a beginning exercise.

Pierre gave talks that were mostly silence, gathering attention to the tremendous warmth of self-remembering presence.

Once Jamil asked him to speak about marriage. After a very long silence Pierre said, "When ten thousand times you have put the interest of your beloved before your own interest, and when ten thousand times your beloved has put your interest before her own interest, you might begin to know what it is to be married."

When we asked Pierre why he came back to visit us several winters in a row, he said, "Because you're already a group!"

Lama was in its glory when the summer program brought the greatest number of people to the mountain. Ram Dass, in particular, gave very generous camps of two to three weeks, bringing two hundred people at a time to the Dome. His camps were called Inward Bound with Ram Dass . . . Laid Back with Ram Dass. . . .

Ram Dass was balder. His beard was white. He was less ethereal and glowing, sharper and brighter. His gift of gab would peacefully permeate the satsang in a unified field of consciousness—and it permeated my mind. For years afterward people would say to me, "You sound just like Ram Dass."

One morning, I could see his aura. He was sitting and talking in front of the Dome window. I could see his aura shimmering brightly all around his body, against the blue backdrop of Taos Mesa. I could see his aura extend and blend with the light around all the people in the Dome. We were all bathed in a blanket of light.

Although Ram Dass was the voice talking inside my head, I still felt uncomfortable around him and tried to avoid contact with him. Many times, on my way home from lunch, I would pass by the Pond Dome where Ram Dass was sitting with his beads and I would walk on by. Finally he said, "Ahad, how come you never say hello?" I realized that I thought he would want to be left alone when really, I was the one who wanted to be left alone. I never could relate to Ram Dass personally. Maybe his light was too bright.

Ram Dass was wide open to humanity, but my personality was too wounded, too limited, to be that open. Living at Lama allowed me ample opportunity to remain isolated while in community.

He said to me, "You're still at a romantic stage of life."

I said, "What do you mean by that?"

"It's as if you're watching yourself living your life, but you're not fully engaged in living your life."

I thought of myself as the detached artist, the steppenwolf, watching life from the outside, making artifacts from my observations, using love affairs to generate poetry. The atmosphere of unconditional love pervading Maharaj-ji's satsang opened my soul to a higher love, but my personal reality still had a long way to go to open up to that love. I may have experienced essential bliss in meditation, chanting, and sacred dance, but the awareness and embodiment of divine presence in everyday life was still very transitory.

Another time he said to me, "I look at you and wonder why this old grouch is still here . . . and then I see you looking at your son and see something wonderful."

Gabe would come up and live with me at Lama during the summers. He ran around the land exuberantly with his little friends. Everyone in the community looked after them. He especially loved Camp Winnarainbow, which was a kid's circus camp run by Wavy Gravy and Surya Singer.

Wavy Gravy was a hippie clown who walked around and called everybody boss. Even the youngest smallest kids he called boss.

One time I asked him, "Wavy, how come you call everybody boss?"

He replied, "When you work for nobody, everybody is your boss."

At that time, Ronald Reagan was running for president. Wavy Gravy was running his own campaign—Nobody for President. He would put an empty chair in the middle of the stage, stand next to it, and wax eloquent about his candidate, urging us to vote for nobody because "Nobody loves you . . . Nobody can do it better . . . And nobody really cares. . . ."

One moonlit night I was carrying Gabe up the hill to my house. The woods were very dark. Eyes wide open, he said to me, "Dad, what is the scariest animal in the forest? Is it the wolf?"

"No."

"Is it the owl?"

"No."

"Maybe the coyote?"

"Gabe, the scariest animal in the forest is the one that walks on two legs."

One evening, Gabe and I were sitting on the bed in my cabin playing with Hot Wheels miniature cars, going zoom, zoom, zoom, *crash!* when out of the blue Gabe said to me, "Dad, I love you very, very much!" My heart popped open.

"And do you know why I love you very, very much?" My heart just couldn't get any wider. I held my breath, hanging on his every word.

"Because you give me lots of cars and trucks!"

Mouna was a friend of Lama who lived in Arroyo Hondo. She had studied acupuncture and Chinese herbs at the school of natural medicine run by William Lesassier in Taos. I confided in her that I had a problem with rapid ejaculation and that I knew sex would be better if I lasted longer. She said, "No problem. I treat that all the time." I laid on my back and she put two needles into my belly on the midline. As I laid there the sun was setting and red light was filling the room. I could feel tremendous whirlpools of blocked energy being released and spiraling out from my belly. I was amazed. Since then have never had this problem. I became convinced of the power of acupuncture.

One summer afternoon I was running pell-mell down the path from Lama Central to the ISC. A thunderstorm had been building, it was getting very dark, and rain was just about to pour down. I was running to beat the rain, thinking of nothing, when Mouna, who had been hiding behind a tree, jumped out in front of me, waved her hands and said, "BOO!" At that very instant twenty feet behind her a tremendous bolt of lightning hit the middle of the path with a deafening *BOOM!* We jumped out of our skins. We laughed and danced around. The lightning had struck right where I would have been, had she not jumped out in front of me.

Lama became a place of pilgrimage for Sufis, and the Lama Dome a center for the Dances of Universal Peace. Many Sufi teachers came to Lama every year, Wali Ali and Saadi in particular, and the initiates in the community led the dances at Lama.

The dances and the "pseudo-Sufism" of Hazrat Inayat Khan had been an object of enmity for the Muslims during Lama's holy wars, consistent with the fact that historically and to this day, Sufis have been persecuted by orthodox Muslims. At Lama, love survived and the fanatics vacated the premises.

In the early eighties Saadi and Tasnim founded the PeaceWorks Center for the Dances of Universal Peace, which would later become the International Network for the Dances of Universal Peace. They began publishing cassette tapes and booklets with dance instructions and music, making the dances available to the public. Saadi said to us at Lama, "The dances are given freely to the world forever."

Once the dances were given freely to the world forever, we began holding the dances in the community. We had some experienced dance leaders, such as Sara Morgan, but we worked with a group leadership format, a priesthood of all believers, if you will. Anyone who wanted to present a dance was encouraged to do so and supported to do so. We had extensive rehearsals. We empowered each other. We led dances on Sunday afternoons for visitors, on Friday evenings for Shabbat, and on other occasions.

> *Blessed are the arts which open the hearts and woe when the hearts are sacrificed for the arts.*
>
> MURSHID SAMUEL LEWIS

Dancing in Lama Dome, summer 1976.

After Gabe was born I no longer heard the singing voice that had been with me since college. My muse left me. I was no longer isolating myself to listen to the voice within, no longer singing songs in secret, no longer collecting poems and songs. I could no longer maintain my self-identity as a poet. At the same time creative inspiration flowed more and more into communal music, chanting, and the Dances of Universal Peace, moving out of my mind, more and more into my heart.

I was always the musician for the dances at Lama, always sitting in the center of the circle, playing my guitar and singing to God. Singing Hallelujah is one thing. Singing Hallelujah with dozens of sweet voices and warm hearts harmonizing with each other in a resonant dome is another thing entirely. I would close my eyes and go out into space—although I soon learned that I needed to keep my eyes open and my attention focused on the feet of the dance leader. The role of the dance musician is not to be the shining star but to be the moon reflecting the light of the dancers in the circle and, oh yes, hold the ground while everyone soars.

Sacred dance is not just about invoking God in heaven in awesome impersonal unknowable transcendence. In the sanctuary of the sacred names, in the safety of the circle of love, every aspect of our humanity, every aspect of our God in our humanity, can and does come forth—eroticism, asceticism, celebration, debilitation, enthusiasm, anxiety, fear, anger, attraction, repulsion, joy, serenity, even boredom. . . .

> The dancing leads into the dark flesh, the neural pool, the crucible of perceptions: stone-rimmed cave fires at the base of the spine. The molten voice of the core chants Allah. The bright electron cloud chants Allah, Allah—alla this love asleep in matter becomes whirring flesh, then light . . .
>
> The circle of dancers moves counter-clockwise—Allah Hu—against the magnetic inertia of the Earth—Allah Hu. The one who spins—Hu—in the center, clockwise, accelerates the Earth's magneto, takes all the resistant electricity of the chanting circle and becomes a column of light uniting heaven and Earth . . .
>
> All incarnations unleashed (demons, magicians, lost children, fresh lovers, wanderers)

*surge forth like gardens under the floods of eons of flesh working out
on this Earth, dancing distances, elaborating the solar code until the
only learning is genetic, the only language is light. . . .*

Outside the delicate cat's cradles and cootie catchers of our daily
interactions, we can feel ourselves to be fully human and fully loved in
the sacred circle. And this can be challenging, particularly in the partner dances. To dare to look into the eyes of another human being with
the intention that the pure presence in me recognizes the pure presence
in you—and to witness as well the flicker of fear, the wisp of lust, the
subtle automatic judgments that may arise, the withdrawals, to recognize your own projections, to accept that the other had his or her own
reactions, to forgive yourself and your other and let it go and return
to the simple blessing of sharing presence, all in an instant before you
move on to the next beloved—can be challenging. The practice of the
partner dances supports me in flowing personal love into transpersonal
love. But it's not always easy at first.

The dances can also bring up religious wounds and judgments for
healing. I've known people to leave the circle the minute they hear
"Allah." I've known people who leave the circle because their "Shema
Israel" is too sacred to be chanted in public. I've known other people
who stay in the circle and work with their discomfort around "Allah"
or "Shiva" or whatever.

There are dances that invoke the names of the Goddess in ancient
Middle Eastern traditions, which naturally delight all the goddesses
in the circle. We were doing a dance that invoked the Goddess as the
Celestial Serpent with the phrase, *"Ama Gal Dingar,"* just like ringing
a bell, "Ama Gal *Ding*-ar." When I heard that phrase ring that bell, I
felt sudden abject terror. I almost passed out, and I found a way to leave
the circle. Working with this bizarre reaction, I found traces of past-life
memories of having been a male sex slave in a Mesopotamian Goddess
temple, a boy toy who was castrated and then sacrificed to the Goddess.
The dances bring up all sorts of stuff.

Sitting in the center of the circle and playing guitar, I was acutely
aware of every mistake I made. Every time I made a mistake, I would

almost stop dead in my tracks—but it was my responsibility to keep the dance going, so I kept on strumming. But that egregious mistake would burn in my mind all afternoon and was all I could think of. Afterward, people would come up and thank me for the music and say how wonderful it was, and I wondered what they meant. My mistakes were so obvious to me. Years later when I was once again in the circle of dancers, I noticed how little attention I gave to the musicians. As long as they were in tune and on time, I barely noticed them. My attention was absorbed in the sound of my own voice!

These days when I make a mistake, I don't freak out. I just keep on strumming.

In my last year at Lama, I worked together with my beautiful friend Glory to bring forth a body of mostly Christian dances, as she was mostly Christian. She was a very gifted dance leader: enthusiastic, spontaneous, and inspired. She would come up with movements to melodies, and I would support her with guitar. But, when she presented a new dance to the group, she often forgot her original movements and made up new ones on the spot! In the dances, we are generally concerned with presenting them exactly as they were originated, so this was an education in spontaneity and delight. Some of those dances are done to this day.

Dancing with a big circle in the Dome was hot, sweaty, jubilant, chaotic, and glorious. It was Murshid Sam's genius to give young people a joyful way to praise God in the body and bring the divine out of the ethers into living life. Many people caught glimpses of Sam during the dancing. In the silence after a dance I was aware of a vortex of angelic presence spiraling up and down through the center of the Dome.

Now that Nooradeen was no longer present to bear the brunt of my father projections, now that I was a father myself, I took it upon myself to do forgiveness work around my father, which I understood as asking Allah to loosen those tight angry dark spots in my heart and pour light into it. Forgiveness is something I can ask for, not something I can do. I had a lot of repressed anger and frustrated libido wrapped around my father image.

I wanted to embrace my incarnation and take full responsibility for my life here on Earth. I wanted to imagine my motivation for choosing this birth. Who was I before I was born, and why would I be inclined to take human birth? I wanted to know that this life, no matter how painful or how joyful, is in some way my choice, not just a karmic trap or an accident. I wanted to know that I was conceived in love and raised in love, no matter the limitations of my parents and myself.

My father had stopped speaking to me because he was angry and disgusted at my life choices, at how I was throwing away the fine education he had provided for me. I had my own share of pent-up rage and rejection. After Gabe was born, I did a lot of forgiveness work around my father and felt ready for reconciliation. I wanted to be friends with my father again, no matter how unlikely that was. I wrote and asked him if we could try to be friends. His initial response was not all that promising:

> *So you would like to find a way for you and I to be friends. It is an appealing thought, but I doubt you have pursued the idea very far. I have very little in common with a mystic on a mountain except some genes and past history, most of which is not the kind on which friendships are built. In other words, unless you change your lifestyle, I would find it difficult to believe that you are pursuing this friendship idea seriously. With good wishes, Poppa*

As time passed, we began to communicate again, although we never really became friends. When I visited my parents in Baltimore, I would take walks with and engage in talks with my father. One evening he took me and my mom out to dinner. We all had a couple of drinks before dinner and a couple of drinks with dinner and I was feeling my oats and holding forth on burning environmental issues. My father didn't want to hear about this and asked me to stop talking about it, which just made me wax more eloquent on the subject. Finally he got up, threw down his napkin, and stormed off to the bathroom.

"I really wish you would apologize to your father," my mother said, "and stop talking about this. It's very upsetting to him."

I had to stop and look at myself. I was the one who wanted reconciliation. I asked myself what was more important, my ideologies or peace in the family? Ideas or feelings? What was more important, pushing my ideas on unwilling ears or respecting my father? There was no way he could hear me, so what was the point?

When he came back to the table I apologized to him and spoke no more of save the whales or hug the trees or whatever had been so important. I kept my peace. Life went on. I got out of my head and into my heart.

At Lama I relied on the Biblical verse, "Remember thy Creator in the days of thy youth." I had set foot on a path from which there was no turning back.

My personal mantra was "Pain now, light later. Pain now, light later . . ." affirming that devotion to spiritual practice would have a result, that light would come into my darkness.

Forgiveness was given to some degree. The pain in my heart relaxed to some degree. I was ready although unprepared to make a life in the world. Only much later would I engage in personal psychological work to become more fully aware of the childhood traumas still active in my unconscious, still shaping and limiting my life. My soul needed to know God first and would attend to my ego later.

As time went on I spent less time in the prayer room meditating and more time walking in the forest. Lama was surrounded by national forest, old growth piñon, pine, and aspen. All around Lama there was an extensive network of trails, some obvious, some just deer paths. One way I would take led me east up the old logging road through the aspen groves by the stream before cutting south through the steep pine forest to come out on the ridge way above the High Hermitage. The path then descended into the western panorama. Occasionally, I might encounter bear or catch a glimpse of deer, but very rarely. Mostly it was just sunlight and birdsong in the deep forest.

Gradually, my mind would calm down, get quiet, and enter into the mind of the forest. My mind became the mind of the forest. The hills and valleys and groves and clearings and paths were mapped in my brain. Walking through the forest was walking through my primordial prehuman self, walking deep into the collective unconscious.

When I was a child, my sisters and I would play fantasy war games in the forest. We called ourselves the Guardians of Towson, constantly on the alert for enemy troop movements or warplanes flying overhead. Now the forest was my guardian, preserving an ancient dimension of myself as a creature of the Earth, a passing breath in the vast forest.

The mind of the forest is very deep and slow and very green. The thoughts of the forest are like whale songs stretching out over decades. I stopped taking my camera with me. My humanity opened to the mind of the forest. This was the final phase of my spiritual practice at Lama Foundation.

## 1982

I had grown somewhat comfortable and content at Lama, perhaps too content. I felt very well loved and appreciated by the community. But I could hear Gabe calling out to me when he was not with me. "Dad, where are you?" I could not ignore my son calling to me to be with him full time, which meant moving to Santa Fe.

I had originally come to Lama as a refuge from the road, as a retreat from the world, and I had found peace, joy, and love living in spiritual community on the mountain. I thought I could spend the rest of my life here, but now it was time to move on.

There were certain other Lama graduates who also thought I had stayed on too long on the mountain and referred to me as a barnacle. It made me mad to hear this, but I had to admit they were right. I had come to Lama thirteen years ago and had been living there continually for eight years now. My lease was about to expire. The following year we created the seven-year rule, which limited continuous residence at Lama to seven years. Even I agreed that my number was up.

There was a dark side to my life at Lama as well. I was smoking again, hand-rolled cigarettes of cheap tobacco. I was still smoking marijuana. In fact, I had a secret garden in the forest where I was growing marijuana, which I was giving away freely until someone decided to rip me off. I took the unprecedented measure of putting a padlock on my house, which was also ripped off. I stored my remaining harvest under the bed platform in my VW van. But the message was clear: it was no longer cool to grow dope on Lama mountain.

I later found out that my smoke had been stolen by a bug-eyed, bushy-haired hippie who named himself Ram. This false prophet held court around a campfire down the hill, entrancing his sycophants with tales of alien contact, messages from the Pleiades, and, of course, the magic herb given him by the cosmic brothers.

I found this out after he and his girlfriend had moved to Taos. They still came back to Lama to help themselves to food from the larder and oil from the garage. That this went on at all is a reflection of how spacious, trusting, ungrounded, and unconscious the community had become. When I found out I drove down to Taos and confronted these thieves. They stopped coming to Lama, but all my dope had gone up in smoke.

My poetic muse, the singing voice, had abandoned me after Gabe was born. I no longer had rapturous nights of creativity. I had gone from reading spiritual poetry to devouring horror novels. I had gone from Rumi to Stephen King. I began reading into the fringes of reality: haunting, possession, UFO sightings, UFO abductions, ancient astronauts, conspiracy theories, that sort of thing. Living on the fringes of the world for so long I developed a curiosity about and sensitivity to all sorts of unconventional human experiences. I never did see any flying saucers except in my dreams. Eventually, my interest in all that waned.

Life at Lama was glorious, warm, and gregarious during the summer—and cold and lonely during the long winter. Lama became a community of hermits living in huts scattered throughout the forest. It was cold all winter, colder than it is now. A blanket of snow three feet deep covered the land in silence all winter. We could only walk on narrow paths between the buildings. If you went off the path you were wallowing waist deep in snow. We wore cheap cotton thermal underwear all winter, long johns, even when we were sleeping. The only heat other than body heat came from chopping wood and burning wood.

At night, when I came home alone, my cabin was stone cold. I would light the smoky kerosene lamps and make a fire in the wood stove. I would get into my sleeping bag and read in the dim yellow light until the carbon dioxide from the stove and the kerosene fumes robbed the air of oxygen, making me groggy. After I blew out the lights, I would lie huddled in my sleeping bag, listening to the wood stove cool and the mice scampering around the race tracks they had made in the insulation in the walls. When I woke in the morning, everything was absolutely still and freezing cold.

I kept my mind busy with astrology and music, horror novels and mysteries because I could not bear to face my emotional state, which was basically despair. Not knowing what to do with myself, I had embraced the path of meditation, devotion, and service. "When in doubt, serve somebody" was a functional strategy for life at Lama. I had subscribed to the goal of effacing the ego in divine unity and did my best to imagine that.

What I did not know was that in order to abandon the ego, one had to have a functioning ego in the first place. I had pursued my ideals of going beyond the mind and opening to the flow of inspiration, but now, fourteen years after the trauma of college graduation, I still had no idea where I was going or what I was doing with my life. I was discouraged, disheartened, depressed, and in denial. My son had been taken away from me by his crazy mother. My poetry and lyric inspiration had stopped coming to me. I was hiding out from the world in a communal dream that could not last.

On top of it all, I had fallen in love with a married woman, Glory, and I was burning in the agony and ecstasy of impossible romantic love. It was a burning, yearning, soul passion I could not resist. Glory and I were twin flames, souls born of the same light, the same star. That was our myth. I could not violate her marriage nor could I reject her love, so deep was my need to be loved. We loved each other for years, but we could never be together.

At Lama, they wanted me to take on the role of Coordinator. It was definitely my turn. But my mind was too unstable and my heart too ashamed to take on this role of service at a time when my behavior was threatening to tear apart a marriage and create a rift in the community.

## October 1983

After a year of ecstatic walks in the woods with my beloved, alternating with deep dark depressive nights, I packed up all my belongings in my van and moved to Santa Fe. I was thirty-six years old. I rented an apartment on Alto Street, two blocks away from Gabe and his mom, and became a full-time, half-time dad. I left my beloved in the forest.

> *At last you vanished*
> *silent and swift*
> *like a deer into the forest*

*and I drove away*
*to exile among the traffic*

Had I found God? Had God found me?

I had surrounded myself with lovers of God, trusted in their belief systems, and took on their practices. I had found deep peace and presence in solitude, into which I kept withdrawing. My mind was still hyperactive, my mood often depressive, but the door of my defenses was open to the light of the heart, sharing with friends and beloveds in community. I could be transported for hours, chanting the names of God. I found communion and ecstasy in the Dances of Universal Peace. I was aware of a strong voice of guidance that overrode and redirected my ego.

I was addicted to a self-medication that seemed to lift me to a higher level and then put me to sleep. Union with God was a grandiose fantasy I allowed myself.

*I am no me no more I am*
*an idiot of God I am*
*a ruminant of Ram I am*
*YOU*
*always everywhere*

My faith was not firm. My practices were shaky. I was not able to hold on to my beloveds, so I wrote poems and sang songs about transpersonal love that were, again, well-intended idealistic fantasies.

*I love every one I meet now*
*every one any one*
*Names change The face is the same*

Then an impossible love for a married woman blasted open my heart and shattered my ego.

# 7

# SANTA FE, 1983–2006

My first night in Santa Fe, Jesus knocked on the door to my apartment. At least that's who he said he was: Hey-Zeus, as they say *en español*. Where I had just come from, if someone told you he was Jesus, you accepted that as being real for him in the moment. Of course the next day he could be Krishna or Buddha.

The young man standing in my door had large eyes, clear olive skin, an oval face, and long crinkly black hair that fell below his shoulders. He looked like a Mexican Jesus. He said he lived across the street. He asked if he could come in and use my phone since the phone in his house was broken. It is a great honor to have Jesus come into your house and use your phone—of course I let him in. As he walked across the one room of my apartment his eyes darted back and forth checking everything out, perhaps looking for what could be boosted. He got on the phone and began talking rapidly about an ounce of this and a gram of that, still looking nervously about. Jesus was making drug deals on my telephone!

The next night he showed up again. I asked him to go somewhere else to find a phone.

## November 1983

Within a month of moving to Santa Fe I met Joanna Walsh at a Thanksgiving dinner. She was the most extroverted and talkative person

193

there. She had a crown of white hair, a glowing face with smooth youthful skin, and sparkling blue eyes. She was dressed in a gold wool suit and wore an amber necklace. Though in her seventies, she had the vivacity and enthusiasm of a much younger woman. She seemed delighted to get to know everyone who was present and was especially delighted with herself. She had an effervescent quality of joy that was in no way silly or giddy.

The next thing I knew she was asking me if I remembered having come from another planet and if I remembered what it was like on my home planet. I said as far as I knew my home planet was Earth. She thanked me for my knowing and continued merrily holding forth.

Her husband Hadron was sitting across the table from me. He had barely spoken a word all night, which later I would find out was due to advanced Alzheimer's disease. He had the husky build of a former athlete, a handsome face with a prominent forehead, thick bushy eyebrows, and shimmering green eyes. His face suggested love of beauty, refinement of thought, and nobility of spirit. I felt a little uncomfortable with him sitting across from me saying nothing. But he seemed content to be sitting there next to his wife, probably out in space somewhere, hardly there at all.

Every now and then he would appear to focus into the present moment, pick up his head, look alert, and say something unexpected and humorous, such as, "This sure is a strange planet." Joanna would repeat what he said. Everyone would laugh. Then his head would droop and once again no one was at home.

At one point everyone was sounding off about politics, airing their opinions and feelings. Hadron picked up his head and said, "War is business. Business is war." Joanna repeated this and everyone laughed. "That is one of his Hadronisms, which everyone used to appreciate so much," she said.

Then a most unusual thing happened. Hadron raised his gaze, looked me straight in the eye, and said softly but very forcefully, "Sell DuPont stock now. Sell DuPont stock now." Then he nodded off again. That was the only thing he said directly to me that whole evening.

This shocked me. How could he know that my sole source of financial security was some DuPont stock that I had inherited from my grandfather almost twenty years previously? It had not occurred to me until that moment that my karma was to have homeopathic ownership in one of the vilest corporations on the face of the planet, a major contributor to warfare and armaments, chemical and nuclear pollution. But here it was, plain in my face: "War is business. Business is war. Sell DuPont stock now."

Joanna told me she would like to work with me on my inner life, to help me remember where I had come from and what I had gone through to get here. She offered to take me back to my home planet. I was impressed by her charismatic exuberance, but suspicious of anyone wanting to "work on me," which I interpreted as wanting to enlist me in their belief systems. I was deeply disillusioned and depressed after the train wreck of leaving Lama and abandoning my one true married-to-another love. I had no reason to consider working with Joanna. The last thing I wanted was to let someone else into my psyche. It took a dramatic, spontaneous event a year later to demonstrate to me that past-life recordings were an experiential reality for me.

## September 1984

This spontaneous past-life memory came on Truchas Peak with Glory, who was a Christian with no belief whatsoever in reincarnation. She merely asked me a question that I was asking others at that time.

At the time, when I was reading horoscopes, I would ask the person to close his or her eyes and do a brief meditation. "Remember what it was like before you were born," I would say. "Remember that impulse, that desire, to come to Earth this time, to choose your parents and your incarnations."

That was really my question for myself, but someone else had to ask me for me to answer it.

After a day and a half of backpacking, Glory and I were on the summit of South Truchas Peak, one of the highest and most sacred mountains in the Pecos Wilderness. To be so high in the thin air on the top of a twelve-thousand-foot sacred, pyramidal mountain guarded by strange markings, rain, mist, and remoteness was an awesome experience. I was probably in an altered state already. I did what seemed to me to be the natural thing. I reached for my pouch of Bull Durham tobacco, rolled a cigarette, and began to smoke it.

"Ahad, what are you doing?" Glory exclaimed. "Here we are on top of this most sacred mountain—and you are smoking a cigarette! Put out that cigarette! Now! Come over here and sit next to me. Sit down and close your eyes."

I did what she asked without questioning why. I sat down and closed my eyes.

"Now I want you to remember what it was like before you were born," she said, turning my own question back on me. "I want you to remember why you chose to come to Earth this time."

I let the question resonate within my being and opened to receive. I saw the face, the head, and shoulders of a European Jewish matriarch, her gray hair pulled back in a bun, her eyes large and piercing, stern and loving. I knew this was my grandmother. Now I was not born into a Jewish family, nor did this picture resemble my grandmother. But the information was very clear and I didn't question it. I told her what I saw.

"That's good," she said. "Go with it. What more do you get?"

I saw a dining room and my family seated around the table for Shabbas. It was an inner room, no windows, dark wooden paneling, big wooden table set with silver and brightly glowing candles. We had lit the candles of Shabbas. I remember feeling, "We are the Chosen People, illuminated by God's light." I was a young man sitting with my grandmother, grandfather, mother, father, and sister at that table. It felt warm, safe, and secure.

"That's good. Go deeper. What more do you get?"

Then my body started shaking, and I was sobbing from the deepest part of my being, weeping uncontrollably. This was unexpected and shocking. I rarely let emotions overcome my intellectual front, and such deep feelings were unknown to my conscious personality. But my body was overcome by the emergence of memories I could not yet articulate. This traumatic heaving went on for a long, long time. Glory put her arms around me and held me. I was unable to say anything for what seemed like an hour, overwhelmed by the release of grief and terror.

When I was finally able to verbalize what was written in my soul and released through my body I said, "They destroyed my culture. They destroyed my family. And I lost my life."

This was the information I was given. Immediately many strange things about my life became clear—my attraction to Jewish women and Jewish culture, my soul recognition of Jerusalem as home, my marriage to a Jewish woman, my aversion to fanatical Islam, and the nightmares that had terrified me throughout my adult life, dreams in which I was a fugitive, a stranger in the everyday world, pursued by shadowy groups of men who were gangsters, fascist thugs, or Nazis.

Apparently I had been a young Jewish man in Europe in the thirties. I had seen my family and my culture destroyed by the Nazis. I had become a fugitive and lost my life. Once out of the body I had not returned to the spirit world but stayed around on the Earth plane until the war was over and then sought a new life in a new body with parents in America, which seemed to be a safe and secure place. This is why, when Glory asked me to remember choosing my birth when I came to Earth *this time* around, I remembered images of my family and my life in Europe, for I had not been away from the Earth since coming to birth in a Jewish family in Europe in the twenties.

Though I had read books about reincarnation and past lives and such, I had no actual experience of past-life memories up to this point and was skeptical, but also open-minded, about the subject. Because Glory's belief system was fundamentally Christian, and her theology had no room for ideas about past lives, she was playing with me a game of inner imaging that I had played with her. There could be no question of her projecting her belief system on me and suggesting that I go into previous lives. This gave the experience a more objective quality. No one was doing a psychic reading for me. The images had arisen spontaneously. The power and depth of the emotional release left no doubt that these memories were real down in my soul, without answering the question of how they had got there and why they had remained buried for so long. My best working assumption was that these were deep memories of my immediate past life that now were ready to emerge.

The very next week I called Joanna Walsh and asked her if she would work with me on my inner life. I would engage in inner work with

Joanna over the next ten years, becoming very close friends with her in the process.

Joanna and her husband had been immersed in Scientology in Los Angeles in the fifties before breaking free to bring forth their own realizations and methodologies under the banner of the Church of Totality and Totality, Inc. Joanna was a spiritual maverick, unaffiliated with any spiritual tradition. Although she took some perspectives from Scientology, her realizations and methodologies were all her own.

My motivation for working with Joanna Walsh was to resolve my impossible love for Glory and to remedy my inability to have healthy relationships with women. The focus of our work together was the dissolving of the limitations and frustrations I experienced in romantic relationships through releasing the deep soul impressions (*samskaras*) of past-life recordings restimulated by these relationships.

Joanna was not into giving psychic readings or suggesting or projecting images into my mind. She facilitated my own discovery of imagery buried deep in the unconscious. She had a great deal of patience, given that I work very slowly. She was more interested in developing my ability to see for myself than in any picture I came up with. She was more interested in triggering me to the realization of being superconscious.

I uncovered and released a whole chain of memories of lust, jealousy, passion, romance, love, and death, all the way down through my human history, starting with the caveman bashing in the head of his woman while she was having sex with another man, and ending with the frustrated lust and sublimated passion of a village priest in the remote Swiss Alps.

Working with and dissolving these affect-laden images effected a permanent change in my inner and outer life, releasing me from what seemed like a chain of curses, trauma, and tragedy that had darkened my soul and frustrated my every love. On a deeper level the self-revealing imagery gave me a pure origin myth and solved the conundrum of my tortured identity.

All this time, I had been searching for identity through romantic relationships. Each beloved gave me the gift of a certain dimension of myself. The continual loss of intimacy seemed the price I had to pay for love. I had no idea how hormonally driven I was. I had no idea that I needed a stable, functioning ego in the material world to sustain a mature relationship. I was romantic, idealistic, dysfunctional, and ungrounded. I was identified with being a lover and a poet. Spiritual community was just the backdrop for my relationship dramas to play out against. My spiritual journey was happening while my ego was busy making other plans.

The nitty-gritty details of my work with Joanna Walsh, of past lives, entities, and relationship dramas, as well as Joanna's own life story, therapeutic methods, and metaphysics, is recorded in my book *Superconscious: Releasing Past-Life Recordings.*

The beginning of the work with Joanna was the experience of being aware of being present as the space within one's body, the empty space between the molecules and atoms of matter/energy that comprise one's body, of being aware of being present as the space not only within but also around one's body—and of gradually expanding that awareness until one is conscious of being present as the space within and throughout the entire universe. The end result of the work is being aware of being Totality, of being Superconscious.

Each time Joanna would lead me through this Total Meditation:

Be aware of being present as the space within your body. Within the matter and energy comprising your precious body, between the molecules and atoms you are ninety-nine-plus percent space, empty space. Be aware of being present as the space within your body right now.

Be aware of being present as the space within and around your body, including your astral and etheric force fields.

Be aware of being present as the space within which this room exists. These bodies, this furniture, these walls are existing within the space that you are.

Be aware of being present as the space within which the city of Santa Fe exists. The breeze is blowing through you. The birds are flying through. The people and cars are moving through you. And you are present as unbroken, continuous space in which all of this exists.

Be aware of being present as the space in which this whole region of the country exists. The mountains, the rivers, the trees, the sky, all exist within the space that you are.

Be aware of being present as the space within which the whole country, the whole continent exists. All the vastness of the land, the rivers, the sea, the sky, all exist within the space that you are.

Be aware of being present as the space within which the planet Earth exists, a beautiful blue-and-white ball floating within the space that you are. See the planet in peace and harmony and love floating within your space.

Be aware of being present as the space within which the whole solar system exists. The sun and all the planets whirling around it exist in the emptiness of your space.

Be aware of being present as the space in which the whole galaxy exists. Millions and billions of stars, dark clouds of matter, infinite life forms, all exist within the space that you are.

Be aware of being present as the space within and throughout the entire universe. Innumerable galaxies, whirlpools of light, dark clouds of matter, infinite life forms, all exist within the space that you are.

Be aware of being the stillness.

Be aware of being vastness . . . of being motionless . . . of being timeless . . . of being foreverness.

Be aware of being Totality, whole and complete, within and throughout the whole universe.

Be still and know.

The reality of being present as the space, which is also called ether, *akasha, purusha,* and *sada shiva,* among other terms, is permanently established in my being. The work with Joanna confirmed every spiritual reality I had experienced and banished my skepticism—precisely *because* it was unorthodox and unconventional. Spiritual reality is not dependent on the form in which you experience it, is not dependent on any form of experience, even though, paradoxically, essential presence *is* experience in the present moment.

Being aware of being Totality, of being Superconscious, was the goal in and of itself. Superconscious has the ability to create and uncreate realities to experience. If a person lacks the ability to create and uncreate realities, it is because there are traumatic imprints from this life or previous lives in the subconscious that are interfering. As Superconscious one has the ability to look at these recordings in the subconscious without reacting to them, to erase and release these recordings, and to put new recordings in their place.

Joanna would direct me to be aware of being Superconscious, outside of time, with total ability and total awareness. Then, as Superconscious, I would establish a line of communication with the subconscious and ask to be shown those past-life experiences that are interfering with my ability to function as Superconscious in the present moment.

Joanna would then direct me to release those pictures from my body, using the universal vortex energy within and around the body—and then, most importantly, to give my subconscious a new blueprint of positive pictures for the future, telling the subconscious, "This is my new reality for my body." Superconscious will take whatever is held in the subconscious and manifest it in the time stream.

My Jungian analyst calls these past-life fantasies. The soul contacts affective imagery in the imaginal realm. Fantasies are as real as anything else to the psyche.

If you want to know more about how to do this, read *Superconscious: Releasing Past-Life Recordings*. Suffice it to say that this work was very effective in clearing away a lot of psychic darkness, traumas, entities, curses, and so on—and that my dreams of love, happiness, and prosperity really did come true, although it took a long time for them to manifest.

One day Joanna and I set the intention to uncover and release my karmic pictures around my father. Some people work quickly and get psychic images rapidly, but this was not the case with me. Joanna was very patient with me. It usually took me a long time, eyes closed, to concentrate my attention and wait to receive images in the gray nebulous interior mind field. This is what I saw that day.

*I see myself living in the cliff dwellings, one of the ancient inhabitants of this land. I was an important and powerful man with a long nose, not a warrior but a priest, a keeper of songs and ceremonies for the tribe. We lived in peace and harmony with the land. I was happily married and lived with my wife in great harmony in one of the stone buildings. I asked who this was—and found out that my wife in that life was my mother in this life!*

*The one flaw in this perfect existence was my son, with whom I was not pleased. He was a young soul, slow, simple, and dull. He had no fire, no passion. He was not like me at all. He brought no honor to me. He made me feel ashamed among the tribe. As he grew to be a young man and showed little interest in anything, I was hard on him, pushed him, challenged him, and talked down to him. "Be a man. Do something with your life. Make me proud of you." I was invalidating and unkind.*

*He was humiliated and angry at me. Determined to show me up, trying to do something heroic, he stole a pony when raiding a neighboring tribe and got himself killed.*

*I was devastated. I did love him very much. He was my only son and I had pushed him into getting himself killed. I withdrew from my wife, from the tribe. I spent months sitting alone and brooding. Grief, anger, and frustration. Finally, in despair I did the manly thing and single-handedly attacked the neighboring tribe to avenge his death. I was wounded, suffered, and died.*

*We lived in a peaceful culture. There was no reason for my son or me to get ourselves killed other than my blinding pride. It was an exercise in futility.*

*Coming into this life, the tables were turned. He was the father and I was the son. He was not pleased with me. I brought no honor to him. And so forth. . . .*

All the work in uncovering and releasing past-life recordings would be an exercise in futility without visualizing a new blueprint for my life, a vibrant image imprinted on the subconscious, held there as a living picture for superconscious to create in the time stream. Joanna would instruct me to visualize my body radiant and healthy, and to give my body a beautiful wife, a beautiful house, and lots of money, to visualize every detail.

"Then, turn the image around," she would say, "and breathe it into your body. Tell your subconscious: 'This is my new blueprint for my body.' And let nothing invalidate the blueprint you have made for your new life."

This was difficult for me to do, but I did my best to cooperate with the instructions. Everything I had visualized was indeed realized in my life—a good twenty years later, long after Joanna was gone.

At one point Joanna asked me to imagine holding a big bag of gold in my lap. My whole body turned red with resistance to this idea! I had so many judgments around money.

Having grown up in what I experienced as the coldness of wealth, I felt that having money created isolation from other people and separation from reality. This was the gestalt I felt in my family. I saw how people with money could buy their way through life and have everything the way they wanted but never actually experience life itself. For whatever reason, my soul needed to experience poverty, vulnerability, reliance on something other than money in the bank, to be dependent on divine grace or luck or fate, on the kindness of strangers and the goodness of humanity. . . .

I lived in relative poverty for a good twenty years, learning my lessons about money through accounting and managing other peoples' money, first for the Lama community, and then for a series of business employers. Even astrology was karmic accounting. It was time to prepare to come out of voluntary poverty and into prosperity.

Joanna kept trying to get me to go to my home planet. She said that most of the people she worked with came from another planet and did not feel at home on Earth. I tried to see what I could see but never got any reality on being from another planet.

Glory had told me that we came from a great light deep in space and I had seen this with her. Now in session with Joanna many years later I asked to go home.

> Glory appeared to me in her light form and said, "Come on, honey, let's go home." Her light form was bright, pure, radiant, joyful—no burden, no sorrow, no age, no pain. She took my hand and led me out through a vortex, a time/space tunnel, back to that great light deep in space, the sea of light.
>
> "Yes," I said, "I've already been here. I know this place, but I'm supposed to find a home planet. I want to tune in to that reality."
>
> So I cleared my awareness and opened myself up again—and once again Glory came to me in her light form, like Beatrice in The Divine Comedy, to lead me back to the sea of light. Hard-nosed, skeptical, I kept testing what I was getting, clearing my space again as many as six times.
>
> Every time I kept seeing Glory in her light form. She kept saying to me, very gently insisting, "Come on, honey, let's go home. This is home for us. This is our home." She was very patient with me.
>
> How many times could I question my beloved? What else was there to do? I went home with her.
>
> What followed is beyond the ability of words to describe.
>
> The great light deep in space, the sea of light, is a vast plasma that science might call the center of a galaxy.
>
> Within this vast plasma are millions and millions of beings of light. To Earth-plane astronomers these beings appear to be stars, spheres of light. As perceived by the stars on their own level of awareness, these are living, moving, dancing, rejoicing light beings, whose bodies are fluid, living flames, capable of extension, expression, articulation, all the elements of dance. Not only does each light being have movement, each one also emits sound vibrations (music) and subtle dancing colors far beyond the range of human perception. The

whole vast plasma cloud is bathed in unceasing, ever-changing light, though the overall ambiance seems to be golden white.

Gustav Doré's engravings of the angelic spheres in Dante's *Paradiso* come closest to earthly images that faintly reflect this reality.

In the sea of light, the sea of love, being is always joy and delight, with dancing lights, swells of exaltations, choruses of glory—millions of stars eternally circling around the central light, while within the grand cosmic dance infinite permutations and combinations occur: smaller circles, roses, crosses, triangles, and so on, revolving around their own centers—all as individual beings of light dancing, rejoicing freely, intermingling, interpenetrating. We move freely in and out of each other's forms, delighting in mingling, not bound to each other by anything at all but universal love. This is from where we came forth and where we return to: home.

From home the time line unfolds. Some of us wanted to experience greater individuation, greater freedom, and greater space in which to move, so we left the sea of light and went into outer space. We experimented, innovated, and experienced many varieties of movement in outer space. In outer space our individual lights seem extremely bright by contrast, while in the sea of light all the lights blend together and individuality is more a matter of subtle variation in color and sound.

Then she and I and some others decided to form our own circle of dancing lights. I got the image of lights dancing in a circle, every other one going the opposite direction, interweaving in and out of one another like fish in a grand right-and-left, weaving a crown of light. Our circle got larger and larger until it became immense. Then beings began to drop away to go explore elsewhere, until finally our circle was very small again. We went off to explore other worlds, she and I and our little cluster. We went planet-hopping for a long time and eventually came to planet Earth.

I was attracted by this lovely blue-green-white planet. It seemed so fresh, so new, so full of vitality and potential compared with all the other older worlds we had visited. I wanted to zoom into the Earth sphere and merge into it. Glory didn't. She wanted to stay in her light body, dancing in space. No problem. We had always been together. I didn't give a thought *to what separation might mean. I projected a light beam from my hand and followed it down into the atmosphere, entering the Earth game alone.*

*I am flying freely above the African veldt. I see vast herds of antelope. This world is sensational and beautiful—blue skies, green grasses, flowing waters, and at night the familiar infinity of stars. I find I can move into and out of any life form freely, taking tastes of what it feels like to be in a physical body. The human life forms are dark and dirty, primitive hunters and gatherers. They don't move in and out of bodies like I do. I am a joyful spirit, lyrical, inquisitive, intoxicated with the songs, the vibrations of the myriad life forms. I'm a disembodied spirit, a body of wind, aware of embodied thoughts, feelings, and sensations, without being trapped in them. I play games with animals and people, making energy phenomena happen, sometimes mischievous, sometimes helpful, reveling in the joy of experience. Some people can see me and hear my voice, others not. I'm a spirit playing at being a god.*

*I immerse myself in earth, water, and air, moving through mountains, rivers, winds, and storms for a long time before I take the plunge and dive into a human form. At first, I'm just moving in and out of human bodies, vicariously experiencing human realities. Then I go the full route and come in through conception. I remember the gradual involvement with human conditions, the gradual forgetting of who I really am. I am aware of automatically recording my human experiences, automatically identifying with them, weaving myself into the web of karma. Then I hang out too long in the body of a caveman and end up popping the head of my woman who is having sex with someone else. Now I'm really caught.*

⊙〜⊙

We all need our origin myths, whether religious, cultural, national, familial, or individual. Plunging persistently into the imaginal world, I had discovered imagery that satisfied my need to know where I come from and who I really am.

Glory was my guide in this vision, my guide to a great light deep in space, a whirlpool of bright lights were dancing around the center of a galaxy. This was not an image of twin flames in eternity but of an assembly, a cohort of lights, my cosmic siblings, my stellar tribe, rejoicing in the glory of unity before streaming out into the cosmos, into worlds of experience. I remembered launching out into the universe and exploring many worlds before coming to this beautiful planet that I now call home.

Our experience at Lama, perhaps of our whole hippie tribe, could be seen as a coming together of a cohort of souls to renew our connection with love, peace, and joy, before flowing back out into the greater world of human history.

My recall on Truchas Peak with Glory in 1984, at age thirty-seven, had been very vivid and undeniable: I had been a young man when I died in my previous life in the Holocaust in Europe. However, throughout all my work with Joanna I had not recovered *how* I had died at that time. I sensed that I had been a fugitive, not immediately killed with my family, but I didn't know for how long, nor whether I had been murdered, committed suicide, or what.

Then on Christmas afternoon in 1992, in my forty-sixth year, I fell into a reverie and was shown: the image of the waystation by the railway late at night with deep snow falling all around, shining in the light of a single street lamp. The image haunted me in my early twenties, then came back again, and I knew that this was the picture of my previous death. I knew now that I had been a fugitive from the Nazis, running, hiding, wandering, perhaps with a companion, and finally had reached the end of the line. Starved, exhausted, cold, I had sought shelter in this waystation by the railway in the middle of a big snowstorm. Too exhausted to move any farther, I had simply let the snow and the cold embrace me and had left my body.

My soul recall had come around full circle. I had no doubt that when I was experiencing this image in my early twenties, *end of the line* echoing in my head, seeking out empty railway stations in the middle of the night in the cold and the snow, fantasizing about abandonment, homelessness, helplessness, being a fugitive, that the impact of my previous death was restimulated in present time at exactly the same age at which I had lost my body before.

The subliminal resonance of my previous death radically altered my life in my early twenties. My inner and outer state went from being identified with being a successful, well-dressed, well-to-do college student to being identified with being a homeless vagabond with torn and tattered clothes. Living in the material world was no longer real for me. I sought refuge in the only place I could, in spiritual community and the search for a spiritual path. I outlived the trauma of my previous death, and true grace granted me the blessings that life has to offer for those no longer young.

My work with Joanna shifted me from cruising the spiritual beltway, singing along to the old songs with the magic words, to walking the mean streets of the inner city of my psyche and asking the denizens of the unconscious night to come out and show themselves. I had thought that absorption into divine unity, emptiness, whatever was the ticket to ride, but how can one surrender to the divine will when one's inner world is mucked up with unacknowledged, conflicting feelings?

Joanna's working model was unconventional, to say the least, but her meditations were genuinely spiritual. Engaging in the work of releasing past-life recordings, I was seeking to relax the grip of psychological complexes in the unconscious by becoming aware of the archetypal figures (in the form of past-life fantasies) that were generating these limiting and defining complexes. Although there was the promise of magical solutions through creative visualization, Joanna was compassionate and patient, spending years with me peeling away the layers of the onion of my psyche.

However, the purest gift that Joanna gave me was the awareness of being present as the space within and around the body, being the space pervading the whole cosmos, pure consciousness, vastness, stillness, foreverness, akasha, purusha, sada shiva, ahadiyat. . . .

New Mexico was my home now. I had found my tribe and the landscape of my soul. I was blessed to have lived on the land with my people, to have lived every day under the bright blue sky, in the high mountain light. Santa Fe too was a vibrant community with many visionary artists, musicians, and mystics. I thought of the east coast, where I had grown up, as the Old Country—gray, rainy, crowded, and oppressive.

New Mexico is an ensouled landscape, vast and spacious. The Native Puebloan people have lived in the same place with their language and culture intact for a thousand years. The Spanish were living on the land for two hundred and fifty years before the Anglos came. There have been struggles, conflict, and bloodshed between these peoples, but not broad ethnic cleansings. Today the Native, Hispanic, and Anglo people live side by side with respect, in peace and harmony. The land is in the soul of the people who live here, the actual land with its rivers and fields and mountains and streams, and humanity has honored the landscape with sacred shrines and *moradas,* monasteries, and stupas.

I had no idea how to make a living in Santa Fe, so I put up posters promoting myself as an astrologer. I felt uncomfortable charging money for readings. I was still learning at other peoples' expense, still uncertain of the accuracy of my readings. But I bravely put myself forth as a professional astrologer working for a fee. That rapidly backfired. I gave several readings that left me strangely drained. Then there was the rancher from Colorado, with Uranus (sudden change) transiting his seventh house of relationship, who wanted to know if he should divorce his wife, which he was going to do anyway. He left me with an empty promise to send me the money later. That sealed the deal. This was not for me.

I have great respect for many professional astrologers who devote their lives to serving humanity in this wisdom tradition. I have no judgments about anyone else earning money in this way. But at that time, I made a firm decision for myself to practice astrology as a spiritual study and service and to neither ask for nor accept any money for doing readings.

The Ark Bookstore, owned by my friends Joanie, Jamil, and Arielle, downtown on Johnson Street, had a healing center, several rooms downstairs where practitioners could offer free sessions as a way of promoting themselves and bringing people into the bookstore. People would sign up for sessions at the front desk upstairs. For several years I showed up every Wednesday afternoon, went downstairs, and did three one-hour readings for whoever had signed up. Someone would walk in, sit down, and hand me a chart. I would open my mouth and speak whatever came to my mind as my eyes roamed around the chart. It would have been a great way to meet people, but I never saw any of these people ever again.

What I got out of this was a tremendous affirmation of the depth of this wisdom tradition and of my own ability to communicate something insightful and hopefully useful from a blind reading of a chart. This was not me coming in by the back door and reading charts for people I already knew, as I did at Lama. People walked in the door, sat down, and handed me a chart. I had no time for preparation or reflection. The reading was instantaneous and mostly non-interactive. Most people would sit in silence for the whole reading, stone-faced, until the very end, when they would burst forth with enthusiastic appreciation. . . .

"That was so amazing!"

"You described my life perfectly!"

"This is exactly what is happening!"

"I can't thank you enough!"

The affirmation and appreciation were uniform and consistent and, I suppose, to be expected. After all, if you're not paying for something, what else can you give in return? I did get to see that astrology functioned well on the street in a series of blind studies—but that raised certain problems in and of itself.

We are all, to one degree or another, narcissistic, self-centered, and self-absorbed. We all need some degree of reflection of our image in the world, some degree of validation of our sense of self. My fragile sense of self needs to know that someone else senses me as well. So, on that extremely rare occasion that someone else focuses entirely on giving me a reflection of myself, I am, of course, pleased that someone is paying attention to me, I am easily flattered by all the positive things that person says about me, and I am thrilled that he or she has caught a glimpse of the depth of my suffering. The result is that I am inclined to identify with pretty much anything he or she says about me. Imagine the following statements all made to the same person.

"You are courageous and pioneering"—*Yes!*

"You are anxious and fearful"—*How did she know?*

"You are passionate and loving."—*Absolutely!*

"You are detached and wise beyond your years."—*What a relief she can see this!*

"You have artistic gifts."—*That long to be expressed!*

"Oy vey, how you suffer!"—*Oy vey, how I suffer!*

As long as the astrologer is describing character traits that we all have to one degree or another, it is very difficult to evaluate the accuracy of such statements.

"You are very generous."—*Absolutely!*

"You are very thrifty . . ."—*You got it!*

". . . to the point of being stingy."—*I'm not paying for this!*

Flattery will get you everywhere. I harbor the suspicion that popular astrology is a form of self-indulgent entertainment, that no matter what an astrologer or a newspaper column tells you, you will believe it—for a fleeting moment.

Astrology has a long and checkered career in the West, having fallen in and out of favor, of use and disuse, many times, including being totally lost during the Dark Ages. The recent revival of astrology at the turn of the twentieth century was coincident with the rise of the art and science of psychology. Modern astrology has a very strong psychological orientation and presents itself as a useful method for psychological self-understanding. As such, the basic paradigm is that character equals destiny. Describe a person's character and you describe his or her destiny. That was the paradigm I was working under.

*Astrology is 100 percent accurate—in hindsight!*
MURSHID SAMUEL LEWIS

I worked in Santa Fe doing accounting in the business world for twelve years. I chose this means of livelihood through the use of a pendulum.

I was confused about the lack of any relation between vocation and livelihood in my life. I had developed many refined skills pursuing the things I loved: poetry, music, dance, photography, and astrology. But these vocational callings seemed unrelated to making money, at least in the ways I practiced them. Material success in these areas seemed to require a good deal of self-promotion and chutzpah, which was not in my nature.

I was coming to the conclusion that my vocation and my livelihood might not be the same. I might have to work for a living doing things other than my soul's calling. But what to do? How to know what to do? How to make a choice? My thinking mind was too reactive and uncertain, overburdened with conflicting rationalizations. I could not figure it out nor get any sense of direction. But I had to start doing something.

So, for the first time in my life, I used a pendulum to dowse out my situation, to bypass my conscious mind and get what answers I could from Superconscious.

I wrote down a list of all the vocational skills I had or could imagine developing: accounting, astrology, bookkeeping, poetry, photography, and so forth. I took a recent picture of myself and the largest piece of money I had (a fifty-dollar bill) and laid them together. Since I wanted to check out various vocational skills in relation to Ahad and money, the picture and the money would serve as my witness. I would hold the pendulum over the picture of Ahad and money and then hold the pendulum over the various options on my list one by one to see what kind of a reading I would get.

Using the pendulum allows the unconscious to speak directly, bypassing the conscious rational mind. Pose a yes or no question. If the pendulum swings in a clockwise circle the answer is yes. The bigger the circle, the stronger the yes. If the pendulum swings in a counterclockwise circle the answer is no.

Accounting and bookkeeping came up with the strongest positive responses, with only very weak responses in other areas and definite negatives in areas such as poetry. Based on that I decided to enroll in the community college and take courses in accounting. Somehow it made sense to me to make money by keeping track of other peoples' money. It was no coincidence that this was my father's profession.

Simultaneously with the psychic clearing work I was engaged in with Joanna, I was making a living, earning an income, paying rent, buying food, getting grounded, and raising a son.

I learned a lot of mundane wisdom from working in the business world. I learned that most people in the business world were honest people making an honest living. And, yes, Virginia, people really do lie, cheat, and steal. That's considered normative behavior in the business world, although it helps to be delicate about the way it is done. In the manufacturing firm I worked for, it was accepted that a full 10 percent of our receivables, the money owed to us, would never be collected. That was the normal cost of doing business. And that was before our firm went bankrupt after selling a quarter of a million dollars of stock!

I had to stop smoking marijuana to work in the business world. I needed a crisp, clear, rational mind to crunch all those numbers and keep all that data straight. It was simple survival. I could not smoke dope and hold down this kind of job.

One immediate effect of ending my use of marijuana was a tremendous flood of dreaming. Marijuana use suppresses or reduces REM sleep, dreaming, and dream recall. I have had several dreams in which I smoke dope in my dream state and then cannot keep my dream eyes open to the dream that continues to go on all around me. Just dreaming about smoke turns my dream eyes sandpaper dry and stuck shut.

Since 1971 I had been writing down my dreams for their magical and aesthetic value. Dreams are the poetry of the unconscious. Many spiritual and romantic encounters take place in dream time. And yet from 1975 to 1984 I did not record one dream. Dreaming again was recovering a lost part of my soul, the dream dimension.

I have filled voluminous dream journals for the past thirty years. Ideally, I write down my dream immediately upon awakening, writing down everything I remember with no attempt at understanding or interpretation, as if I'm taking dictation from the unconscious. I have had prescient dreams, prophetic dreams, dreams of the afterlife and the other world, and extraordinary dreams, but mostly ordinary dreams. I stopped trying to evaluate whether the dream was worth writing down and just write them all down without question. If I find myself having an association or an interpretation, I let that happen as part of the process, but in general, I'm not prone to interpretation. I'm on the same page as Bob Dylan when he sings,

> *At dawn my lover comes to me*
> *and tells me of her dreams*
> *with no attempts to shovel the glimpse*
> *into the ditch of what each one means*

East DeVargas Street, Santa Fe, New Mexico.

*Classic dream . . .*

*We are driving through the snowy woods late in the afternoon under an overcast sky. We come up a circular drive lined with trees alongside a large field deep in snow with a vast thick forest on the other side. We come to a stop in front of a large institutional style building . . .*

*We enter the building and move into the brightly lit laboratory where the walls are lined with cages full of various species of animals who are there to be experimented on. The animals are restless, uncomfortable in their confinement, and grow more excited and hysterical as we approach. In particular the monkeys howl and shriek and throw themselves at the bars of the cages, monkeys with pink faces and big eyes looking very much like babies. The chaotic tortured atmosphere is too much for us and we leave . . .*

*Outside it is darker now, kind of a snowy gloaming. Silence is deep and snow is beginning to fall again. We pull the car forward slowly but then stop as we watch two deer silently moving through the deep snow at the far side of the field. They do not notice us nor are they aware of the wolf who emerges from the forest at the far-right side of the field and begins cautiously stalking them . . .*

*Now we are walking along a country road in a glorious New England autumn, the sky a deep cool blue, the trees vivid red, scarlet, orange, gold, yellow, burnt umber. We walk up the road to a farm house. There are horses grazing in fenced pastures. There are chickens in the yard. A friendly russet Irish setter comes up to greet us. A fluffy cat snoozes on the window sill. A rosy-cheeked elderly woman greets us warmly at the door . . .*

*She welcomes us into her kitchen and serves us tea and homemade cookies. She is radiating well-being, love, joy, and peace. She tells us about her wonderful life, her wonderful husband, now passed on, her wonderful children, and more. She seems to be saying that she has loved and been loved, has gone for what she wanted and given what she had, she has fulfilled though not exhausted her*

*passionate love of life, and now she is happy to love and give, seeking*
*no return for herself . . .*

When I moved to Santa Fe I was disoriented, depressed, overweight, and without any spiritual practice. In my last years at Lama I had stopped meditating. I had stopped sitting in the prayer room. I read horror novels instead of chanting late into the night. I went for long, lonely walks in the woods, tuning into the mind of the forest. There was nothing for me in the prayer room. Meditation had nothing for me.

The first discipline I engaged in while in Santa Fe was jogging in the park, forcing my fat body to huff and puff and exert and sweat. When I had some money, I joined a gym and became a devotee of high-impact aerobics, running and jumping and lunging with a room full of sexy ladies. I could feel the burn and the endorphin rush on a daily basis. I called it my evening attitude adjustment. After fifteen years, though, the high impact became too stressful on my body and I shifted to sweating it out on the stationary bike.

I engaged in fasting to reduce and control my weight. I would drink only water for three, five, seven, ten days at a time. As I understood, when the stomach is given nothing to digest, it stops producing gastric acid and physical hunger ceases. I had to deal with a lot of mental and emotional hunger, such as cravings, food fantasies, and so on, but if I put my attention on my body, there was no physical hunger. My body was actually relieved to take a break from processing all that shit. Having no new calories to fuel its activities, the body activates autolysis or self-digestion, drawing on the calories that are stored in the fat cells.

At first I had fears that I would have no energy, with no food to give me energy, that I would have to lie around listless all day, just wasting away. At first, I indulged in such fantasies, along with the food fantasies. Imagine my surprise when I found that I actually had more energy than before, that I could function longer and with greater concentration without always thinking about eating and taking time for eating, which of course involves shopping and cooking and cleaning, as well as eating and shitting.

In my desire to lose weight I had inadvertently discovered fasting as a spiritual practice. I experienced that my body was enlivened, not by calories, but by spirit. I found that I could work all day at my job in the business world with no lack of energy or concentration. I might take more time at home to rest, rather than eat, but I could work on the job nonstop and feel great. Man does not live without food. But man does not live by bread alone, either. Life is breath. Life is spirit in the body.

Water fasting is not for everyone. It worked well for me. There is, of course, the likelihood of putting back on all the weight that was lost once you start eating again, unless you change your eating habits. Nevertheless, I effected a permanent 15-percent weight loss over several years of intermittent fasting.

On the job, when I was not fasting, I found that if I took my lunch hour and ate my fish sandwich and fries I would be nodding off and struggling to keep from falling asleep all afternoon, as my blood rushed out of my head and into my belly. I found that if I went out to my van at lunchtime, lay down, and took a brief nap, I would be energized and alert for the rest of the day.

I joined a group of mostly Lama beans—Rahaman, Kate, Subhana, and Surya—in leading the Dances of Universal Peace at the Unitarian Church in Santa Fe, in a wonderful, sparkling white, high-ceilinged sanctuary. We had big, glorious, monthly dance meetings all through the eighties. I continued sitting in the center of the circle, playing guitar, at first. Then they asked me to lead dances as well, as I had a large repertoire of dance music. At first, I was reluctant to get off my butt and out of my comfort zone, but it didn't take long for me to enjoy leading dances.

Leading dances is not only instructing the group in the words, the music, and the movements of the dance, but also giving an attunement to the meaning of the dance, transmitting an appropriate atmosphere in as few words as possible. The dance leader needs to be both hierophant and traffic director, literally head in the clouds and feet on the ground, absorbed in the refined divine presence and calling out directions like a kindergarten teacher at the same time. The dance leader must engage not only outer listening to the music and inner listening to the heart, but also what Saadi calls active listening, hearing all the voices in the group and allowing the group breath to guide the direction of the dance. Dance leadership, like the motto of the state of New Mexico, grows as it goes.

I have always led dances in a group leadership format. Sometimes advance planning is needed, especially for larger events, but it usually works for each leader to show up with a couple of dances to offer and just see how it flows. There was one time and only one time when I was the only dance leader to show up. I was not at all prepared to lead the whole meeting. But one dance just led to another, and I found out that I could lead a whole meeting with no preparation.

We had a problem with one of our drummers. He was a great drummer—too great to support the dance leaders. He would interrupt and correct the dance leaders. His drumming would take over and control the rhythm of the dance, overriding the instructions of the dance leader. He really was a great drummer, but more into the art form than the heart form of the group. As he was my friend, it was my painful duty to inform him that we were choosing another drummer, maybe not as great a drummer, but someone with more attunement, to be our primary drummer. He never came back to our dance circle.

While the Unitarian Church was undergoing renovation, we moved downtown to the social hall of the Episcopalian Church of the Holy Faith. With a high-pitched cathedral roof and great acoustics, this felt like a sacred space. We were happy there until one day a woman called me and gently inquired about our philosophy. The next week we got a letter from the minister of this High Episcopal Church informing us that we were no longer welcome in the church. When we tried to have a discussion with him, we got papered with a bunch of quotes from St. Paul about worshipping idols. These Christians were no more tolerant of universality than the Lama Muslims had been.

The dances moved to the Church of Religious Science and then, for some reason, to the basement of a television studio. We were losing magnetism, with fewer and fewer dancers all the time. Finally, one snowy night, no one showed up to dance. Rahaman and I looked at one another and admitted that it was all over. We stopped holding dance meetings.

But the community was not ready to let go of the dances. For the next year we held discussion groups at private homes to find out what went wrong. No dance, just talk. It turned out that there were a lot of hurt feelings and a lot of bruised egos, and a lot of issues centered around the dances. The upshot was that if we were going to start up the dances again, the leaders would need to commit to monthly meetings at home to process with each other so that our unprocessed emotional offal would not pollute our dance meeting. We had run for seven years on grace. Now it was time to pay attention to our humanity.

We started the Santa Fe Dances of Universal Peace up again in 1992 with a new constellation of leaders that would include myself, Maboud, Tara Andrea, Dena, Shems, and Judi, and of course, regular monthly home meetings. Soon enough we were also back at the Unitarian Church.

I would go back up to Lama most every year for dance camps. One year, Saadi announced to us that the dances were getting out of hand, beginning to lose consistency and identity. I knew what he meant.

A fragrant young hippie girl named Strawberry Moonshine had denounced our dance meeting in Santa Fe. "These aren't the Dances of Universal Peace!" said she as she stomped away.

"Well, what are the Dances of Universal Peace?" we called after her.

"The Dances of Universal Peace are when you dance around a fire and raise the cone of power!" said she.

Saadi said that they were asking us all to join a Mentor Teachers Guild, which would provide mentored training and certification for dance leaders and ensure an unbroken chain of transmission back to Murshid Sam. At first I bridled at the idea of a hierarchical organization. "Think of it more as a friendship," Saadi told me, "a companion in dance leadership walking through life with you, someone to check in with." Wali Ali agreed to be my mentor and grandfathered me into the guild.

Our revived Santa Fe dance meeting was humming along. Accommodating six dance leaders every month was something of a stretch, and there were the inevitable personality conflicts. But the issue that split up the leaders' group was chemical sensitivity. Without any discussion, Tara Andrea had put "please come fragrance free" on our posters, which caused Dena, who was fond of her perfume, Shems, and Judi to revolt—in part at what seemed like a pseudo issue and in part at what seemed like an authoritarian coup. We had heated meetings and even hired a mediator, all to no avail. Those opposed thought that chemical sensitivity was a psychological issue that they did not wish to accommodate. Perhaps it was just a pretext for personal animosities to have their way.

Although I had no firsthand experience, I could plainly see that some members of our community were extremely chemically sensitive, including our drummer, and that perfume could make them ill. I cast my vote for fragrance free.

When the smoke cleared it was me, Maboud, and Tara Andrea who carried forward the Santa Fe dance meeting. Maboud and Tara brought big energy to the dances, focusing on community building and outreach. Maboud has been a real inspiration to me, as he receives melodies in dreams, which he uses to develop very powerful dances together with his wife, Tara Andrea, who is an excellent musician. We led the dances together in Santa Fe for sixteen years until I moved to Albuquerque.

I also took refuge in weekly *gatha* classes, focused on the teachings of Hazrat Inayat Khan, led by Shirin. She led us in Sufi prayers and practices and read the gathas. I loved the depth of these classes but never stayed for tea and cookies, always eager to get back to my familiar aloneness.

After ten years or so, Shirin stopped giving the classes but the rest of us continued to gather for zikr practice, first at Hamid and Cleo's, then at Ananda's, and finally at Joseph's home, where we held full-moon zikrs. There was silence and deep reverence in these gatherings, but also an atmosphere of spontaneity and enthusiasm around chanting zikr. Each month I drove due east, straight into the full moon, for zikr at Joseph's home. By this time, we were intimate enough with each other to allow improvisational freeform chanting, sitting or standing, and to let the lead voice pass around the group, making for some exquisite harmonies.

The rhythmic meetings of the dancing hearts of the lovers has continued unabated for close to fifty years now. If my life were a string of beads and each bead were a location, a relationship, a friendship, a job, a study, an activity, an identity, a book, a song, and on and on, the string on which these beads are strung is breath, meditation, sacred chant, zikr, and the Dances of Universal Peace. Being human, there are politics involved, but these are just blips in the continuum of ecstasy.

I did return to Lama for dance camps and retreats in the summers. At the conclusion of one Ram Dass retreat, there was a fire ceremony in which people were encouraged to find pine cones, invest them with karmic bonds they wanted to burn, and toss them in the fire while the group chanted a mantra invoking Kali the Destroyer of Illusions. Normally I only watched, but this time, I felt called to participate.

The cock, the snake, and the pig at the center of the Tibetan Kalachakra represent the three root causes of suffering: lust, anger, and ignorance. I translated this somewhat obliquely into contemporary terms as attachment to or obsession with money, sex, and power. I thought these would be good karmic bonds to work on releasing.

I found three pinecones in the forest and meditated with them, investing them with my attachments to money, sex, and power. As I concentrated on this, I realized that, by and large, I had much more aversion to money, sex, and power than I had attraction to them. I especially had judgments about money and power. Then I realized that resistance, repression, and denial of money, sex, and power were equally attachments, that negative hang-ups were as binding as positive clingings.

I saw that I wanted to give up all pushing or pulling, attraction or rejection, all judgment on money, sex, and power and simply let them be what they are, energies tumbling in emptiness. I had to give myself permission to deal with money, sex, and power without craving and without aversion, simply allowing them to be in life, and to continue developing compassion in emptiness.

That night under a full moon we stood in a circle around a large blazing fire, chanting a complex mantra to Kali. One by one people came forward clutching their pine cones invested with intention, and tossed them into the fire. Ram Dass as *pujari* (priest) would sweep his hand upward and pronounce *"Swaha!"* (So be it!) with each offering.

Conscious of the full light of the moon, the light of the fire, the impersonality of the ceremony, I came forward and tossed my three pinecones—my attachment to and rejection of money, sex, and power—into the fire. I was ready to begin a new cycle.

∞∞

Sometime in the late seventies my mother ended up on psychiatric medication. The story we were told was that, after all her children had left the nest, she began acting crazy, acting out in certain ways. She may have had a psychotic break. I don't know. I wasn't there. Personally, I believe that the only thing wrong with her was that she had too much energy and awareness for my father to deal with. The fact is that she was briefly hospitalized, and then my father, backed by family friend Dr. Magruder, gave her a choice: institutionalization or medication. She chose the meds and ended up on Haldol, an extremely strong drug used to treat schizophrenia and acute psychosis, for ten years.

My mother continued functioning as a wife, cooking and cleaning and all that, but there was no light in her eyes, no sparkle, no merriment. She had been reduced and subdued. I was shocked. In my eyes there was nothing wrong with her other than a repressive husband and a complicit doctor. But I wasn't there. I couldn't do anything about it.

When my father was dying, Mom got off her meds and the light returned to her eyes. My sister Lucy was shocked that Mom was so happy after my father died. Now she was free to be herself, without soul-deadening medication. She survived my father by a good sixteen years. Her mind was lucid and alert to the very end.

My father took a forced early retirement in 1979 at age sixty. My impression is that, once he stopped working, he didn't do all that much with his life—mow the lawn, take walks, and play golf. He didn't really have any friends to speak of. My sense is that he was bored with living. When cancer came for him in 1989 at age seventy, he didn't fight it. He felt a pain in his leg in the spring and by summer he was consumed. The last three days of his life he turned his face to the wall, stopped communicating, and would not eat. He refused to allow any of his children to come home to say goodbye to him, so I stayed in Santa Fe and kept on working. I had been a disappointment to my father and he was a disappointment to me.

The day my father died, I was making love with my girlfriend Melinda. On the bright, sweaty morning sheets we were reaching another peak of sexual ecstasy when the phone rang and rang and rang. I knew my father had died at that moment.

That Sunday afternoon, we hiked up Big Tesuque Creek, high above Santa Fe, up through the aspen forest and meadows to the ridge above the top of the ski lift. I felt an aching, throbbing, stabbing pain in my lower back. I imagined it was my kidneys, the seat of fear, metabolizing my body's fear of my body's death now that the body that had embodied me proved to be dead. After a couple of hours of walking through the pain we got to the ridge and sat down on the rocks in the sun. Small gray birds clustered on the rocks around us. The pain calmed down . . . but returned every Sunday for many months.

Melinda was a lovely young woman from Tennessee, tall, willowy, and blonde, with big brown eyes. A massage student, she was renting a room in a house where I was staying. One night, I had a dream that she came into my room, lay down with me, and made love with me. The next night she really did come into my room and lay down with me. She asked me to just hold her. It felt wonderful and blissful. The next night she came into my room again, lay down with me, and made love with me. Effortlessly, love came into my life again.

Melinda and I reached sexual maturity together. Melinda was the first woman who had completely surrendered herself to me in physical love, with no blocks or controls, internal or external. I was the first man she reached orgasm with and did so repeatedly, time after time. Together we reached very high states of unitive energy and awareness, beyond thought, beyond mind, for long periods of time. We would make love for hours on end, sometimes all day. Our romantic passion lasted about two years.

Melinda was a gentle, loving soul, spiritually open, focused on establishing herself professionally—and tragically on the verge of mental illness so severe that she would end up taking her own life. I was work-ing full time and raising a son who was bursting into adolescence. I was present to her process as much as she would allow it, but I could not navigate the devastated territory she was entering into.

The first signs of trouble were when she became moody, discour-aged, depressed. She was sucked into negative emotions that rendered her unable to keep appointments and work on the clients she did have, let alone bring new clients into her practice. She became agitated and anxious about her career. Her radical mood swings moved her deeper into depression, despair, futility, and suicidal thoughts. She began hear-ing conflicting voices inside her head that tormented her with mental agitation that would not stop. She became distracted and confused.

Our relationship became unbalanced and inconsistent. She would push me away from her and cut herself off from me. She would cling to me and not let me go, weeping like a terrified child. She would become angry and abusive and punishing. She would distance herself from me, hide from me, and cut me off. Then she would pull me in and start cycling through the changes again.

During our time together I had used Joanna's methods of psychic clearing to keep on dissolving the painful reactions that kept coming up inside me, feelings of rejection, abandonment, and confusion. Instead of letting myself be overwhelmed by all these familiar feelings, I would go out and take long walks, working with the energy vortex within and around my body to release these limiting feelings back into space. And it worked! For the first time in my life, I could recognize and take charge of clearing away negative emotions. I came back from these walks clear, calm, invigorated, and inspired.

I also used vortex energy for psychic birth control, as we never used any physical form of birth control. While we were making love, I would be aware of the vortex of energy surrounding our bodies and put into the vortex this information: *No conceptions, no pregnancies, no births. No conceptions, no pregnancies, no births.* I did not have to repeat this mantra for very long, but I did do it with absolute certainty, knowing on every level that this was true.

But none of Joanna's methods would be of any help to Melinda.

There were certain times when I was overtaken with grief and sorrow deeper than I had ever felt before. One summer afternoon, I lay on the couch and wept nonstop for at least three hours. I cried deep, racking sobs and shed more tears than I have cried in my entire life, while Melinda held me and the landlord was trimming the Siberian elm bushes outside my window. I never cried in front of anybody if I could help it, but this time there was no help for me but to let the deep sorrow well forth. I had no idea of why I was so emotional. Melinda might be withdrawing from me as a lover, but we still had our relationship, our friendship. Here she was holding me. Where were these tears coming from?

As her mental disturbance developed, sex became the only way that she could get beyond the torment of her agitated mind. But as her inner fragmentation grew deeper, even sex could no longer take her beyond her mind. "No more sex," she finally told me. "It just doesn't work anymore."

On our last night together, sleeping in separate rooms by that time, just before I fell asleep, I saw a bright point of light pass very slowly above my bed, just like watching a satellite orbiting way, way up in the sky. I knew that this was the spirit that wanted to come in to me and Melinda, but I knew that this was not the right time for this to happen.

I had suffered what I thought was schizophrenia in my twenties. I had heard many levels of voices singing inside my head and endured repetitive suicidal thoughts. It was part of coming to wholeness, according to R. D. Laing in *The Divided Self*. Through spiritual practice, spiritual community, spiritual guidance, and inner work, I had moved through this fragmentation to a greater wholeness. I felt confident that Melinda would also, in time, move through this dark period and come to greater wholeness and peace.

I couldn't have been more wrong.

Melinda was suffering the adult onset of congenital schizophrenia, inherited from her mother's side of her family. Schizophrenia had overtaken her mother at about the same age as Melinda was now, in her early thirties. Her mother was hospitalized when Melinda was nine years old. Her father divorced and remarried. Her mother has been institutionalized or on medication ever since, with a manageable but incurable condition. Apparently her mother's mother had suffered the same illness.

Delusions, voices, irrational destructive and self-destructive behavior— her madness was much more virulent than anything I had experienced. She lost her clients. She packed up all her belongings. She moved out of her house. She spent the summer wandering around the Southwest desert, sleeping in the camper shell on her pickup truck. She stayed with friends. She checked herself into a rehab center but found no help there. She asked me to drive her and her truck back to Nashville on Thanksgiving 1991.

On the three-day drive back to Nashville, we sometimes talked as normally as possible, given her darkling depression. At other times she would howl and scream like a caged and tortured beast (the male entity), her blood-chilling cries of agony and rage destructive to the passivity of her body. At other times she was completely limp and lifeless, silent and uncommunicative. I was heartbroken and helpless before her madness.

She ended up moving in with her crazy mother in Nashville. We continued to stay in close touch, having long telephone conversations late at night. As winter turned into spring, Melinda became more and more passive, lying in bed and watching TV all day and all night with ever briefer spurts of manic activity in between. Sometimes she claimed to be Jesus ("I mean THE Jesus," she would say), filled with divine light and healing for the world. "You know he died at thirty-three, the same age as I am right now," she would say. But most of the time, she was sunk in a bottomless dark pit of despair and could find no light.

She refused all medications and was phobic about how they might affect her. She realized that this was an inherited genetic predisposition to schizophrenia. She felt that her body was "damaged goods," no use to her nor anyone else.

On the week of her thirty-third birthday, in August 1992, Melinda surprised me by saying that she was going to come out and visit me. Her daddy had bought her tickets, her daddy was going to drive her to the airport, and she was excited about seeing me and being back under the wide blue skies of New Mexico. The night before she was to come, she called and we talked late into the night, excited and happy to come together again.

The next morning, I got a call from Melinda's brother. It was hard for him to speak and hard for me to hear what he told me. He had left a hunting rifle lying around in his mother's house. That morning Melinda had put the barrel of the rifle in her mouth, put her toe on the trigger, and blew her brains out.

The world stopped for me then, and a certain part of my heart shut down. Shock, horror, sorrow, grief, anger, denial, despair. At least now I knew why I had felt such profound grief the year before.

At the funeral, her father said, "Melinda has made many choices since she became an adult. I have not always agreed with her choices, but I have always supported her in her choices. And I support her now in this choice she has made."

I was amazed at the wisdom and compassion of her father's words. It was a daring and courageous act to free herself from the bonds of an irreparably damaged body. But at that moment there was no way I could support her in the choice that she had made. I was in shock, I was hurt, and I was angry, very angry.

The psychic activity in my dreams immediately before and after her death was awesome, revealing, and to some extent, healing. I felt Melinda's spirit coming into my space, just as she had promised, clinging to me. I could not allow her to "reside" with me. I spent long hours in meditation clearing my space of her spirit, clearing her spirit of all the anger and despair that kept it attached to the Earth plane.

Melinda always loved the dark, dry seed pods that fell from the carob tree. She loved to use them as shakers when she danced. I had a big bag of those seed pods that she had given me. That fall I took those seed pods up to a long, flat, deserted mountain top and spent the afternoon dancing, shaking those pods, singing spirit songs to Melinda, loving her, blessing her, releasing her, throwing the shaken pods into the four directions and finally, finally, saying goodbye to her. It is the deepest song I have ever sung in my life, one that I can never sing again.

My heart shut down. My eros withered. It would be thirteen years before I would be intimate again.

I was lonely most of the time. My refuge was walking in the mountains around Santa Fe, particularly Atalaya, the mountain on the eastern edge of the city and closest to it. Atalaya, which means "watchtower," is nothing remarkable to look at, kind of like a battered green bread loaf with a few crusty cliffs edging the top, rising to two thousand feet above the city beyond St. John's College. The much higher peaks in the Pecos Wilderness are far more awesome to behold from the city. You might not even notice Atalaya. Access is through an exclusive subdivision and public parking is very limited, so there are never many people on the mountain.

Atalaya was my most intimate mountain sanctuary for two decades. I knew her ridges and valleys, her edges and curves, her birdsong and creature rustle, her winter desolation, springtime bounty, summer glory, and fall colors as well as a husband knows his wife.

At first it seemed like there was only one way up the mountain, about two hours of steep climbs and ridge walks to the high ridge. Over time, I discovered a delicate web of trails penetrating every area of the mountain: the moist valleys, north and south summit trails, adjacent peaks, and the back country sealed off as the Santa Fe Watershed. I could take an hour or a day to hike Atalaya. There is one lovely peak rising up on the south side that a movie actress bought to build her house on. She carved a road up to the peak, but then relented under community pressure and gave the land back to the people.

Atalaya was unremarkable from a picture-taking point of view but absolutely exquisite as the territory of my soul. I knew every part of her, and she knew my every mood.

Cerro Gordo, Santa Fe, New Mexico.

One Easter morning on the path, I held silent conversations with the souls clamoring to be born through me and Melinda and made it clear that this could not happen.

One crisp fall afternoon, walking up a shady valley, I suddenly was called to lie down in the grass and say goodbye to my Aunt Bee, as if she were lying right next to me, at the very minute she was dying in Washington, D.C.

One summer afternoon I was cruising along the summit when, glancing out over the city, I saw a plume of smoke rising from my neighborhood. I wondered if it was my home going up in flames and for a brief moment felt free of all attachments and worldly cares. I knew that it would really hurt if I came down off the mountain and found that it really was my house burning down. But for the moment, I couldn't deny that I felt elation and release, a clear lightness of being.

One stormy spring afternoon, before I had a regular job, I took some LSD and climbed Atalaya alone. When I got to the high ridge at the top, the winds were howling and raging with gale force, obliterating my mind. I listened to all the voices of the wind, sang into the wind, and howled and whooped and yelled all afternoon until the rain came pouring down.

## Winter 1993

I decided that I was ready to buy a house for the first time in my life. I spent nine months house hunting but found that I had a strong emotional resistance to buying a house. On a glorious day in June, after viewing one of the last remaining hilltop lots in Santa Fe, a gorgeous building spot, I went for a drive in the country to celebrate. Immediately a feeling of darkness and gloom descended over me—fear, terror, and despair. To build a house there, anywhere, would be to be trapped, doomed—that was all I could hear.

These feelings were so intense and irrational. I began to realize that they must be due to the restimulation in present time of negative emotional complexes hidden away in the subconscious. I had carefully considered this move and explored its consequences. I had made a rational decision that seemed supported by higher consciousness, and I was approaching it all in a very business-like manner. But subconscious reactivity kept being restimulated and getting in the way. I knew it was time to ask Joanna for help.

In session, Joanna guided me to look at various contributing factors—the loss of my beloved through suicide, my early childhood alienation, and my immediate previous life as a fugitive from the Holocaust. This alone took many hours of concentrated work. Though resonant, none of these recordings seemed primarily causal, and we asked to be shown the picture that was the root cause of my not being able to buy a home.

I maintained awareness of being in space, it seemed for eternity. I asked to see, to be shown, and waited, waited, waited. Finally, in the gray ethers of my vision, there was a small opening through which I could see flames. It was a lightly constructed house, as in the tropics. The roof was on fire and collapsing in on me.

Joanna said, "Where are you?"

I heard, "India."

And immediately my rational mind tried to invalidate me, "Oh yeah, sure, India, that's fantasy."

But I had learned to discount the resistance of my rational mind to seeing, and said out loud, "India."

Joanna said, "Good, go into the picture deeper. Get more information."

I sensed that there were men standing outside my house, men who had set fire to it to destroy me. I got a clear picture that I had been an astrologer living in an Indian village, a small man with a white beard, a good man, a Sufi, and a lover of wisdom. Joanna told me she saw that I had a wife and a small child who were also destroyed in the fire. I tried to identify the men who destroyed me. My mind said that maybe they were Hindus who hated Muslims. Having identified the causal picture, I released the picture and all the feelings associated with it using the vortex energy, dissolving all the light particles back into space until nothing remained. Then I replaced that picture with my new blueprint for a home, family, love, and security. Now I was clear and ready to proceed.

I related this to David Frawley, a Vedic scholar friend. He asked whether this incident was in recent times, after the partition of India and Pakistan. I said it seemed to be in an earlier century. He remarked that

Hindus were not known for their violence but that Sunni (orthodox) Muslims were known to persecute Sufis and other heterodox believers.

When he said that, it all fell in place: my Sufi heritage but aversion to orthodox Muslims, my love of astrology but reluctance to promote my profession to the public. The bottom line was that the last house I had owned had been burned to the ground, myself and my family along with it, and this had been the memory that caused the arising of fear and terror at the prospect of owning a new house. Several years later I would immerse myself in the study and practice of jyotish or Vedic astrology, reclaiming some of my past-life wisdom.

## August 1994

I found a beautiful affordable house to buy in a quiet neighborhood by the Santa Fe River, just in time for Abe to move in with me at the age of sixteen. He had been living with his mother for a while, but now her new marriage and her new household were dissolving. Abe came to live with me for the next eight years. Although he had dropped out of high school to be snowboarding, he gradually found his way back into education. By the time he moved on at the age of twenty-four, he was well on his way to getting his life together and becoming a paramedic and a firefighter.

To my dismay Joanna had little knowledge of or use for spiritual traditions. She was a spiritual maverick. Her realizations were based on her personal experience, not on traditional wisdom. When the Jehovah's Witnesses came to her front door wanting to talk about God she said to them, "You want to talk about God? How about talking with God? I'm God! What do you want to know?"

Joanna and I remained close friends until her death in 1998 at age ninety. In the long run, our love for each other was just as important as any metaphysics. She trained me in her methodology and wanted me to carry on her life's work. I did work with some other people for a while using her methods and found them very effective. But working with people in this way is not my calling. As she was not connected with any tradition, her philosophy and methodologies perished with her personality.

I did edit and publish her husband's masterwork, *Totality Concept* by Hardin Walsh. Their life work survives only in the two books I published.

I had decided that meditation had nothing for me long before I left Lama. I could and did sit with the community, but sitting meditation had lost its juice for me. More and more I would spend hours walking in the woods alone, immersing myself in the mind of the forest's deep, very slow, prehuman thoughts. Meditation was nothing, I thought. Nothing happened. There was nothing for me in meditation.

Over time, my life became full of a lot of worldly concerns that I had largely avoided while living on Lama mountain. But after years of immersion in telephone, traffic, and business, my mind became full of so many things that I began to miss that nothing I had experienced in meditation, that space behind the mind, between the breaths. I wanted to have that spaciousness, that peace and quiet, that serenity, back in my life.

Once again I established a meditation practice in my life. I found an old black office chair whose seat was broad enough to sit cross-legged

in, whose back was tall and flexible enough to support my body, and this became my seat, my asana, my tiger skin. Every morning, before anything else could happen, I sat in my chair, no longer on the floor, and concentrated on breathing in and breathing out, concentrating on the stillness behind all the phenomena of my mind, which would rise and fall and eventually quiet down.

I lived in ten different places in my first ten years in Santa Fe. But my meditation seat was always next to my bed, and first thing every morning, I would sit in silence, watching my breath, aware of rising dream and falling dream.

All sorts of mental and emotional activity arises in this space, as well as mantra, wazifahs, and zikr, and no matter what needs to arise, there is no need to repress or suppress it, the practice is to honor whatever comes up to awareness and return awareness to breathing in and breathing out. The utmost simplicity of this practice becomes the accommodation for everything else in life to arise and pass on without disturbing the simple presence of awareness.

> *When that practice is done for a long time, uninterruptedly,*
> *and with sincere devotion, the practice becomes a firmly*
> *rooted, stable and solid foundation.*
> YOGA SUTRAS OF PATANJALI: 1.14

There came a time when I was deeply immersed in the teachings of *advaita* (non-dual) Vedanta, in particular the illuminating discourses of Ramana Maharshi and Nisargadatta Maharaj. The fundamental teaching is that the soul (*atman*) is the same as the ultimate reality (*brahman*).

> *All that is required to realize the Self is to Be Still. What*
> *could be easier than that?*
> *Take no notice of the ego and its activities but see only the*
> *light behind it.*
> *The ultimate truth is so simple; it is nothing more than*
> *being in one's natural original state.*
> RAMANA MAHARSHI

The advaita masters engaged in brilliant dialogues with any and everyone who appeared before them, with the certainty that the same essential reality exists in each and every being. There is no separation between self and reality because, ultimately, there is no limited self.

I would sit out on my porch, smoking, reading, drinking beer at night, being aware of the truth of these teachings, being aware of essential presence, and yet also being aware that something was missing, that I was fooling myself by pretending that simple presence is the ultimate truth. It is—but it isn't. Something was missing.

I call this my period of advaita solipsism. Solipsism is the theory that the self, one's own mind, is all that can be known to exist. Am I all that is, as advaita seemed to be saying, or am I just fooling myself? In retrospect I can see that what was making me so uncomfortable was that I did not know myself fully, although I thought I did. I did not know my repressed rage and the roots of my addictions and all sorts of other unconscious material filtering and distorting my experiential reality. For simple presence to be truly simple and not just partially delusional, the gates of the unconscious would have to open and all the poison come to light.

A correlation of solipsism (my mind is the only reality I can know) is that anything outside my own mind is uncertain—the external world and other minds cannot be known and might not exist. There is only one reality and I Am It.

"I think therefore I am" is a great place to start but a lousy place to end up. I am aware of being present as the space in which everything exists, and specifically, as being present as the space in which the luminous, self-absorbed whirlpool of self-awareness answering to the name Ahad appears.

Although I did have moments, even hours, of being present in essential reality, in which I realized the truth of unity, my "normal" state of relentless mentation persisted for most of my waking hours. Even though I finally acknowledged a state of contentment in my life, buffered by smoking and drinking and ample leisure time, I could not discount vague feelings of depression and loneliness. It was the writings of A. H. Almaas that demonstrated to me that my realization of essential self could be, and indeed was, very real, even at the same time as unresolved psychic patterns persisted.

*There have been many cases in which a highly acclaimed teacher or guru behaves in a disturbed manner which does not accord with what is known about spiritual development. Some people take these situations to mean that the particular teacher (or guru) is not really spiritually developed. However, the truth of the situation might be that the teacher can experience and manifest very deep spiritual states and insights, but his development is incomplete because his realization is obscured when certain unresolved self-representations (and their object relations) arise in his consciousness under certain circumstances, and he cannot disidentify from them.*

A. H. ALMAAS, THE POINT OF EXISTENCE

Over time it became clear that there is a more autonomous dimension of my being that is constantly speaking, singing, and guiding me, which I become more aware of when I quiet my mind and listen—the still, small voice of calm. But this "voice that sounds like God to me," as Leonard Cohen sings, can also be insistent and intrusive, until I pay attention to it.

The singing voice of my youth, which gave me so much poetry, had its own wisdom and agenda quite apart from my conscious ambition to master my craft and be recognized as a poet. It was not under my control. It had its own rhythm and timing. It would repeat a key phrase in my mind until I gave in and wrote it down—and then, when I was paying attention, it would give me the rest of the poem. It was like taking dictation. All I had to do was show up and write.

There is an autonomous voice that is with me constantly in everyday life, letting me know what to do and how to do it, so that often I don't think about what to do next—I just do it. And it can be very persistent if I don't pay attention to it.

One Christmas Eve I was getting the prompting to go over and visit my friend Adrienne and give her some money. I rarely touched base with Adrienne, who lived on disability in Section 8 housing, but I enjoyed her sharp mind and her Christian heart. I kept on ignoring this prompting all day, but it just would not let me be, it just kept bugging me until I surrendered and went over to visit her and bring her some money.

Her story was her gift to me. "I'm getting older," she said, "and my health is not so good, but I wanted to experience love once more in my life. So, I asked God, I prayed to God to give me someone to love. And God answered my prayer. While I was on retreat at Pecos Monastery, I fell in love with one of the monks there, Brother John. He is so beautiful, and I love him so much, but he can't love me in return, because he is a monk, married to God. You see I asked God for someone to love and he gave me someone to love—but I forgot to ask for someone who could also love me in return."

God does answer prayer, so be careful what you ask for.

I went to Ram Dass's public darshan in Santa Fe in October 1996. He was sitting on stage at the center of a crowd of people. I watched the sparkle of the crystal mala beads (prayer beads) as they passed through his fingers, remembering Ram, Ram, Ram, as he talked on and on and on.

He said that, in his thinking, he was coming to speak of three levels of being: ego, soul, and awareness—awareness here meaning eternal consciousness beyond time and space. As usual, Ram Dass had the gift of being able to formulate, with elegant simplicity, the realizations that had been nudging around in my head for some time now.

So then and there someone asked him, "What about reincarnation? Is that real or not?"

And Ram Dass replied, "From the point of view of awareness, there is no reincarnation for there is no identification, only pure awareness. However, there may be and often is some self-identification on the soul level after the body is dropped. So, then, I would say that that which identifies reincarnates."

One evening at twilight, the sun not yet set but behind the ridge, I was driving slowly along West Alameda on my way home. Twilight is that in-between time when things may not be what they seem. My eye was caught by a woman walking on the sidewalk ahead of me. I gazed at her shapely denim-clad butt, her long dark hair, and, as I was passing, her beautiful face. I felt instant attraction. She must have felt my attention because at that moment she turned her head to look at me, revealing the other side of her face, which was horribly burned and scarred. I felt an instant repulsion equal to my attraction. The attraction and the repulsion cancelled each other out, which blew my mind. . . .

Suddenly I was standing face to face with her in a timeless place, witnessing that we were two pure soul lights focused in different physical realities. This recognition took place, as do many essential experiences, in a split-second in eternity, a moment outside of time, which resonates throughout life.

## January 4, 1996

My last day of work in the business world. I had gained much skill in accounting and computer technology, but I was relieved to step out of the arena of quantity, of left-brain information management. Experiential reality is largely the result of where I focus my attention. If I am focused on numbers eight hours a day, my experiential reality is pretty dry. I signed up for courses in graphic design at the community college.

## May 5, 1996

A massive forest fire swept through Lama Foundation, causing all the residents to evacuate, astounding us in Santa Fe with TV images of towering clouds of smoke billowing up from the mountain. When it was safe to return to the land, the residents found that the central dome, the new community center, and the old kitchen had all been spared, but almost all of the other structures and 95 percent of the forest had been destroyed. The residents had lost everything and came back to live among the ashes.

Several weeks later, I drove up to Lama to witness the devastation. The land was ankle deep in soft gray ash. We had to wear breathing masks. I climbed the high hermitage hill with Rahaman and surveyed the surreal lunar landscape left by the fire. Where there had been an endless carpet of green forest there was nothing but smooth gray ash punctuated by the black toothpicks of burnt trees. It was deathly still and silent, with no birdsong, no creature rustle. The residents were charred, black smudged, ash covered, red eyed, and burned out.

Siddiq's wife Sakina started a fundraising office in their home in Santa Fe. I immediately volunteered my services. I was galvanized to action. Lama was my spiritual home. There was no question that I would devote all my time to restoring Lama. I did whatever I could in the fundraising office: mailings, accounting, and a lot of graphic work—newsletters, brochures, flyers, posters, and more. Over a million dollars were donated to Lama after the fire, an outpouring of love that demonstrated how much Lama meant to the world. I played a small part in that fundraising.

The resident community was traumatized, disoriented, and uncertain how to continue functioning. Siddiq and I held numerous meetings with the officers of the foundation to provide support, perspective, and guidance. All assumptions about what Lama is and how Lama functioned had been burned up in the fire. The resident body could no longer handle long-term decision making the way it always had in the past.

Out of this crisis we evolved the Lama Council, a circle of representatives of the residents, the continuing members, and the Trustees, entrusted with making long-term decisions. The greater circle of nonresident Lama beans would now participate in the long-term decision-making process. Since the average resident stays at Lama for only three or four years at most, the Lama Council brings long-term perspective and stability to decision making.

The real heroes of the restoration of Lama were the crews of people who worked on land reclamation for several hot summers under Jai Cross. They cleared away the masses of burned branches and fallen trees and created land contours and barriers to prevent erosion from the rains. They planted thousands of piñon and pine trees. They brought down most of the burned snags. John Murray put up the first building after the fire: he rebuilt the Maqbara Hermitage by hand, using only lumber salvaged from the burned forest. As work was going on to complete the community center, the new Coordinator, Bird Sharples, championed building new residences using straw bales and other alternative building materials. A new and very different residential template emerged after the fire.

Lama Foundation Dome.

At Annual Meeting in 1997, I was elected to the Board of Trustees and immediately, to my surprise, made Chairman of the Board, a role I did my best to fulfill over the next five years. My years on the Board of Trustees were a time of service, of giving back to Lama something of what Lama had given me. It mostly involved driving up to Lama for all-day Council meetings and participating in the politics from a more detached perspective.

Our most significant action at that time was to revise the Lama Foundation's Statement of Purpose. The original Statement of Purpose was idealistic and vaguely Gurdjieffian.

> *The purpose of the Lama Foundation is to serve as*
> *an instrument for the awakening of consciousness*
> *through the harmonious development of the*
> *three-fold nature of man,*
> *and to that purpose found a center . . .*

Forty years and many generations later, no one had any idea what that meant. Money was coming in to rebuild the buildings, but we had no real idea of who we were or what we were doing. In particular the perpetual Lama conundrum presented itself: Are we a community functioning as a spiritual school or a spiritual school functioning as a community? This is perpetually resolved in favor of the latter but nevertheless remains a conundrum.

We invited a skilled facilitator, Kate Brown, to help us. She told us to forget about revising the Bylaws, the "how-tos" she called them, and focus on arriving at a genuine Statement of Purpose. You can't figure out how to do it until you know what you are doing and why you are doing it. She led the whole community in a chaotic and fruitful day of brainstorming, filtering through hundreds of flashes of inspiration to arrive at a new Statement of Purpose.

> *The purpose of the Lama Foundation is to be*
> *a sustainable spiritual community and educational center*
> *dedicated to the awakening of consciousness,*
> *spiritual practice with respect for all traditions,*
> *service, and stewardship of the land.*

This meeting was, for me, the high point of the Lama revival.

After five years of service on the Board of Trustees and Lama Council, I resigned in 2002. I was confident that Lama had stabilized, had reconfigured, and would survive. I was weary of the tedious and encumbered decision-making process. I was in deep disagreement with some of the directions the reconstruction was going in. I felt Lama needed guest housing to serve the profitable retreat programs. The residents wanted to build a cottage industry studio to house the marginally profitable prayer-flag industry. I gave in and withdrew.

Lama had been my life curriculum not once but twice. That was enough. I further resigned as a voting continuing member and am happy to be a non-voting free associate.

One summer, when I was at Annual Meeting, the continuing members gathered in the prayer room to renew membership. Each member lit a tea light and placed it to float in a big bowl of water, resulting in a pool of floating flames illuminating the dark prayer room. I closed my eyes in meditation and was aware of everyone leaving the room. I thought I was all alone deep in the silence, until Asha spoke.

"You really should write down your memories of Lama before you're too old."

That pebble dropped into the still pool of my mind. The waves it made rippled back and forth for several years. My memories of Lama are highly personal. I was not ready to write them at that time. Gradually I came to feel that photographs from my time at Lama would give a truer and richer picture—worth tens of thousands of words—than anything I could write. So, in my own time and in my own way, I began to work on the so-called "Early Lama Book."

I had kept all my negatives, slides, and prints from my time at Lama, leaving copies of everything on the mountain. Everything had burned up in the fire—pictures, writings, and records. Nevertheless, there were some surviving folders of photos scattered around and stashed away, which I collected to use. The book, titled *Early Lama Foundation,* consists of about 70 percent my photos and 30 percent other peoples' photos. I wrote enough text to bear witness to the early days at Lama Foundation, so that future generations can have a fairly impersonal and truthful understanding of those early years. The first printing of *Early Lama Foundation* was gifted to Lama, along with the copyright. It is Lama's to reprint and sell as long as it wishes.

One gray fall day, I was walking down a valley path by a stream in the woods above Santa Fe. The day was chilling and darkening, as if it was going to snow. I could hear the water gurgling behind the dense masses of willow shrubs. I was walking along lost in thought, when I heard the sharp scolding of ravens and looked up to see many ravens flying low overhead, flying together in formation up the valley, big dark birds with wings spread against the stormy sky, like the Luftwaffe blitzkrieg over London. This was unusual and unnerving, but I kept on walking and thought no more of it. . . .

That is, until an hour later, when I was coming back up the path: I rounded a bluff and there, next to the path under a cottonwood tree, was a large congregation of ravens sitting on the ground together, seriously talking with each other—a parliament of big black birds in a circular clearing. I was amazed. They were startled—and immediately flew away with loud complaints. I had no idea what to make of such a sight.

When I got home and listened to the news, I found out that America had just invaded Afghanistan that day, this was the fall of 2001, sending in wave after wave of bombers.

∞∞∞

In 2002 Abe moved away from home at age twenty-four.

Raising Abe had been relatively painless, as I had loved him, supported him, and let him do whatever he wanted, for better or for worse. I would not subject him to the kind of repressive control I had experienced from my father. I threw away the rules I grew up with. Abe was a good kid with a good heart, a mensch, intelligent, and independent. Unlike me, his primary gifts were social and athletic. His passions were snowboarding, river rafting, and all sorts of wilderness sports. Unlike me, he started working at an early age and traveled a good deal with his friends. Indeed, he raised himself with his friends as much as he was raised by his parents.

For a while, it seemed as if he was just an outdoor slacker. My patience was wearing thin. But his horoscope told me that higher guidance and good fortune would kick in at age twenty-four—and it did. A good woman motivated him to get his own place, and she lived with him for a while. He turned his interest in wilderness medicine into studying and getting licensed as an EMT, Intermediate EMT, and paramedic. As of this writing, he works for Santa Fe County as a firefighter and paramedic. Every day he is helping people and saving lives. I am very proud of him.

∞∞∞

In 2002 my mother was hospitalized for seven weeks in Baltimore, effectively beginning her end-of-life process at age eighty-two.

My mother had been having a merry old time ever since my father died in 1989. But now, old age and her bad habits were catching up with her. She was a major alcoholic, sometimes starting her drinking in the morning, and smoked her Chesterfields like it was World War II. We three children were her closest friends, and we rallied to support her as her health grew worse. My sister Katherine, trained as a nurse, was her primary caregiver, followed by my sister Lucy, with me a distant third. After she took a number of falls at home, we persuaded her to accept visiting and then live-in help. In the last year of her life, she surprised all of us by moving to Portland, Oregon, to be close to Katherine. She suffered no mental impairment and was sharp, lucid, and talkative to the end.

I had been sustained by my mother's love throughout my life. She may have been harsh and critical of my sisters, but she was always interested in and supportive of whatever I was doing, even though she didn't always understand what I was doing, nor did she need to. When I spoke to her of spiritual matters, she would say, "Oh, Frank, that's beyond me!" Her love was constant in my life.

I accepted her dying by dying along with her . . . or at least imagining dying. There had been no intimate love in my life since Melinda took her own life ten years before. Abe had left home and was getting his life together. I was chronically lonely, but I was used to it; I accepted it. I was free to do whatever I wanted. My meditation was strong. I felt that my spiritual state was one of contentment.

From time to time, I would lie on my bed in the afternoon and imagine that I was dying. I reviewed my life to see if there were any regrets, unfinished business, karmic debts, or unfulfilled desires. There were none. I was reconciled to my fate, whatever it was. I was content. I was free to go. I was dying along with her, an unusual bardo. Of course, you could say I was just pretending—and I was. You could say that if I stayed with it longer, if I went deeper, if I were in a prison cell . . . and you might be right. But this was my experience at the time. The Sufis say, "Die before death."

There are stages of expansion and stages of contraction on the spiritual path. At times the love, the joy, the enthusiasm, can expand until consciousness fills the cosmos. At other times, all hope is lost and one is all alone in the dark. Some Sufis consider contraction to be the higher state. Lying passive on the bed, shrunk to my own nothingness, I know I am completely in God's hands, "like a corpse in the hands of its washer."

Despite my long association with Ram Dass and Maharaj-ji, I had never understood the Ramayana as sacred scripture. It's a very charming story full of miracles and wonders, not to mention monkeys and bears, and, no doubt, a lot of ethical homilies. But to me, sacred scripture is full of, well, the Word of God, inspiring me and telling me what to do in no uncertain terms, the voice of Jehovah and Jesus and Allah. Not so the Ramayana.

I shared my quandary with Ram Dass, who just smiled and said, "You must not have been with us back then."

Then one fall afternoon in the middle of my life, I was walking up an arroyo in the forest above Santa Fe. The sunlight was sparkling on the brilliant autumn colors of aspen and scrub oak. I was thinking about how many of my contemporaries were coming to full fruition in their fifties, showing their full colors. I was feeling the sunlight penetrating the cells of my body with liquid heat and light. I was feeling sunlight alive in everything, rock, tree, bird, blood, experiencing all life as embodied sunlight, when all of a sudden—I got it!

Rama is of the solar dynasty—Ram, Sun, Ra. If Ram is Sun and all life is sunlight, then every creature in life, every character in the Ramayana, is sunlight, is Ram, is God. It's not just the story of the avatar who loses his kingdom, loses his wife, and forgets himself. That's just the pretext for the story. The Ramayana is a vast and glorious celebration of the divine life, sun, light alive in every living creature. We realize who we are through our heroic actions and remember who we are as we die and merge back into the sunlight. Ram, God, Sun is life itself in all its infinite variety. That is sublime sacred scripture.

Sherry Bishop, my one-time employer asked, "Ahad, do you think we choose our birth or is our birth chosen for us?"

My mind started whirring. Do we have the freedom to choose the form of our incarnation or are we impelled by the momentum of our previous karmas into a necessary life formation? I shifted up out of my dialectical mind.

"Sherry," I said, "I think that both are equally true and even more than that on a soul level."

# 8 JYOTISH, 1998–2010

My first job in Santa Fe found me working in an office in a house built of river rock in the oldest part of the city, the Barrio de Analco. When I went out for my lunch break I would stop and talk with the man who was watering the front lawn. He was a tall man with a long face, long hair, and luminous eyes. He was David Frawley, a Vedic scholar who had written *The Astrology of the Seers,* a book on jyotish astrology. I was drawn to the wisdom that flowed easily from him, and I asked him to read my Vedic horoscope.

Jyotish is a wisdom tradition that has been unbroken for thousands of years and is an integral part of Hindu spirituality. Jyotish has always used the sidereal zodiac. The sidereal zodiac measures the actual zodiacal constellations in the sky and the planetary positions in these actual constellations. The twentieth-century sidereal positions of the planets are about twenty-four degrees earlier than the tropical positions shown in the western chart. (The tropical zodiac shifts over time against the background of the fixed sidereal zodiac.)

When David showed me my Vedic chart, the first thing I saw was that my Moon was in Leo . . . just as I had always known it was! The Moon was in warm Leo, not cool Virgo. The Sun was in intellectual Gemini, not emotional Cancer. And sensual, earthy Taurus was rising. My mind, my heart, and my soul relaxed. This was my true horoscope. I knew I had come home. David said that my chart was a difficult one for marriage. My first and seventh houses (self and other), my first and

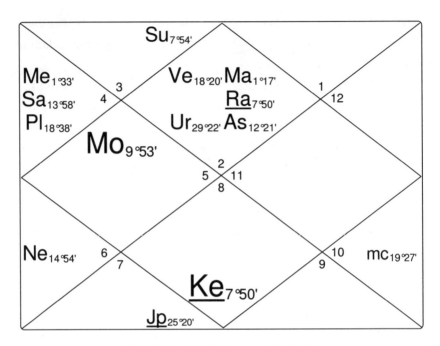

Rashi Chakra, jyotish horoscope, Ahad Cobb.

seventh lord (self and other), and Venus were all strongly afflicted by
Rahu and Ketu, the Nodes of the Moon, which play a major malefic
role in jyotish. They create turbulence and sudden unexpected change
wherever they are located, in my case in the areas of self-identity and
love relationships. At times it feels like life is out of one's control. This
had indeed been the nature of my love life.

Dismayed, I said to David, "Well, what do I do?"

His answer: "Well, you could always worship the goddess."

I had no idea what he meant, but over time I found out.

Jyotish has a unique system of planetary periods, *vimshottari dashas,*
that give a picture of the unfolding of the karmic potential of a horoscope over time. The *dashas* and *bhuktis* (periods and sub-periods) are
considered more primary than even transits as indicators of life events.
If the transits indicate marriage but the dasha/bhukti does not indicate
marriage, it's not going to happen—or if it does happen it's unlikely to
last. The dasha/bhuktis set the stage for what's going to happen and the
transits fine tune the timing.

I took home the horoscope David had given me. I tested it right away. I did a detailed analysis of the timing of the major love relationships in my life to date. Much to my surprise every single one of these relationships had both begun and ended in the bhukti (or sub-bhukti) of either Rahu or Ketu. Every single one without exception! I was astounded. I was converted. Jyotish is the real astrology!

I began to read everything about jyotish I could get my hot little hands on, which wasn't all that much at that time. I got a rudimentary computer calculation program from David. I worked my way through his substantial correspondence course. I studied everything I could for the next ten years and got absolutely nowhere. I had mounds of information that I just could not digest, compute, metabolize, absorb, or make sense of.

Meanwhile I was attending the monthly meetings of the Santa Fe Astrology Forum, a delightful gathering of the astrological community founded by Edith Hathaway, Arielle Guttman, Heather Robbins, and Marcia Starck. I would walk into a house packed full of astrologers excitedly talking to one another. Astrologers are generally very light beings. There was a lot of light in the room. After a while we would focus together on presentations or topics for discussion, often the mundane astrology of politics and current events, sometimes new techniques. Western astrology was always coming up with new planets and new analytical techniques. This was a lot of fun. I made some good friends. But I was no closer to learning jyotish.

One night David invited a few people over to his house to meet K. N. Rao, a jyotishi who had founded a school for jyotish in New Delhi. Mr. Rao was a small man with a very white beard and a very big mind. He was life-long celibate and lived alone. He had worked as a government employee in the tax department. When he came home from work in the evening, he would do jyotish with whoever came to see him until late at night. He never took any money for reading charts or teaching jyotish. Jyotish was his sadhana, his spiritual practice. It was difficult for him to be in America where everyone wanted to give him money for looking at their charts. He didn't want to accept any money but was persuaded that this was the custom in the West.

Finally, I had some validation for my own attitude about money. My astrology was spiritual service in a wisdom tradition, not about buying and selling. I had always felt like a bit of an outcast in the astrological community for not charging money, for not trying to make a living reading charts, but now I perceived a healthy model for my values in Mr. Rao.

Finally in 1997 I resolved to do all my charts in the light of jyotish, to force myself to learn it in practice, with no turning back. I began to make terrible mistakes. The worst was when I was reading for a woman who was concerned about her prospects for marriage. She had Rahu and Ketu in the first and seventh house, just as I did, so I said, as David had said to me, that this was a difficult chart for marriage. I told her that the coming year promised romance and relationship but not to count on it to last. In fact, her affliction was much less severe than mine. In fact, she did get married within the year and her marriage endures to this day. She may have forgiven me by now, but she was pretty distressed by my unwarranted prediction.

I had been a decent amateur astrologer with a good heart and good intentions to help people, but I had also been frustrated at the vagueness and pseudo-psychology of my knowledge from books. It was clear that most people appreciated receiving attention, perspective, and guidance, God willing, from looking at their horoscopes with me. I was always given appreciation and gratitude. But I had no confidence in the accuracy of the information. Jyotish promised to be and indeed proved to be much more accurate and insightful.

I had learned Western astrology through reading books, observing myself and other people and nature, and tracking the movements of the planets with calendar and ephemeris for the past thirty years. I had been trying to learn jyotish that way for the past ten years—but it just wasn't working. I was totally committed to jyotish and I was screwing up right and left. I needed a teacher. I needed to find someone to teach me how to do jyotish.

In 1998 my teacher appeared. Hart DeFouw, who had a reputation as a superb teacher, was teaching a series of three courses on jyotish at the Ayurvedic Institute in Albuquerque, beginning in September.

Jyotish is an oral tradition in which books are not primary source material. Books are backup to the transmission of a living teacher. Hart DeFouw had studied one-on-one with his jyotish guru, Mantriji, for fifteen years. Mantriji refused to let Hart write anything down. If he pulled out pen and paper, Mantriji would abruptly shift to mundane topics. Hart quickly learned to give Mantriji his full attention and only at the end of the day go to a park bench and furiously scribble down everything he could remember. You can read all the books you want about jyotish, but you can't learn jyotish from books.

After I had studied with Hart for a while, I came back to David Frawley and said, "Western astrology is false. All those people in the Astrology Forum are totally deluded."

David looked at me with a gleam in his eyes and said, "Ahad, there are many ways of looking at the sky. We happen to believe that ours is more accurate and insightful."

That set my mind to rest. There are many ways of looking at the sky.

Jyotish is an oral tradition, part of a vaster oral wisdom tradition known as *sanatana dharma,* eternal dharma. The earliest sources we have of this tradition are the Vedic hymns, the four Vedas, which date back to 5000 BCE. Jyotish is one of the Vedangas, one of the "limbs of the Vedas," in fact "the eye of the Vedas."

We are raised in a literate culture where books are the primary source of knowledge. This is all morphing as we enter into global cyberspace together, but for the last two thousand years at least, the written word has been the primary form in which knowledge has been preserved and transmitted in Western culture, starting with the holy books, the Torah, the Bible, and the Qur'an. The teacher teaches from books, no matter what the subject.

We are conditioned to think of oral knowledge as malleable, changeable, and unreliable, as in the game of Telephone where some story gets passed around a circle whispered from mouth to ear, from person to person, and the delight is in how the story gets distorted as it moves. It is inconceivable to us that oral knowledge could be perfectly preserved without error or corruption over thousands of years—and yet that is exactly what happens in India and other oral cultures.

Mr. Gurdjieff, for example, was raised in the Caucasus Mountains of Russia at the turn of the twentieth century. His father would take him to seasonal gatherings of bards chanting traditional epic poetry, epic chanting contests, which deeply impressed the young boy. Imagine his surprise some twenty or thirty years later when he read that the four-thousand-year-old Sumerian Epic of Gilgamesh had just been translated from cuneiform tablets—and the text was exactly the same epic poetry his father and his friends had been chanting!

Oral tradition teaches by repetition and intensity, forming neural pathways imprinted with the preceptor's voice (rather than words printed on a page), forming a living, speaking knowledge. The Vedas were chanted for thousands of years before being written down. Classical jyotish books (*shastras*) are full of pithy, often enigmatic, verses that are meant to be memorized and then unpacked or unfolded by the teacher's commentary. Commentary is necessary to breathe life into the condensed verses, which are ideally memorized at an early age. In India it is said that a book that is not spoken is dead.

In 2012 I was in a carpet store in Jaipur that sold beautiful carpets made by hundreds of families in Rajasthani villages. Some people were making carpets as an exhibit for tourists. I watched an old man sitting at a loom rapidly and unerringly pass the shuttle back and forth, weaving a complex design.

"Where is his design?" I asked. "How does he know what threads to weave?"

"Each line of thread he weaves is a line in a chant he has memorized," said the store owner.

When asked to do so, the old man chanted a verse for each line he was weaving. The whole carpet was a memorized chant of hundreds of lines! Multiply that one carpet by hundreds of carpets in hundreds of families . . . I was astounded. That is how the knowledge of carpet design is passed down through generations of presumably "illiterate" villagers.

∞⌒∞

Hart was a brilliant teacher. He would talk in an organized, focused fashion with no notes whatsoever. Knowledge was fully present without outlines or notes or quotes on three-by-five-inch cards. He was quite well prepared on his topic yet unbound by any agenda, which is to say, he was free to let his mind roam wherever the moment took him, weaving it into the theme of the day or going off on illuminating digressions.

Unlike his guru, Hart did allow us to take notes in his presence, but he himself always spoke from inspiration and without notes. He did distribute a booklet of the core principles he was teaching in each course. But true to style, he didn't necessarily teach everything that was in the booklets and would often engage in major unplanned side trips from the topic du jour.

For me this was breaking out of the confines of the library and entering the stream of the living word, forging new neural pathways in my literate brain.

Although I have a twelve-inch stack of course booklets and a four-foot shelf of notes I have taken from Hart's classes, I rarely if ever refer to any of them. When I teach jyotish I prepare teaching materials, handouts, sample charts, and so on—but I don't need to prepare myself or brush up on the subject very much. The knowledge is fully present as it was given—in awareness, in breath, and in speech.

The first thing Hart said on the first day of class is that jyotish is the study of the lords of light. *Jyoti* means "light." Isha means "lord." Jyotish is the study of the lords of the outer light and the inner light (*prakriti* and *purusha*).

I once asked my guru, "What is the inner light?"

He replied, "Did you have a dream last night?"

"Yes."

"By what light did you see the objects in your dream?"

The goal of the jyotishi is to become a *devajña*, a knower of the divine, a seer of the unseen.

That first day, Hart also did one of his frequent on-the-spot, spot-on demonstrations. "How many of you have Capricorn rising?" he asked. Three out of thirty students raised their hands.

He asked each one, "Have you moved in the last year, changed location, moved to another house?" Each one of the three said that this was the case.

"How did I know this?" he said. "There is a principle that states, 'When the lord of the first house (of the body) is debilitated in the fourth house (of the home) in a moveable constellation, the native will move.' This year Saturn, which rules Capricorn, is transiting in Aries, its debilitation constellation, a moveable constellation, in the fourth house for someone with Capricorn rising. If you have Capricorn rising, you have moved this year."

Such spontaneous demonstrations of accurate insight and knowledge of the unseen were based on the memorization of thousands upon thousands of discrete principles with specific application. Jyotish is not a rational, logical, systematic body of knowledge. Learning jyotish is like swallowing iron balls, his guru would say. And yet Hart did an amazing job of not only presenting the categories of knowledge but also articulating methods of analysis and judgment. Jyotish is preserved in *parampara,* in family lineages. Hart was transmitting to us the consciousness and methodology of his lineage.

Hart DeFouw was not a large man, but his presence and his mind were very large, shining with the light of jyotish. He was intense, fiery and wiry, pitta personified, *brilliant,* quick, illuminating, irritable, insightful, and energetic.

> The best thing about my teaching is that I teach by inspiration. The worst thing about my teaching is that I teach by inspiration.*

Guru stories, digressions, jokes, topical commentaries, philosophy, etymology, stories of *devas* and *asuras* and celebrated personalities, all were as much part of his teaching as the nuts and bolts of astrology. For me it was a re-immersion in the ocean of the Hindu spiritual wisdom tradition whose waters had first blessed me through Ram Dass.

---

*Quotes in this chapter are from Hart DeFouw.

Hart gave lasered attention to any object that came in view. Once he stopped speaking for several minutes to follow the course of a fly that had wandered into the classroom.

*A fly can fly. But can a fly fly to India? If a fly should fly into a jet plane going to India, the fly can fly to India.*

The mind is the fly; the jumbo jet the *jyotir vidya,* the living wisdom tradition.

We soon learned not to ask questions in class. A simple question asking for a simple answer would invariably lead to an exhaustive twenty-minute response that would derail the momentum of his presentation. We learned to hold our questions to the end of class or outside of class, although he did value the occasional *pariprashna,* the illuminating and clarifying question.

Hart required all his students to take the three jyotish foundation courses he offered as a prerequisite to attending more advanced classes. If we are all on the ground with the basics, he would say, later we can fly together. A very dedicated and coherent body of students gathered around Hart during the twelve years I studied with him, many brilliant and luminous souls who became my colleagues and friends.

I had been reading charts as psychological profiles with the tacit assumption that character equals destiny. Jyotish liberated my perception of what is depicted in a horoscope to the vaster paradigm of karma. The horoscope is a karma-scope depicting all the experiences that are ripe to manifest in a lifetime. My karma, as reflected in my horoscope, includes the nature of my potential for success, recognition, wealth, relationship, vocation, education, health, longevity, travel, and spirituality, as well as indications of all my relations with others (mother, father, etc.)—in addition to my psychological profile.

The concept of karma misunderstood and narrowly applied is deterministic and limiting. Correctly comprehended, the concept of karma includes not only the accumulated results of past actions unfolding in the present but also the perception that new karma is continually being created in the free will.

> *Free will is our volitional capacity to act in a direction untainted by our conditioning. Everything we experience is ultimately the effect of our free will, most often free will exercised without full awareness of the consequences.*

I may be driving late at night on a narrow road winding through the forest in the Jemez Mountains. I am probably not aware that there is a herd of elk crossing the road just around the next curve, that this experience is about to happen. I will not see them until I come around the curve. I have free will as I am coming around the curve. My ability to meet this experience is limited only by my momentum, my attention, and my awareness.

This experience may or may not be indicated in my horoscope and it may or may not be "my" karma. In fact, there are three sources of karma: oneself, other beings, and acts of God. I am not the only actor in my world.

Here are some examples.

My wife-to-be was driving us north on the interstate when a red truck veered in front of our car and we slammed into it. The driver of the southbound truck had suffered a heart attack and lost control, crossing the median and coming into our path. Our car was totaled. The man died later that day, while my wife and I came through with relatively minor injuries. The experience of that accident was not indicated in either of our horoscopes—but I am certain it would be there in the chart of the man who died. We were impacted by his karma.

Six years later, my wife was stopped at a traffic light when a texting teenager slammed into her rear end. At the time it seemed like a minor accident with minor damage to her car. She got immediate treatment for her injury. But complications from that accident and from treatments she received developed into four years of painful recovery. At that moment, the transiting planets impacted her chart from every angle, indicating the nature of the karma impacting her personally.

A young woman fell down a ventilation shaft to a horrible death. Her mother came to me and asked if it was murder. Her chart very clearly indicated that other people were involved in her death, although I could not say that it was intentional murder.

Another woman was visiting her mother in a big city. Late at night, she heard people fighting on the street outside the house. As she approached the front door to see what was happening, a stray bullet came through the door straight into her heart. She died instantly. Nowhere was this indicated in her chart. Her death was karma that she experienced, but she was not the source of that karma.

The horoscope is a karma-scope in which the jyotishi sees a symbolic reflection not only of a person's personality and character, but of all of his or her relations, all of life's conditions, successes, failures, gains, losses, and so on. And behind all the drama of life's experiences, there is the pure presence of the soul having those experiences. The concept of karma allows the soul to witness all these experiences in a broader, more impersonal way. We all come to Earth to have experiences and we all ultimately experience everything—the good, the bad, the ugly, the exalted, and the debased.

A woman came to me for a reading. She was a single mother who supported her daughter by working as a bookkeeper. Unfortunately, she had worked for many years for a man who was running a Ponzi scheme, fleecing his clients of millions of dollars. She had to have suspected what was happening, but she wanted to hold on to her job and her income. Now the law had caught up with him, and it looked as if she was going to be indicted in federal court as an accomplice to his crime. She was a very sweet person. She wanted to know if she was going to jail. I was able to look at her chart and say, "The indications in your chart are definitely consistent with spending time in jail," and I gave her the time frame. This relieved her of her uncertainty and allowed her to prepare and put her affairs in order. She did, in fact, spend several years in prison teaching yoga.

I had always been wary of the slippery slope of flattery, of a reading that consists solely of saying good things about people. Now I was finding that when I could articulate the suffering and challenges apparent

in a chart it came as a great relief to the client, the validation of someone else perceiving their suffering, something most of us try to keep
hidden from the world.

◌◦◦◌

Mantra is an essential component of jyotish. Before class we would
chant mantras to Ganesha, Devi, and Surya. Ganesha or Ganapati is
the lord (*isha* or *pati*) of the *ganas,* the categories of knowledge invoked
at the commencement of any study. From the Goddess, Devi, Lakshmi,
Saraswati, all speech and the fulfillment of all desires flow forth. Surya,
the Sun, is the illuminating, shining light, the essence of jyotish.

We align ourselves with the divine source of this illuminating wisdom tradition, the jyotir vidya, which is itself a goddess. The more you
dance with her, the more she dances with you.

I had been in love with mantra ever since I heard John Coltrane
growling, "A love supreme, a love supreme, a love supreme. . . ." My
use of mantra had been entirely devotional: to clear the mind, open
the heart, and let the love flow. To paraphrase Krishna Das, mantra's
essence is not in the words, but in the love we feel in our hearts.

With jyotish study came the practical application of mantra.
Recitation of planetary mantras or deity mantras is a core element of
the *upayas,* the remedial measures jyotish offers. To propitiate, draw
near to, or come into relationship with Mars, for instance, one might
fast on Tuesdays, wear red, and recite Mars's mantra 108 times or 1,008
times. Alternately, one might fast on Tuesdays, wear red, and recite
Hanuman's mantra. There are many specific applications for mantra.

Ganapati is the lord of obstacles, who both removes obstacles from
my path and places obstacles in my way for my awakening and growth.
As pati (lord) of all the ganas (categories of knowledge), he rules not
only intellectual knowledge but actual living knowledge, that is, not
only intellectual knowledge about chemical reactions but the lawful
categorical chemical reactions themselves; not only the musical scales
but the rhythms of the planets. I have many *murtis* (statues) of this love-
able, pot-bellied, four-armed elephant-headed raja with his trunk dipping into a bowl of *ladhus* (sweets). Colorful imagery aside, Ganesha

has shown himself to me in the inner world as the immeasurable vastness of the entire universe.

Now when we're driving around downtown looking for a parking spot, my wife will say, "You'd better pray to your elephant." And before I can say *Om Gam Ganapataye Namaha* three times, a parking place appears. It rarely fails to work. This mantra is potentized by my practice, which maintains a relationship with this cosmic potency.

Ganesha, Hindu devotional poster, artist unknown.

When I was much younger, I had a hard time asking God for anything in prayer. There were a couple of times I lost something and was so desperate to find it that I asked Jesus to please help me find it, the lost coin, the contact lens washed down the drain, or whatever—with instant results. What was lost was immediately found! God answers prayer! I proved this to myself.

However, I felt ashamed at the poverty of my need and embarrassed that I would trouble so august a presence as Jesus with such petty things. I was amazed at such divine demonstrations but so convinced of my own worthlessness that I resolved never to ask for help from anyone, let alone God. I would go it alone.

In my adult life my egoic independence led me to breakdown after breakdown and the inevitable realization that I was totally dependent on that higher power. I can play my guitar until there are calluses on my fingertips, but I am totally dependent on my skin to make those calluses. I could not create one living cell on the tip of one finger.

One cannot go through life completely alone. Help was constantly flowing in from all sides even though it took me a long time to accept this. I still don't have the habit of asking for things in prayer, but when push comes to shove and times are desperate, I will take my cares and concerns, my needs and desires, and turn them over to the higher power that creates and animates all and everything. I no longer pretend that I'm bothering someone. God has infinite capacity to respond to everything for God lives in everything.

꩜

Jyotish not only provides insight into the karmas playing out in the time stream of our lives, it also offers upayas, or remedies that may serve to alleviate our conditions, fulfill our desires, and strengthen our abilities.

The classical upayas are spiritual remedies: fasting, mantras, and charitable acts. Typically, one would perform upayas to propitiate the planetary deva who is the lord of the planetary period one is running, especially if it is difficult or challenging, typically fasting on the day of the week ruled by that deva.

At that time, I was running the eighteen-year period of the great malefic Rahu, the North Node of the Moon, the Serpent's Head. Rahu brought me many gifts but much sorrow as well. Rahu has no body and rules no day of the week. But Rahu is like Saturn, so upayas for Saturn work for Rahu as well.

I chose to fast on Saturn's day, Saturday. Nothing but water would pass my lips until the sun set. I also kept silence as best as I could: no telephone calls, no email, no errands, no running around, no busyness. This brought a calm still center to my weekly rhythm. I was actually observing something similar to the Jewish Sabbath.

I integrated recitation of Saturn's mantra into my daily practice. I fed black ravens and black ants, Saturn's creatures. I gave money and offered kindness to homeless people. I was not trying to get something from Saturn. I was trying to come into a greater alignment and conscious relationship with Saturn.

On occasion I gave the upaya of feeding ravens or crows to people running Saturn periods. One man, who had an exalted but very problematic Saturn, chased all over the Southwest trying to find ravens to feed. It was difficult and took a long time. Finally in the middle of a snowstorm on the rim of the Grand Canyon, just as he was about to leave after three days of waiting, the black birds accepted his offering. It took him great effort to feed his ravens. Another woman, who had a strong and

comfortable Saturn, found it easy to feed her ravens, simply putting offerings under a tree in her neighborhood. She told me the food they loved best was peanuts in the shell.

The classical spiritual upayas (fasting, mantra, charitable acts) are all forms of prayer that serve to place our karmas, our cares and concerns and desires, into the hands of the gods, the deva, the divine.

By contrast, the wearing of jyotish gems specifically strengthens the influence of particular planets for better or for worse. Gems are expensive, not for everyone, and can be seductive. Gems must be prescribed very carefully, based on the natal chart. Wearing gems can be beneficial and life-enhancing, but wearing the wrong gems for your chart can strengthen the destructive potential of malefic planets, as I found out.

My mother had given me a beautiful star sapphire ring that had belonged to my grandfather. Blue sapphire is the gem of Saturn. Strengthening Saturn in a person's life is very tricky. Only certain people can benefit from wearing sapphire. Wary of wearing it, I kept the ring hidden away in the back of a drawer for a very long time. When I finally decided to put it on, right at the start of a Saturn period, it was a total disaster.

We were booked to fly to Europe at the very time that the Moon was conjunct Saturn. Big mistake. The flight was delayed and then cancelled due to heavy snowstorms. We arrived a day late. We were on a river tour through Germany. Limiting conditions from my childhood and past-life echoes of the Holocaust were reactivated. I became severely depressed, beset by fear and anxiety. I began making lots of mistakes and experiencing undue amounts of delays. I couldn't think clearly. But when I took several bad falls, the last one down the steps in front of a museum in Vienna, I took off the ring, never to wear it again. It was as if Saturn was giving me a full-on darshan. "You really want to see how bad I can be, buddy? Well, here I am, in your face, twenty-four seven."

*When we are truly in jyotish we are devajña, knowing the divine. That which is beyond our ken is deva. That is why you can never be certain of the results of upayas. When the blessing comes, it is deva. The idea behind an upaya is to be a giver, not a taker. If you receive a blessing, this is deva.*

⌀⌀⌀

By 2003 my social life was largely taken up with sharing commutes to go to class in Albuquerque, giving readings, and hosting or attending study groups with my brilliant fellow students.

> *A student obtains one-fourth from the acharya (scholar),*
> *one-fourth from his own thought, one-fourth with other*
> *students, and one-fourth from time (unfolds over time).*

Hart was not just teaching us jyotish. He was teaching us how to be astrologers, how to give readings. He taught us how to discern definite objective facts about a person's life from a chart and how to use gentle questions to inquire about the validity of these perceptions.

The light of jyotish began attracting many people to come to my home for readings. The most universal response to having their first jyotish reading, to learning their planetary positions in the sidereal zodiac, was, "This feels much more like me than my Western chart. This feels like my real chart." My sentiments exactly.

There is an instant intimacy that occurs when one is looking so deeply into another person's life, due to the penetrating insight of jyotish, a genuine appreciation of how amazing each one of us truly is. In that moment, it was almost like being in love. Then she or he would walk out the door. I found myself wanting to keep on letting the insights pour forth, to call them up and say all those things that never got said. But I knew that whatever was said in our time together was exactly what was meant to be heard. The results of the reading were for the client, not for me. I had to practice not only letting each one go, but also forgetting about their charts and their karma. I became a master of detachment—confidentiality guaranteed.

I was still a student. I was still not asking for money for my services. But somewhere along the line, the idea of reciprocity crept in, the idea that it would be good for people to give something for what they were receiving, to balance the exchange. So, I began asking for a love donation, whatever they wanted to give.

~~~~~

In 2003 Hart moved from Albuquerque to San Rafael, California, where he would teach for the next seven years. I spent a lot of time with the beautiful people in magic Marin, studying with Hart. What he was teaching us was priceless and we knew it.

Hart did not pretend to be a guru, although he talked extensively about philosophical and spiritual matters. He got up at four o'clock in the morning to do his practices and prepare for the day's class. He ate a spare vegetarian diet. He was very pitta, fiery, brilliant, sharp, incisive, hilarious, and withering in his criticism of those he saw as distorting the tradition. His sun was shining all the time. He never stopped teaching. In addition to jyotish, he taught us palmistry, Sanskrit, and Yoga Sutras.

Hart began teaching us *prashna,* which opened up my paradigm of reality in a major way. *Prashna* means "question." Prashna is the art of giving a specific answer to a specific question based on interpreting the horoscope cast for the moment the question is asked of the astrologer. In the West this is called horary astrology. Although it has some skilled practitioners, it is no longer widely practiced in the West. Hart said that prashna is the most widely practiced form of jyotish in India, and it is his own personal favorite.

If the birth chart reflects the sum total of karmas ripe to be experienced in this life, prashna reflects the present moment, a moment beyond birth, and measures where the unfolding karma has arrived—a karmic update, so to speak. For prashna you don't need to look at the birth chart to answer a question for someone. You don't even need to know the birth chart.

It can't be an idle question or a vague inquiry. It must be a specific question asked with a strong desire to know the answer. It doesn't matter if it is a big question ("Will she marry me?") or a small question ("Where is my lost ring?"). What matters is the *prayatna,* the will, the strong desire behind the question.

A man once came to Mantriji to ask about the health of his nephew. Mantriji replied, "Have his mother come and ask me. She will have the prayatna."

The prayatna is crucial because each question can only be asked and answered once for the answer to have validity. Prashna is not like playing with the Magic 8-Ball or flipping a coin enough times so that you get the answer you want. Reality reflects the real answer in the present moment.

If the prashna and the birth chart do not agree about the matter in question, most of the time the prashna will prevail, because the prashna is an indication of what has been done since birth to lead to the momentum of the present moment. If the birth chart is benefic and the prashna is malefic, the person is experiencing results of evil karmas done since birth. No matter what your previous karmas, you are always creating new karmas.

After thirty-five years of studying birth charts, I find that the answer is right here in the present moment. The sky reflects each moment with great precision, the current situation experienced in life, and the answer to every question. This brings me totally into awareness of the present moment in this holographic cosmos.

Oh, yes, and the astrologer must have a pure mind.

John Frawley, probably the best author on traditional Western horary astrology, writes that he would go on radio shows and publicly predict the outcome of soccer matches with uncanny accuracy. After he had done this for a long while, a friend suggested that he bet on his predictions and make some money at it. As soon as he placed his bets and brought desire for money into the equation, the accuracy of his predictions took a nosedive and remained very average until he gave up betting.

I was on fire for prashna, doing it every chance I could. When someone asked a direct question, I would look at the chart of the present moment rather than the birth chart. Here is a sampling of the questions one friend asked me in the course of a year . . .

"Should I buy this car? Should I go to India? Should I do a facelift? Should I cancel the hysterectomy? Should I rent my house or sell it? Should I delay moving? Should I sue my brother? Is my son using drugs again? Is the lost dog going to be found? Will my son find my lost cell phone? Where is my wallet?" There was a lot of prayatna behind each question.

Another friend was looking to buy a house on the east coast. Every time she found a house, she would call me all excited: "Is this the one?" Ten times the answer was no. When she finally found the house she bought, she was so certain that she did not call me for a prashna. Unfortunately, that house burned to the ground a few years later.

Going back to March 5, 2003 . . . a jyotish study group was meeting at my house in Santa Fe. Hart had not taught us prashna yet, but we knew enough to play around with it. As was my habit, I had made a chart for the start of the class (18:00) so that we all could see where the planets were on that day. At that moment George W. Bush was amping up our country to invade Iraq, spreading lies about weapons of mass destruction in Iraq to justify his intentions. There was great uncertainty and anxiety about whether we would go to war or not. Not a single one of us wanted our country to go to war.

We decided to use that chart I had prepared for the start of the class to ask the question, "Will America go to war?" It was a truly amazing chart that unequivocally stated that we would go to war very soon, that America would bring war to Iraq, and that it would be a protracted destructive conflict with no clear victor. It would take the Sun (us) seven days to complete its ninety-degree aspect with Saturn (them). We concluded that we would go to war in one week. As it turned out it was two weeks before America invaded Iraq, on March 20, 2003.

This was not the answer we wanted. We didn't like what we saw in the stars, but we did agree that we all saw the same thing. It was an amazing demonstration of the power of jyotish.

Hart says that the mind is smart enough to realize that it can't know everything and it can't control everything. This generates anxiety. Anxiety is a natural condition of the mind. The mind is too small to really know everything. The remedy for this anxiety is for the mind to take refuge (*sharanam*) in something greater than the mind. Living wisdom tradition, *sampradaya*, is that something greater than the mind. Jyotish illumines, enlightens, and broadens one's perspective on what is happening.

Sampradaya is a gift bestowed when two or more people, the one who has the gift and the other who receives the gift, meet together for the transmission. It is a gift embedded in an established sublime tradition, a noble transcendental universal tradition.

Four things are necessary for a sampradaya, a spiritual tradition, a gift that is shared:

(1) a gift of sublime knowledge, a living wisdom that is noble, true, and illuminating;
(2) a giver, someone who has the gift;
(3) a receiver, someone who can receive the gift; and
(4) a process of transmission.

The teacher must own the gift, must have the gift to give, and the student must be able to receive the gift and must match the qualities of the gift.

People rarely want to have a chart reading when things are going well, life is good, and people are great. Although some people come for knowledge, out of curiosity, or for a periodic update, mostly they come for a reading when life is challenging, when big changes are imminent, for better or for worse, or when there is some crisis. Big changes are about to happen or are happening, but the outcome is unclear and the direction unknown. Often some significant decision is looming, whether to get married, buy a house, make a move, that kind of thing. Often the decision is already made, and the person wants to see his or her situation from a broader perspective. Sometimes the question is: "What can I do to change this?" or "How long is this going to go on?"

Since the ego values homeostasis, lack of change, according to its own nature, and since reality is nothing but impermanence and change, most astrological readings will focus on indicators of change affecting, for better or for worse, the person's reality. The astrologer will often weave a story of astrological momentum: how things have led to the present moment and what the direction forward is.

The changing planetary periods give reliable indicators of change. It is amazing how many people come for a reading coincident with a major change in planetary period. And inevitably, the transit of the great malefic, Saturn, which represents the necessity of change, generates ample insight into the challenges facing the person. One could give an entire reading based on Saturn alone.

One bright summer morning at Lama a woman came to me and said, "Ahad! Last year I saw an astrologer in Boulder, and he said that by this time all my suffering would be over and—Waaah! It's worse than ever!"

I told her that I thought this was an irresponsible thing to say. Astrology can indicate when certain experiences will be experienced and when they will move on into something else—but not that they will never be experienced again.

For instance, Saturn transiting in the second house (mouth) signifies, among other things, the necessity to deal with the neglect of dental health that led to this moment and the necessary change that is happening, that is, either proactive dental care to improve the situation or the teeth getting much worse. What I can't say is, "All your dental problems will be resolved once Saturn leaves your second house. All your suffering will be over."

What I *can* say is, "Now is the time to focus on taking care of your teeth, even if it is very expensive. If you don't, it will be much worse in the future." What I can say is, "If you give this matter the attention it requires, this matter will come to some degree of resolution in such-and-such a time period, maybe not a total solution, but enough resolution that you can move on to other considerations."

As an astrologer, I often find myself put in the role of the Wizard of Oz by clients seeking oracular pronouncements on their manifest destiny from behind the green curtain, while I feel that what is more meaningful is a dialogic inquiry into the nature of reality as experienced by the person. I do provide an initial download of jyotishical insight to impress the person with the uncanny accuracy of the tradition. But then we seek to harmonize the astrological information with the person's actual experiences and expectations. Usually, we are able to arrive

Statue of Ganesha

at a good sense of the karmic momentum in the near future along with remedial measures that may be helpful, which often come from what Hart calls the shastra of common sense.

Some people can't get out of bed in the morning without consulting their horoscope. My goal is not to control reality through esoteric knowledge, no matter how much my ego may wish for that control, but rather, in the words of Hazrat Inayat Khan, "to be in rhythm with life's conditions and to be in tune with the infinite."

There is no single standard way to read a horoscope. Although there are certain approaches that generally work, each reading is in the moment and of the moment. Working with a horoscope is like holding an exquisitely complex crystal in your hand and ever so slowly turning it around over the course of time, continually revealing new facets and new insights.

Most crucial to a reading is the question or questions, conscious or unconscious, that the person is bringing. I always ask my clients to bring their questions to help focus the reading. A more accomplished jyotishi might know the client's question without asking, based on the chart of the moment when the person walks into the room. But, as my mother used to say, "It never hurts to ask."

⚭⚭

Hart always said that jyotish reflects life, life does not reflect jyotish. Astrology reflects life. Astrology is a cosmic mirror in which we see our life reflected in a larger perspective. Life does not reflect astrology. We are not ruled by the stars.

We are not ruled by the stars—but we are subject to necessary identification with any number of conditioning factors, including place, time, genetics, and culture—summarized as *desha, kala, patra:* the place where we are, the time when we are, and the circumstances we are in (body, psyche, family, culture).

Most of the time, most of us operate with limited awareness of the conditioning factors with which we are identified, let alone the karmas flowing forth from the unseen unconscious. We assume we are operating with free will. Free will is a healthy hypothesis, which needs to be continually tested, to be measured against the reality of the results we experience.

Paradoxically, the more we are aware of our identification with defining conditions, the freer we are to operate within and beyond them. The aim of the jyotishi is to see the unseen, to catch a glimpse of the drift of karma, and to communicate this in a compassionate and helpful manner.

Before Hart stopped teaching, he told us, "I no longer believe in astrology. I believe, to the best of my ability, in grace. Astrology is useful, a way to make a living. We live by grace. I employ no gems, no rings, no upaya (remedial measure) stuff. My upaya is to find my way to my guru and cry."

# 9

# MARYROSE

In the summer of 1998 I went to a dance camp that brought many dancers from South America to Lama Foundation. At the end of the week there was a ceremony in which we broke out into groups and each group came up with movements to express particular words of Chief Seattle. My group danced, "The Earth does not belong to us. We belong to the Earth." Unfortunately, my group's movements were very lame compared to the other groups. I felt ashamed at our performance.

The next day I was sitting in the shade of the trees behind the Old Kitchen moaning about my distress to a friend who set me straight.

"Ahad," she said, "there is no right way to pray."

I met MaryRose for the first time at that dance camp. I was walking downhill in the twilight just after sunset when I met a beautiful young woman with long dark hair on the path. We stopped to talk, about what I don't recall. All I know is that there was nothing in that charred landscape, that burned meadow set in a broad vista under the darkling sky, nothing but her luminous eyes. I was enchanted. She was married. I had been down that road before. The moment passed.

MaryRose lived in Albuquerque, where she had a private practice as a psychologist. She began to come to the dances in Santa Fe and before long was training to be a dance leader under Tara Andrea. She was very feminine, alluring, erotic, and veiled in deep devotion. I was strongly attracted to her, but I did not come on to her. It is unethical for dance leaders to take advantage of the magnetism of their function to become romantically involved with members of the dance circle. Besides, I am very shy. At some point during her training, I became aware that she was no longer married.

Over the years, we got to know and appreciate one another. There were times when I drove to Albuquerque to play guitar for her as she led dances. There were times when she came to Santa Fe for guitar lessons or jyotish readings. We talked on the phone. But I couldn't permit myself to love her or desire her.

At the end of one reading, she said, "I have just been proposed marriage. What should I say?"

Saturn was transiting her seventh house of marriage. This usually means a big fat no. I just said, "I think you already know what to say."

In fact, she had already decided she wasn't going to marry.

We kept setting the intention to go for a walk in the woods together and kept on being too busy with our lives to follow up on that intention.

Then one day, MaryRose called me on her cell phone as she was driving back from the Painted Desert. She kept me talking with her from the Arizona border to her front door. She told me how wonderful I am in so many ways and wondered what courtship might be like. She expressed so much love for me that I was blown away. I felt like the gates of heaven were opening up above me. Angel choirs were showering down white light, pure love. For years we had had the intention to go walking together. We agreed to meet.

## June 3, 2005

We drove up into the Sandias to hike on a trail through the high forest out to the Sandia Crest, the steep cliffs that overlook the city of Albuquerque. It was a glorious blue sky, summer day, cooled by high winds. MaryRose was very fetching in a turquoise tank top and navy shorts that barely contained her petite, full figure. Sunlight glittered on her long dark hair that swayed down to her waist. Love light sparkled in her eyes.

The wind was very strong when we reached the edge of the Sandia Crest, so we sat back under the bushes and each smoked a cigarette. She told me everything that was happening with her. We talked about our lives and the great mutation that was occurring in humanity, opening up to each other, feeling out what it might be like to be together. On the way down she told me that if I was attracted to her to be open about it. Repressed desire surged through me. Here was the most desirable woman in my reality, asking me if I was attracted to her. After considering my words, I told her I found her extremely attractive. There were very high winds all day. My world was beginning to shift.

A week later, MaryRose fed me a beautiful dinner of chicken and spinach in her backyard. We hung out in her living room, sitting across from each other. I told her that sometimes I feel lonely, but I am used to it.

"My loneliness is like a ceiling fan that is still turning even though it has been unplugged," I told her.

"You can forget about that!" she said.

At that moment I saw the image of Wendy, the first woman who had ever loved me, shimmering in her face, the same long dark hair and loving eyes.

All of a sudden my heart opened. It was as if there had been a rusty cage around my heart, like a mouse cage, a have-a-heart trap. I didn't even know it was there. All of a sudden, the cage around my heart opened, and I heard my heart say, "the Sufi path of love."

I picked up her guitar. We sang, *"Allah Hu El Allah Hu"* and the descant *"Pour upon Us Thy Love and Thy Light."*

We chanted, *"Inshallah, Mashallah, Alhamdulillah, Allah Ho Akbar."*

A week later we were hanging out on the mattresses in her backyard gazebo. After a while, she moved the mattresses together and we began touching. I felt like a child, and said so, open to touching a woman for

MaryRose, Depoe Bay, Oregon, 2005.

the first time in forever. After a while I pulled her back to my chest and held her as her heat sank into my space.

Driving back to Santa Fe on the interstate, I could hardly recognize where I was. I was rushing down the road to the unknown, into the bardo of falling in love.

Love came to town in a very big way. I had not been with a woman in thirteen years, living like a funky monk in Santa Fe. MaryRose was fourteen years younger than me, beautiful, erotic, spiritual, more woman than I had ever dreamed of.

I had always told Allah that I could not be with any woman who was not absolutely beautiful—and look what happened!

> *When new life arises it*
> *surprises like morning*
> *dew on desert grass like*
> *light blooming before the dawn*
>
> *Measuring mind wants*
> *to name and form it*
> *like expecting parents*

*naming the baby*
*before it is even born*

*All I know*
*is your scent on the wind*
*filling the sky behind my eyes*
*and the cavities of my body*

A week later, MaryRose came up to Santa Fe and we hiked the Rio Tesuque. Walking through the woods along the river, she described herself as both grounded and ecstatic. My impression was that she was both a conservative businesswoman and an earthy, loving free spirit.

That night, we did Sufi practices in my living room by candlelight. She lay down on the bed in the guest bedroom and we began hugging and kissing deeply. It was a cool night. She slept soundly, while I went to the other room and lay awake in my bed all night, beyond thought, flooded with light, with presence.

We called this our Night of Power. Light upon light all night. Peace until the rising of the dawn.

In the morning I said, "You are such a joyful lover."

On my fifty-eighth birthday, June 23, we went for a long walk in the bosque, the woods by the Rio Grande in Albuquerque. We felt very comfortable with each other, holding hands at times. We shared our processes. MaryRose told me of forming the image of Mr. Clear to replace the dark image of her previous love. Then, she said, it became "Mr. Clear is near" and just days ago "Mr. Clear is here." We walked with our arms around each other down the bike trail.

As the sun was going down, we sat on a bench by the river. The warm wind was full of cottony seeds from all the cottonwoods in the bosque. She told me these were wishes floating in the air and to make a wish. I wished for just this—this love. We went to a down-home little Mexican restaurant just off Central. We sat outside on the patio. She gave me a feng-shui mirror curtain for my birthday. I felt so loved. We slept together in her bed that night, although I didn't sleep at all.

*Silence in the bosque*
*warm wind off the river*
*blowing fluffy seeds*

*Come to me my ripened wishes*
*Have I died and gone to heaven*
*or gone and died to heaven*
*Do you remember how in heaven*
*you saw us standing in a flower*
*its petals our faces raying*
*white soft flames*
*lovers in the rose*

A week later MaryRose fed me another beautiful dinner. We went to her room and began loving each other deeply. But I sensed a hesitation and pulled back and asked, "Is it all right that I am doing this?"

We went out on the porch and talked. I told her the stars were in a perfect place for us to make love. She questioned me about any lingering attachments to any other women. I told her that she was the most beautiful and desirable woman in the world, that she perfectly embodied the goddess. After a while she said she believed me. I got down on my knees and began to pray. We went back to bed and made love for the first time. I knew I was home. I slept a little for the first time in weeks.

In the morning we went on her morning walk around her neighborhood, mostly silent in prayer.

One night at my home in Santa Fe, she woke from a terrible dream saying, "Ahad, why are you so angry at me? And who is that blonde woman?" She told me her dream and we smoothed things down, but

I did not sleep very well. I knew the blonde woman was Glory, who was still in my dreams now and then, although I had not seen her for twenty years. She had to go.

In the morning I meditated and cleared the space with the vortex energy, until I could not sense the presence of any other spirit, blonde or otherwise.

We went for a magical walk down Little Tesuque Creek in the late afternoon. At the trailhead an older couple stopped their car to ask us directions.

The woman told us, "Don't get lost!"

MaryRose said to me, "Lost? We've been drunk all weekend—blissed out on love!"

We meandered down the charming river valley. At one point, she said, "What is Allah telling you right now?"

"Allah is telling me it's time to move to a new level."

That night we were very tired, and for the first time I slept deeply beside her.

She evoked for me a past life when we were gypsies together. Even though she doesn't believe in reincarnation, she evoked the gypsy life quite vividly. She said that we were madly in love with each other, never stopped making love, and she never stopped having babies. I could see us laughing, clapping hands, making music around the campfire, in our colorful gypsy clothes, surrounded by children in front of our gypsy wagon.

She told me I was giving her the best loving ever. I told her she was the best woman ever in my life, way beyond the fulfillment of the wildest seeds planted in God so long ago.

"Ahad, do you believe we were together in the light of the stars we come from?"

I said, "Yes."

I tuned in with Momma and Katherine in Portland. Momma had been declining for some time, but now it was really serious. She had been diagnosed with small-cell carcinoma in her lungs, a fast-spreading cancer, the only cure for which is chemotherapy, which her debilitated body was too weak to endure.

We drove out to Rio En Medio to go hiking. On the way out, MaryRose tried to elicit my feelings about Mom's impending death, but I was driving and pretty much stayed in my head. We walked up the magical river valley and deep into the forest. An hour in we stood at the bottom of a forty-foot waterfall, which was gorged full of water from the heavy winter. I took off my clothes and, bracing myself on the rock, stood underneath the power of the waterfall, hyperventilating. The plunging waterfall impacted me deeply with the power of life, the power of time, bringing forth all things, taking all things away, awesome, irresistible.

MaryRose crouched down and let the spray blow in her face, blow her hair back like the wind. I sat down and began a deep prayer, offering up all the people we had been talking about, all of our relations, our own selves, into the flow of the rushing river. On the way out I finally connected with my deep feelings of loss and grief—I'm going to lose my mom—and began sobbing and weeping as MaryRose held me.

I always told my god that if I was going to love someone, if I was going to open up and come out of the fortress of my solitude and actually love someone in a more intimate and vulnerable way than just fleeting moments of transpersonal unity, that if I was going to love someone, she had to be beautiful. And, my god, was she beautiful.

MaryRose surpassed all my expectations, all my hopes and fears, when we fell in love. With her sparkling eyes, long dark hair to her waist, and goddess-y body, she attracted me like no other years before we ever came together. Maybe my soul knew that she could be my lover and my wife—but my conscious personality didn't have a clue.

We were both Earth walkers and peace dancers, inclined to elevation and ecstasy, particularly in nature, dedicated to exploring the inner life, and shared a similar spiritual path. MaryRose was highly educated, having an M.A. in counseling and a Ph.D. in depth psychology, and highly accomplished, having run service agencies, taught in universities and churches, and maintained a private practice in Albuquerque for the past twenty-five years. She had deep emotional intelligence, insight, sympathy, empathy, and, most challenging to me, direct intuitive knowledge, that is, knowing without thinking. Time and time again my rational thinking mind would see things differently from her knowing, only to find out that in the end she was right—not infallibly, always right, but most of the time her knowing was spot on. I would also discover that she was a great cook and homemaker, but that's not why I fell in love and remain in love with her.

*When I see Thy glorious vision*
*I am moved to ecstasy . . .*
*Beloved . . .*
*Waves rise in my heart*
*and my heart becomes the sea . . .*

HAZRAT INAYAT KHAN

When I fell in love with MaryRose, I plunged into ecstasy, bliss, anxiety, and panic. I became hyper-alert, hyper-vigilant, restless, and sleepless. I was elated at loving and being loved, really loved, after so long alone, and terrified at the thought of inevitable loss. I was constantly agitated. I lost 15 percent of my body weight, twenty-five pounds, without even trying.

I was concerned about my ability to sexually satisfy such a youthful, erotic woman. But an inherent sense of essential trust and spiritual unity was just as important as sex. The trust was so deep that she would fall asleep in my arms. I would lie awake all night, blasted with the love light, awakening but barely moving at all lest I disturb my beloved's sleep.

One morning we went for a long walk and talk in the neighborhood. We were singing chants to the goddess. Back home, MaryRose changed into a sexy black sheath dress and we danced the goddess dance on the lawn until the sprinklers came on. Then we went inside, into the bedroom, got naked, and made love.

Afterward we were sitting on the screened front porch, looking into each other's eyes, as everything around us dissolved into luminous space. She saw a luminous triangle full of colors surrounding my head. I saw her primal presence, bright like sunlight, joyful, glorious, exalted, her pure soul presence. I saw her as a being of fire and light. I had never had such an awesome darshan with anyone before.

Then we went out shopping, to the meat market, the farmer's market, and the Owl Café for lunch. The day changed from sunny to stormy and there was a nice rain coming down by the time we were home.

Albuquerque, which had always been a big bland city to me, became the radiant City of Love that I eagerly embraced each weekend. And every weeknight, we were on the phone talking with each other for hours. We agreed to keep our new love secret and private throughout that first summer.

*Dream . . .*

*Guided by a soft feminine inner voice, I go into a subterranean warren of tunnels, a mine shaft, in search of unknown treasure. There is some sense of time pressure and inimical forces competing with me. I finally find the treasure, a large golden plaque with a rose engraved on it. I put it in my sack and go . . .*

*MaryRose and I are carrying the treasure. We have to deal with the harassment of diverse vampiric entities who want the treasure. They are annoying but not frightening . . .*

*The golden plaque has been shattered into pieces, for concealment and ease of transport, and wrapped in a velvet cloth. But all we have to do is open the cloth and toss the fragments into the air and the golden rose immediately comes together again in our joy of being together. We are happy together . . .*

*I am alone now down by
the ocean, on the beach in a seaside resort town. Ignoring everything else,
I am drawn to the ocean, to the breakers coming in. The whole scene is
bathed in a luminous powdery-blue dusk. I walk toward the ocean . . .*

The very first person I told about my new love was my old friend, Asha, who had first welcomed me to Lama. She said, "That is fabulous! That is so great! Being in love is the closest thing on Earth to being in heaven. I am so happy for you!

"But, Ahad, just remember—life as 'we' is very different from life as 'me.'"

She had this piece of advice: "Prolong the courtship. Even if you get married, courtship should be lifelong."

Next, I told Abe, and then I told his mom. I asked Varda to give us her blessing. She hesitated and hemmed and hawed, finally saying, "Well . . . I would be willing to give you my blessing if only . . . you could find a way to spend more time with me."

Can you imagine that? We had been divorced twenty-five years ago—and she was still clinging on to some fantasy of wanting greater intimacy with me, using this as a bargaining tool. Varda did not, could not, give us her blessing, and is no longer part of my life.

MaryRose and I went out to dinner with Shirin, who said, "Our work is to create a network of love and light. What is happening with the world is not our business. Take good care of this woman. Don't let her out of your sight."

MaryRose invited me to come with her to the Oregon coast. Driving down from Portland we stopped in Otis to sample their famous molasses bread. We stayed by the sea at the Trollers Lodge in Depoe Bay. We walked the misty bluffs and the foggy beaches, talking freely.

MaryRose suddenly pulled the car to the side of the road and got out to see an eagle soaring overhead. She said, "My rules for being on vacation are: Don't plan anything and do whatever you want to do. There are no rules."

We spent one afternoon in the seaside town of Yachats, engaged in a quest for a hot dawg (what she wanted), which proved to be remarkably hard to find and engendered much comic dialogue and drama until we finally found a place that would grill a dawg. The hot dawg was okay. Finding it was all the fun.

We spent a week walking the Oregon beaches by the ocean surf. On the way back to the airport, we visited my mother at her apartment in Portland. We went to my sister's house first and then over to Mom's for lunch. Mom was very beautiful and sparkling, her eyes a bright sky-blue. Katherine made a nice lunch for us. My mother was gracious but had little to say about MaryRose other than, "She certainly is well-educated."

Afterward, MaryRose told me that aside from appreciating the classy aesthetics of the apartment, she was stunned by how much light came from her eyes. When she said that, I realized I could see it, too: a brilliant diamond-like light sparkling in the dark depths of her eyes in her wasted body. Her light, her sparkle, had always been there. We were both having Mom's darshan. We were both seeing and being seen by my mother.

We were sharing high sex, tantric sex, beyond our experiences, beyond our expectations.

The key to sacred sex is for the man to retain his semen and refrain from ejaculation as long as possible so that both partners can ride the waves of endless bliss.

"Making love with you is a spiritual experience," she said. "I see the moonlight glittering on the water, the stars of the cosmos in your eyes.

"Ahad, I'm married to you—for only my husband could make love to me this way."

"Ahad, I believe you really did have past lives. I don't have past lives, but I really believe you did have past lives. Were you an East Indian saint?"

MaryRose and Ahad, Abiquiu, New Mexico, 2005.

"I don't know." I replied. "I only recall the past lives that were painful in order to release the karma."

"Well, you always smell of cumin."

*Her ecstasy, her poetry, her raving in praise of love . . .*
*She verbalizes such ecstatic love . . .*
*I am deeply silent, beyond words . . .*
*silence, stillness, depth . . .*
*as her waves of poetic bliss washing over me . . .*
*Her states change and flow so rapidly . . .*
*She has so much energy . . .*
*I am nothing but pure awareness in her vast energy field . . .*

She looked into my eyes and said, "I remember you. I remember you."

"I remember you, honey," I replied.

"Ahad . . . I'm so glad I didn't miss you."

*Oh Mother I tried so hard to discover*
*if you were anything other*
*than what I had always known you to be*
*The mystery of your euphoric babble*
*receives the geometry of my names*
*The ceaseless surge of your maya shakti*
*embodies and consumes all my forms*
*The trance formations of our dance*
*pulse at the speed of light*
*Oh Goddess you are eternal energy*
*and I am eternal consciousness*
*You are eternal delight*
*and I am the light of all your dreams*

One weekend we drove up to Durango just to get out of town. We checked into the Best Western Durango Inn, into a nice suite with a living room and a balcony in back. We went to eat at the restaurant next door, which was noisy and had poor food. I felt a growing aversion to being there, energy shaking in my body, making me want to run out the door. Finally, we did leave, paying only for the drinks, and went to a local café for another meal of not-so-good food. When we returned to the inn, she was exhausted and fell asleep.

Along with loving me, MaryRose had been giving me reflections on my behavior patterns. For the first time in my life, I was seeing myself in the eyes of another who could really see my mood swings, my muted meltdowns, my stunned silence when confronted with angry outbursts, and in general, my inability to express my feelings. That very night, I had hated being in that restaurant, but I had gone into emotional paralysis rather than verbalize my aversion. She was in touch with my feelings, even if I was not.

I lay awake that night, restless and agitated, finally realizing that a lot of my bizarre behavior had to do with being emotionally abused by my father, paralyzed in front of his anger, repressing my own anger and vitality. I woke her up around four in the morning, confessed

View from Heaven's Gate above Ouray, Colorado.

all of this, and stated my intention to seek psychoanalytic help.

"Now," she said, "it's time to go home."

But I held her, swayed with her, took her back to bed, and made love with her. We made love deeply and intensely, riding on crests of ecstasy. She said she surrendered to this because she trusts me. She said she was taken into the cosmos, close to the gates of heaven, all the stars, and all the galaxies. It was our most profound lovemaking to date. We were glowing with satisfaction and gratitude and love.

*Whatever happens to me today*
*tomorrow or yesterday*
*I thank you for loving me today*

*for sharing in my bliss*
*witnessing my rage*
*and staying on the page with me*
*as I am polished to shine*
*inevitable death*
*I love you more than I can*
*. . . each breath*

I got the message that Mom was definitely declining and wanted us all to come together for a last powwow with her. I flew out to Oregon to find her just flesh and bones, lying in her bed in her blue bedroom with all her family photos on the wall, breathing oxygen through tubes, surrounded by her children and her caregivers. The atmosphere was very sweet and peaceful and painful.

At one point Momma looked at all the people around her bed and said, "How much of an army does it take to keep me alive?"

### November 1, 2005

It was pouring rain in Portland. I was booked to fly out soon. When I went into Mom's bedroom, she was sleeping. I sat with her and imagined that I was doing a life review for her, seeing all the vivid life pictures of her lifetime, from being born and growing up and parenting until now. It felt complete.

I said, "I love you. Goodbye," and kissed her on both cheeks.

She woke up and mumbled, "You know . . . I don't like all that. . . ."

It was too much kissing for her. We were not complete yet.

I sat a little longer and flowed love and gratitude to her for this life she gave me and that we have shared, all the beauty, all the glory, all the pain. I bent over her. She looked at me, that brilliant diamond glance, very faint now, and pursed her lips for a kiss. I kissed her on the lips and on the hand. It was complete. Ending in love as it began in love.

I stood outside on the porch in the darkly pouring rain and chanted, "*lokahah samistaha sukino bhavantu, lokahah samistaha sukino bhavantu, lokahah samistaha sukino bhavantu, om shanti shanti shanti.*" May all beings in all worlds be happy. Peace, peace, peace.

I went to the airport to fly home. My mother died later that afternoon.

The contrast between my detachment, dispassion, and dying with Mom, and my passionate, glorious life and love with MaryRose had a deep impact. It made me realize how long I had accepted death in my life. To have my mother, Mary, leave my life at the same time as my lover and wife, MaryRose, was coming into my life was like seeing the sun setting over the western ocean just as the full moon is rising over the eastern mountains.

MaryRose's heart love gave me an opening that I was eager to move into. My own experience had been that every time I took the initiative with a woman it failed or ended miserably, whereas every time a woman came on to me, something good happened. Despite my constant, indiscriminate lust (men are always thinking about sex), I had resolved not to pursue women no matter what I felt . . . or at least wait until someone gave me an opening.

I had cultivated transpersonal love and friendship. There was a great deal of opening up to love in our dance circles, but again, my ethics as a dance leader were to not come on to anyone in the dance circle.

My ideal was to live welcoming all, to love everyone equally, and show no preferences. In the dance circles, I tried to give equal attention to everyone and play no favorites. If I had to join the circle from the center, I would back into the circle without looking to see whom I would join with.

When I was lonely, I would pick up the phone and talk with my friends, mostly women. Estrogen loves conversation. Part of the conversation was astrological, implicit or explicit, since that's where my head was at. I got a lot of practice doing prashnas for friends. But it was all just chit-chat, nothing romantic or passionate.

Now, with MaryRose, I was plunging into the most intimate personal relationship with someone who not only opened her heart love and body love to me, but was also acutely aware of the inner life, having both a Ph.D. in depth psychology and initiation on the Sufi path.

Now that I had a gorgeous and passionate young love, lover, and beloved, I had to engage in relationship reeducation, letting go of old habits and learning new ones. Here are some elements of my learning curve at that time:

Give all my attention to my beloved. Do not give any attention to any other women. No matter how innocent it may seem, the potential for flirtation and seduction is always there. No more phone buddies.

Be jealous and possessive. Stake out my territory. Be aware that other men are always sniffing her out. Be prepared to defend what is mine.

Stay together. Don't lose contact. I want you by my side. Don't let anyone come between us.

When we walk, we walk together. When we eat, we eat together. When we sleep, we sleep together. Just because we're mad at each other doesn't mean we can't sleep together.

Get in touch with my feelings. Don't hide my feelings. Don't pretend I don't have my feelings. Express my feelings, no matter how trivial or ephemeral.

It is not enough just to be present and listen. My beloved wants me to express sympathetic understanding and a clear reflection of her feelings.

It all comes down to what Pierre Elliot told us at Lama: "When ten thousand times you have put the interest of your beloved before your own interest, and when ten thousand times your beloved has put your interest before her own interest, you might begin to know what it is to be married."

The most challenging thing for me about living in constant intimate companionship with another being, with MaryRose, is the undeniable existential reality that her experience of reality and her expression of her experience, of her reality, is just as real as mine, like it or not. Not only do you have just as much a right to exist as I do, your experience of reality is every bit as valid as my experience, no matter how different they are. All experience is relative, and intimate relationship is the acid test of how real that relativity is.

One advantage of living alone was that no one challenged or disturbed my subjective reality. I could hear myself think. I could be as grandiose or as lachrymose, as self-disciplined or as self-indulgent as I pleased, and there was no one else to see me. I could be the gleam in Ramana Maharshi's eye or the last breath in my mother's body. I am whoever I think I am from moment to moment, for better or worse. I was more or less content to be whoever I was from moment to moment.

To be in relationship is to be in constant conversation, to be giving and receiving continuous reflections, conscious or unconscious, particularly if one is married to a psychologist. Actually, few people in the world offer me any conscious reflection of self. What passes for conversation is generally dueling monologues. People talk at me about themselves, rarely asking about me, and I accept that this is the way it is. If I don't need to talk about myself, no one seems to notice. Not so with MaryRose.

I am an intellectual, a thinking type. MaryRose is definitely intuitive and feeling. I can't get away with feeling anything without her picking up on it and wanting to know about it. To me, they may be passing moods to be endured. To her, they cannot be ignored. My nature is to engage in intellectual conversation, to exchange and examine ideas, constantly seeking a fresh viewpoint. MaryRose would like to receive what she gives—empathic and sympathetic reflections of a feeling nature. In Joe Miller's famous words:

> *You can get more stinkin' from thinkin' than you can from drinkin'—*
> *but to feel is for real!*

Impacted with the intensity of passionate love, my long-repressed feelings came steaming to the surface, exciting, exalting, tormenting, and confusing me. It has been said that there are only two powers in this universe or any other: love and fear. To my dismay, along with great love came great fear—fear of intimacy, fear of abandonment, fear of losing myself, fear of losing her, fear of being controlled, fear of being out of control—but mostly nameless, faceless irrational fear that would keep me awake all night, lying as stiff as a corpse next to my beloved, terrified to move for fear of disturbing her. . . . And I'd have panic attacks that would jolt me awake in the middle of the night.

This fear was no stranger. It had sung in my bones in my twenties:

> *Fear hangs up a fist for hours*
> *behind the flowered wallboard*
> *then knocks and runs to the kitchen door*
>
> *Blows of bright volted SMACK*
> *feed dream hunger, stun us sour*
> *(soul withdrawn hair by hair)*
>
> *Fear tumbles on emptiness*
> *What scares America scares me*
> *(the little man who isn't there)*

Between meditation and self-medication, I had managed to keep the fear at bay. But now panic was threatening to tear apart this precious love.

∞∞

After our weekend in Durango, I began working with Jerome Bernstein, a Jungian analyst who lives in Santa Fe. The challenge of psychoanalysis is to look at oneself, something I was not used to doing. In fact, I had become very skilled at hiding myself from myself and others. I had become habituated to sympathetically listening to others, offering some reflection of their narrative, especially with astrology, and keeping myself concealed behind the mirror I held up to others. I never looked at myself in any mirror. Now I had to take a deep look at myself, starting with my relationship with my mother.

My mother's death impacted me more than I had realized. She had been my primary self-object, love object, my entire life. My relationship with my mother was emotionally incestuous. I had become her son-lover through our intimate conversations in my teenage years, as we washed dishes and she talked with me about leaving my father. I became her surrogate husband. To be with any other woman was seen by my psyche as betrayal. No one could be as good as her. No wonder I could never have a successful relationship, nor choose to fall in love with someone with whom that was possible. I felt tremendous relief and freedom from the bond with my mother. Now I was free to love someone real.

I did not come to these conclusions on my own. I had a lot of help.

Jerome helped me work through my relationship issues with MaryRose. He helped me to get in touch with my feelings, to express my feelings, in fact, to know that it is healthy and necessary to express my feelings no matter how messy they are. Apparently, I had been on a spiritual bypass, avoiding feeling feelings for a long time. I would replay incidents and analyze conversations with Jerome, and my feelings about incidents and conversations, just as MaryRose was doing with her patients in her office. Jerome had an extraordinary ability to capacitate and reflect my emotions to me, sometimes supportive, sometimes challenging, always beneficent.

Jerome challenged me to define what my ego goals were for this relationship. He said I was vacillating between the polarities of withdrawal into myself and abandonment into the relationship, that is, withdrawal into the defense structures of my ego and abandonment into the vast energies of this wild woman, as is my pattern. MaryRose was very supportive of my work with Jerome.

The much larger issue was becoming aware of the impact my father had on me. Domineering, controlling, explosive, punishing, my father ran the family like the commander of a military base. When MaryRose got angry with me, my automatic response would be to freeze, to not respond, and certainly not to express the anger I could not allow myself to feel. Alternatively, my response would be flight: walking away, going to my room, taking a walk outside, getting in my car and driving away.

In time, I learned to allow myself to feel my rage and yell and scream and say all sorts of mean and nasty things I didn't really mean but certainly felt. I don't know that it made our relationship better, but it certainly made it more real. Only by being real with each other could we start to be kinder to each other.

Jerome asked me if I remembered what I said when I was angry.

"No, I don't remember," I told him.

"That's because you were in traumatic restimulation," he said. "Trauma is a specialized condition. It is not depression, not anxiety, not panic, though it can include these. One of the hallmarks of trauma is dissociation. Trauma has an on/off switch. Trauma is either on or off. When the switch is on you get the whole program. There is no rheostat, no modulation possible. It takes over the autonomic nervous system. A child in a traumatizing situation is helpless, overwhelmed, powerless. Those traumatizing moments, especially in childhood, are freeze-framed."

Locked in my room as a child, outraged at having my natural spontaneity and joy not only unappreciated but suppressed and punished, I was wailing and yelling and screaming at the unfairness and indignity of it all . . . until I calmed down enough to realize that I had to eat. So, I had to get myself under control, suppress my anger, suppress my breath, and behave myself in order to be fed and eat. This is when I resolved, "I'll never do this to anyone."

When my father made me take down my pants and bend over to take a strapping, I cried and screamed at first . . . but then I resolved not to give my father the satisfaction of making me cry. I transferred the terror into defiance, which was healthy. I'm in touch with my defiance, but I suppress the terror and the pain and a lot of my feelings in my relationship with

MaryRose. I never had language for any of my feelings before.

They say that too much analysis leads to paralysis, but it's still alive and kickin' for me ten years later. Analysis does not provide behavioral solutions. Analysis brings greater awareness of the activity of the psyche, and that greater awareness or awakening of consciousness is healing and liberating in and of itself.

The epitome of Jungian analysis is dream analysis. I am a very active dreamer and dream recorder. I have always loved my dreams for their aesthetic value alone. Jerome has shown me all sorts of ways to let the dream speak to me. The dream is an objective message from the unconscious.

He would say, "Let's ask a third party. . . . Let's see what the third party has to say. . . . What is your soul trying to tell you? What is your soul saying to you?"

For instance, I brought this dream to Jerome:

*I am swimming in a huge swimming pool with lots of children and young people splashing and playing and making a lot of noise. I am enjoying swimming in the pool although I don't particularly feel part of the action. After a long while I get out of the pool and walk into a shady alcove where my father is sitting under the branches of an evergreen tree looking at some large art books. I look closer and see that these are books of collages I made from comic books and other art work when I was in college. He is not only looking at the images but adding his own text to the pull quotes and quote balloons . . .*

*I say to him, "I made these books . . ."*

*He says to me, "You made these books and now I am completing them . . ."*

*Then he looks up at me and I see him face to face. He looks not like my birth father but like a gently aged white-haired version of Robert Young from* Father Knows Best. *He smiles at me with kind crinkly eyes and says, "Lately I have been absorbed in the resonance of the Name of God." Tears fill my eyes. For the first time in my life I feel at one with my father . . .*

Jerome had this to say:

"This dream indicates that the dark spots in your psyche from childhood are healed, the dark spots that isolated you from others. Your father, who has been a blank spot in your life, now is looking at your images with you, acknowledging the validity of your life stance, and filling in the blanks of the collages you made to express what you could not otherwise express, a kind, knowing, wise father archetype. Your psyche has been saying that reconciliation with your father is hopeless, you have to go down other avenues, but now reconciliation with the father is real. Quite a dream, quite a transformation."

He has some amazing interpretations. He doesn't always see the same things I see in my dreams. I don't always agree with his interpretations. But he is educating me to hear the language of the soul as it speaks in images in dream time. He sees certain themes, such as lack of curiosity or desire for extroversion, and I have no idea how he's seeing them. When I say I don't agree with him, he says, "If you agreed with me, you wouldn't have to come here."

My inner journey had started with hearing the voice singing inside me and writing down what I heard as song and poetry. (A good deal of the chants came with melodies.) I was inspired by the surrealists to let the unconscious speech flow forth unhindered. I began taking dictation from dreamtime, thrilled by the vitality and beauty of the imagery. At the same time, I was seeking to quiet the mind and open my heart through devotional chanting. Then I worked with Joanna on consciously contacting imagery, moving pictures laden with emotion, and dissolving these "past-life" pictures in order to release karmic patterns. Now I was listening to the oracle of my dreams and, with Jerome's guidance, learning to hear what my deeper self was showing me.

The goal, or at least *a* goal, of Jungian analysis, as I understand it, is not absorption in unitive consciousness, but rather maintaining an ongoing dialogue between the conscious self (ego) and the deeper self (Self), living in the creative dynamic tension between the inner and the outer worlds. Individuation is not an end-product ("Look, Ma, I'm individuated!"), but an ongoing process that includes inner and outer conversation and even conflict.

I experienced a lot of resistance to the recurrent prompting to write these memoirs. "It's not worth the effort. No one will even read it. I'll just give it away like all my other books. Nothing's in it for me."

I brought my concerns to Jerome and he said, "You have a goal orientation toward making a book. Valuing is not producing. Valuing is appreciating the difference between having a story that is trying to tell itself—the process of storytelling—versus product orientation. Writing for an audience is ego related. Writing it down because the story wants to tell itself is different. There is a certain arrogance in assuming you know what is in the story, the story that lives you."

"I experience frustration."

"The urge to write this is coming from within. It's not coming from your ego and your ego doesn't like this."

"My ego feels cranky."

"It has a right to."

I came to recognize the depth of my suffering and the persistent imprint of trauma. I had always tried to avoid feeling my suffering through meditation and chanting, spiritual bypass, and self-medication with marijuana, alcohol, and cigarettes. My suffering isolates me, sets me apart, and makes me unique. Yet this suffering is something I have in common with all humanity. We all suffer experience and experience suffering. My own suffering is miniscule compared with much of humanity, yet my suffering is overwhelmingly real for me, beginning with the inevitable separation from essence as a condition for being human in the first place.

The traumatic impact of my father's wrath is like a target painted on my back, my butt, or wherever he hit me. Even if most of the blows were emotional rather than physical, they hammered black holes in my psyche, dark spots on my heart. When something, no matter how innocent, triggers that traumatic impact, I am out of my mind, falling into that black hole again.

My father is dead and gone some twenty-five years now. I have forgiven my father over and over until I'm blue in the face and washed in the blood. When I can make the unconscious conscious, what I am dealing with is not my father himself but the imprint of him that remains in my psyche. As a child I evolved defense mechanisms to protect myself. I found ways to adapt to the situation and try to get my needs met.

I couldn't express anger. But I could be passive-aggressive, delaying, undermining, undercutting, a sarcastic saboteur. . . .

Demanding to get my needs met didn't work, but I could try to fulfill them by placating, pretending, concealing, lying, and subterfuge. . . .

MaryRose, on the other hand, had no problem expressing her anger, so it is natural that I would unconsciously project my father complex on to her. It is not that I see her as being my father or even being like my father. I see that I react to her anger or any angry person in the same ways as I reacted to my father.

Even more shocking was to witness the ways in which I am exactly like my father, even though I have tried my whole life to be the opposite. I can be cold, rigid, controlling, and withholding, much more than I realize.

I can't eliminate these psychic structures, neuroses, psychoses, whatever, and start all over with a new deck of psychic cards any more than I can get a new set of genes and start over with a new physical body. But the more I bring awareness to the unconscious roots of my behaviors, the more I dissolve the soul's identification with ego structures, the freer I am to simply "be loving awareness," as Ram Dass suggests.

As Hart's guru, Mantriji, says, the ego has to be present in order to function as a human being, but the ego should be like the moon in daytime, visible but pale, not dominating the scene.

## November 10, 2006

A year and a few days after my mother's death, MaryRose and I were driving up north on I-25 to meet some friends at Tent Rocks. It was a bright, blue sky New Mexico morning. We were talking happily, anticipating the dance meeting that night. MaryRose said she was feeling a little frisky. She was only driving about 65 mph, whereas she is usually driving 90 mph or bugging me about driving too slowly. I teased her and kept asking her why she was driving so slowly. We were just past Algodones. I heard her say, "Oh my God." I looked up and saw a red truck right in our path, a wall of red coming at us head on. She braked and steered to the left. There was a tremendous impact. Everything turned white. Everything stopped and was deathly still.

We didn't move for a moment, until I said, "Get out of the car! Get out of the car!"

We got out of the car and stood by the side of the road, praising God for our life, for protection, for delivery from death. MaryRose was holding her hands straight out in front of her. She sat down. She kept asking about the man in the truck, was he dead, was he alright. What she had seen was a pickup truck with a man hanging out the passenger side window, a dead man, while a shadow was still holding on to the steering wheel. A dead man coming to kill us. . . .

Cars pulled up. People stopped to help us, to call 911. Two women held her and comforted her. One woman prayed to Jesus and prayed in tongues in her ear.

The EMS people came from Cochiti. I was ambulatory, but MaryRose was in such a state of shock that they strapped her down to a board and put her on a stretcher and into the ambulance. I rode with her to the emergency room at UNM Hospital. Whenever I was separated from her, she kept asking for her husband. She was put in a corridor station under a wall of drawers in the emergency room, since all the rooms were full. Their concern was that she might have suffered a spinal injury, so they gave her numerous x-rays, cat scans, and an MRI. They kept her flat on her back, in an uncomfortable neck brace, on a saline solution drip with lots of morphine, but would not let her eat or drink anything. It was a chaotic, surreal experience. I stayed right by her side the whole time, finally lying down next to her at the foot of her hospital bed.

The next morning, we were given the good news: the MRI was clean, there were no fractures. She was discharged around ten o'clock, after twenty-four hours on her back in a neck brace with no food, no water, but plenty of morphine. She did have a splint on her right hand for a suspected fracture in her wrist.

The rest of the weekend was a blur of driving around, shopping, eating, talking, decompressing, watching TV, sleeping. We both were resonating with the impact of the accident, the bam! of slamming into the truck, the mystery of the dead man who almost killed us. It turned out this man had had a heart attack, lost control of his truck, and died. We kept experiencing the accident over and over and over again.

We were extremely bonded throughout all of this. This was the moment we realized that we really are married. We've been through death and now . . . 'til death do us part.

## December 28, 2006

Death came again on a snowy day seven weeks later. At sunset MaryRose called me to tell me that her brother, James, had been taken to the hospital and might be dying. She asked me to come down right away. I drove to Albuquerque, plowing through a heavy snow storm in an endless line of tail lights. It took three hours to get to UNM Hospital instead of the usual one hour.

MaryRose and James grew up together like two very different peas in the same pod. He grew up to be a career criminal and spent time in prison. She became a Ph.D. and a professional counselor. When James got out of prison he came out to New Mexico, where she helped him to rehabilitate and to get on his feet again, working in cleaning services and construction. He had a house on the West Side, a lover and business partner (Byron), six dogs, and a nice life. He had just completed a big job and deposited $11,000 in the bank that very day.

He had been having flu-like symptoms and had been diagnosed as having the flu the week before. In fact, he had a myocardial infarction, caused by an infection in the blood that had gone straight to the heart.

MaryRose and Byron were with James in the cardiac intensive care unit. He was unconscious, sedated, intubated, on a respirator, and on three blood-pressure medications. The doctor explained that the infection in his heart had eaten away at the aortic valve, so that the blood the heart was pumping flowed back into the heart and the heart could not keep the blood pressure up. There was also an abscess in his heart and the infection might have been carried to the brain. There was very little chance that he would survive. This was shocking in the extreme.

We stayed with James, touching his body, talking to him, sometimes singing to him. MaryRose called in a priest to give him the last rites. She saw the angel of death walking around the ward in a black raincoat. James was in intense pain, calling out, "Jesus, take me!"

We were singing softly, "Alleluia, Glory, Glory," and "Rockabye, Sweet Baby James."

James was passing away quickly. He squeezed Byron's hand and looked him in the eye and then he was gone.

We asked the nurses to leave us alone with the body for a while. MaryRose saw the light leaving the body, light filling the room, then heat filling the room, and finally coolness. I sensed the tightly focused presence of his spirit expand and fill the room and all space. Two hours later we left the hospital. It was snowing heavily now.

When someone dies, especially suddenly, there is often a halo effect whereby the goodness of the soul is remembered in a glow and the rough edges are forgotten. So we remembered the goodness of James. He was living for today with no long-term future plans, taking cash advances from credit card companies to live on. He was on top of his game, with good work, good home, and the man he loved. He died $11,000 ahead of the game. For us it was two deaths and two near deaths, all in a year.

Early one spring morning, after spending the weekend together with me in Santa Fe, MaryRose drove back to Albuquerque to go to work. The love was flowing abundantly. My soul was flooded with tempestuous passions the likes of which I had never known. The intensity of the feelings was unfamiliar, scary, unbearable . . . anxiety . . . panic . . . I didn't know what to do with myself. I felt like I was losing myself. I paced around the house and rushed outside into the bright sunlight streaming through the green canopy of the huge elm trees that were blown about by the gusty winds, silently calling out for relief, for this tumult to

MaryRose, 2014.

cease . . . and I heard a voice from above, literally a voice from above, a vast calm voice saying, *Trust this love.* . . .

I heard it only once, but I repeat—*Trust this love!*

Another time later on, we had been fighting about something—agitated egos yelling and screaming at each other like little children having tantrums. It's all *your* fault! No, it's all *your* fault! It was late at night, and we were sleeping apart. I was totally devastated. I felt like my world was ending. My mind would not stop defending myself and arguing with her. I could not go to sleep. Finally, after several long hours of self-torture, I did something I have never done before—I called out to Neem Karoli Baba, the only one I know as guru, and begged, "Maharaj-ji, please help me to go to sleep!"

Instantly he was with me. I saw him leaning on his elbow, smiling at me with divine delight, saying to me, "Remember the love. Remember the love."

This calmed me down, and I remembered the love behind all the drama. This calmed me down, feeling the love was real.

After a while I went to MaryRose in the dark and said, "I just can't get to sleep."

"Just get in bed with me," she said.

I got in bed with my beloved and slept like a child.

When I told this to my friend Van, he said, "We forget that we need to ask the gods and goddesses if we want their help. They will not intervene in our lives unless we ask them to, Otherwise, they will just let us be."

After MaryRose and I had been together for two years, we decided to look for a house where we could live together—a house in Albuquerque where her clients lived, in Albuquerque where we could get more house for the money. We drew up a blueprint for our new home. It would be close to nature, by the river or in the mountains. It would be beautiful and in good repair. No fixer-uppers. It would have an office with a separate entrance so that MaryRose could see clients at home. It would have a large room for community gatherings, dances, and workshops. It would have several guest bedrooms. It would all be on one level (that was my consideration) and it would have a swimming pool (her consideration). She could hear the laughter of the Sufis swimming in the pool.

We had been looking since spring, looking more intensely in the summer. We made an offer on a lovely house down by the river. Then it turned out that someone else already had an offer on the house and the realtor was using our offer to force him to close. The realtor never should have showed it to us. We fired him.

This house had a great kitchen but no swimming pool. We would have had to dig the pool in the backyard, right across the fence from a horse barn and horse flies. It was just as well there was an obstacle to buying it.

We made an offer on another, smaller house but backed out over-night. It would have felt like living in a sardine can. And it only had access to a community swimming pool. We had not met our blueprint yet.

Summer was over. Winter was coming on. MaryRose gave me until

September 30 to find a house for us or she would not move until spring. We were on our third realtor. I was definitely feeling pressure.

"Have you been praying to Ganesha?" MaryRose asked.

"No."

"Well, you'd better start praying to your elephant."

So, I began doing rounds of *Om Gam Ganapataye Namaha* on my Hindu mala beads while sitting in meditation and walking down in the arroyo. I did this many times a day: *Om Gam Ganapataye Namaha, Om Gam Ganapataye Namaha.*

"Ahad, maybe you should revise your considerations," MaryRose said, "and look at two-story houses as well. It would create more opportunities."

I said I was open to that.

I kept on looking. I knew that my Moon bhukti (sub-period) was about to begin. I thought this should give me the house I was looking for. Both Saturn and Ketu were coming to exact conjunction with my natal Moon, further activating change of home. I kept on looking: *Om Gam Ganapataye Namaha, Om Gam Ganapataye Namaha.*

### September 29, 2007

MaryRose was on the east coast visiting her dying auntie. I drove down to Albuquerque to look at more houses. The realtor took me right up to the house at 13301 Manitoba Drive.

As I walked through the iron gate and in the front door, I entered into silence and peace. I could hear only the sound of the wind. I loved the way the house looked, all full of arches and windows and exquisite touches. It was located right up against the mountains, a five-minute walk from the Sandia Wilderness. It was located on the edge of Bear Canyon Open Space. Nothing would ever be built behind the house. There was a big mountain view to the north and a big, blue swimming pool in the backyard.

There is an enormous cliff face on the northern end of the Sandias. If you look at it with the right eyes you can clearly see the profile of an elephant with one big ear, a winking eye, and a long trunk. We would have the darshan of Ganapati every day.

And, oh yes, it was a two-story home. I had bypassed looking at it in the spring, when it was listed for $100,000 more than it was listed for now. Now it was in our price range. I felt deep peace and harmony here. I felt that MaryRose would love this house. I called her and told her I had found our house—one day before the deadline. She was skeptical, but she said she would look at it.

## September 30, 2007

I went to look at another house but came back to the house on Manitoba on Sunday. I sat in front of a large Ganapati altar at the Ayurvedic Institute where Hart DeFouw was teaching a class on *vastu* on a very rare visit to Albuquerque. After class, he showed me a new ring he had been given, Ganesha carved in amber. He let me touch the ring and gave me his blessing.

Sunday was a travel nightmare for MaryRose. She got up at five in the morning on the east coast but didn't get home until ten at night. She was pretty gone.

It was not until Monday morning that we went up to the house on Manitoba. The realtor opened the house for us. MaryRose was charmed, enraptured, and enchanted. She kept on discovering new things at every turn. For every problem that appeared there was something even greater to compensate for it.

"This house is a shape-shifter," she said. "It keeps on changing. I am going from room to room. When I see something I don't like, it shifts and I see it from a different perspective. It keeps changing. Then, when I walked into the master bedroom and looked out the door and saw Ganesha looking straight at me, I knew that this was our house. My favorite thing about the house is that there's an elephant in the backyard!"

We offered a ladhu to Ganesha and chanted *"Om Gam Ganapataye Namaha"* in gratitude. A month later we were moved in.

After we got settled into our new home, we began hiking up the Embudito Trail into the Sandia Wilderness and soon discovered a huge *swayambhu murti* of Ganesha on a promontory only half an hour walk from our house. *Swayambhu* means "self-arising, self-generated"—arising in nature, not man-made. A murti is a statue of a deity. This swayambhu Ganesha is as big as a two-car, two-story garage, an elephant carrying a burden on its back. There is a huge ear flap for listening to prayers and a slightly open mouth cavity to receive offerings. On closer look there is a second baby elephant behind him and a large stone mouse, a *mushaka,* his *vahana* or vehicle, sitting right in front of him. This swayambhu Ganesha has become our local shrine. We bring our friends up here for his darshan. I come up here when I am in distress. I come up here when I am full of gratitude and praise. We come up here before dance meetings to bring our prayers and our sweets to this beloved form of the One.

## December 2007

When we moved into our house on Manitoba it rained all night. It sounded as if we were taken up in a whirlwind.

At our housewarming, we took a line of Sufis all through the house chanting *"Allah Allah Allah Allah, Ya Allah Allah Allah."* Photos from that night show numinous orbs of light floating over the dancers.

Over the years we have hosted Sufi teachers and friends. We have had community gatherings, dance meetings, workshops, pool parties, and family holidays at Manitoba.

Soon after we moved in, I had a very real dream of my Grandpa Patterson, my mother's father, who was my favorite grandparent. An inventor, businessman, and philanthropist, he was a bright, warm presence in my life. Later in life, he was debilitated by a form of Parkinson's disease that progressively immobilized his body. He became almost paralyzed. It took great effort for him to speak a few words, which rumbled like gravel in his mouth. He never complained. My grandmother took good care of him. What impressed me was that when he did make the effort to speak, it was always to say something cheerful or to make a joke. A portion of the wealth he created came down to me on my mother's death and helped me buy this house with MaryRose.

*Dream . . .*

*I am sleeping with MaryRose in our big bed in our new house. In the middle of the night Grandpa Patterson comes into the room. He is clearly a ghost, a spirit. He has been dead for over forty years. I get up out of bed to greet him warmly. He greets me warmly. He seems taller than in life, ruddy, healthy. He looks down at MaryRose in bed and admires her beauty. He says she is very beautiful, I am very lucky, he approves of her, tells me to take good care of her. She looks up at him with a wary eye, but she doesn't want to see this, so she rolls over and goes back to sleep. He says he has come to get his gun, his shotgun and his hunting gear, from the closet. He is going hunting. I ask him what he does in the world he is in. He says people mostly play golf and play bridge to pass the time. But he remembers hunting and the hunting camp and he wants to go hunting . . .*

When MaryRose and I moved in together, we became very real to each other in ways I could never have anticipated. The depth of her love, of this love, nurtures, enlivens, and expands my soul. Her ever-changing moods keep me alert and flexible, less set in my ways. The existential challenge of marriage is accepting that the reality she lives in is every bit as real as the reality I live in. Both of our relative realities are equally real and equally unreal.

I choose to surrender my compulsive need to be right and to be in control all of the time. I choose to admire, affirm, and appreciate her perception of reality, her needs and desires and passions. I choose to be open to continual change, which after all, is the nature of reality.

We serve our community through sharing Sufi teachings and practices and the Dances of Universal Peace. We travel around the world together, continually expanding our life experience. We are deeply married to one another.

This is where my story and her story merge into our story. The inner life story I am telling mingles with her inner life story and becomes a treasure we hold together.

In the Holy Qur'an it says of husbands and wives, "They are an apparel for you and you are an apparel for them," or, "You are their garments and they are your garments" (2:187). In his translation, Muhammad Ali comments, "They are a means of protection, comfort, and even embellishment for each other, and the weakness of one is made up by the strength of the other." We share our life together with each other—under the cover of our marriage.

Now I close the doors of our house on the narrative of our intimacy, for the alchemy of our marriage is not my story to tell . . . it is our life to live together.

Our cat Mela.

# 10 SUFI PATH

On the cold November morning of my mother's funeral in 2005, I walked alone around the shores of Lake Wesauking, outside of Towanda, Pennsylvania, trying to collect my thoughts to give the graveside eulogy I had volunteered to do. My mother had spent her summers here as a child. There were patches of morning sunlight shining on the ice melting on the road. I had no idea what I would say. I opened myself to inspiration. I kept hearing, "the Divine Light and the Spirit of Guidance, the Divine Light and the Spirit of Guidance, the Divine Light and the Spirit of Guidance," over and over as clear as the daylight. These words are from Hazrat Inayat Khan's prayer Salat and correspond to the sacred names Ya Nur, Ya Hadi.

The Sufi Path was opening up for me, the Sufi Path of Love, as I had clearly heard that first night with MaryRose. Ya Nur, Ya Hadi . . . "The Divine Light shining in Thy Heart . . ." was calling my heart. I gave no further thought to what I would say. The eulogy went off without a hitch.

I had been initiated by Pir Vilayat but then asked to resign the Sufi Order. The Sufi Ruhaniat had always been my spiritual family, always welcoming to me, with no mention of initiation status. MaryRose had been going to Sufi class in Albuquerque, had been initiated into the Sufi Order, and had been given the Sufi name Shahida. She talked extensively with me about spiritual guidance and the benefit of a spiritual guide. After eight years in the world of jyotish, Sanskrit, and Vedanta, I was ready to reconnect with my spiritual family.

## January 2006

MaryRose and I flew to California to attend a ten-day Sufi sesshin at the Institute for Noetic Sciences in Petaluma. We arrived late at night in the aftermath of massive storms and flooding. I took the exit off Highway 101, missed the turn on a dark country road, tried to turn around, and got our rental car hopelessly stuck in the mud, not exactly in the middle of nowhere but close enough. We had come a thousand miles to get stuck in the muck on a moonless night. We sat there in the dark.

MaryRose started praying to God for help—and out of nowhere an angel appeared. Before I even had a minute to worry and fret, she stepped out into the road and was talking to a great big guy in a great big truck who had miraculously appeared that very minute. He pulled out a chain, wrapped it around our axle, and pulled us out of the mud. Ganesha again, looking like Hanuman.

We drove back to the institute's gates, which were locked. We left our car on the road and walked all the way up the hill, only to find that no one was home. We realized we must have arrived a day too early. I was dumbfounded, but MaryRose was quite happy that we would have the next day free. We walked back down the long steep road, seeing deer, sniffing skunk, and hearing frogs.

We spent the night at the Panama Inn in San Rafael. The next day we drove out to Point Reyes, maneuvering through mud washes that had flooded the road. We walked an hour up the beach, alongside huge glistening ocean waves, and found a quiet place to enter into the white space of a nap before driving back to the institute.

The institute is located high on a ridgetop in the lyrical farm country of Petaluma, all lush green hills and ancient oak forest. Pir Shabda, the head of the Sufi Ruhaniat, opened his arms and gave us a warm welcome. "My favorite dervishes!" he said.

My friend Peter, from the summer with Ram Dass, had been a mureed of Murshid Sam and eventually his successor when Pir Moineddin died and passed the mantle to him.

Sufi sesshin is the group practice of sitting and dancing, sitting and dancing, for ten days straight, maybe sitting for twenty minutes and dancing for twenty minutes at the beginning, then gradually sitting longer and dancing longer. It is not a guided meditation, just simple sitting meditation.

The weather was cold but mostly clear. After lunch we would go walking in the hills above the institute, the charming rolling hills pastured by cattle, wandered by deer, overflown by turkey vultures.

At first, my meditation was unfocused and difficult. My normal routines were not working. I put my awareness on my breathing and watched the mental clutter clear away and then, in the emptiness, the spaciousness—I didn't know what to do! And I had ten days to sit with it! I tried doing various practices and holding certain concentrations: *Ya Rahman, Ya Rahim . . . Ya Nur, Ya Hadi . . . Ya This, Ya That . . .* But nothing was working. . . . Anxiety and boredom. . . .

Then, taking a cue from MaryRose, I switched to a simple concentration on Allah in the heart and everything smoothed out. If I just listen to my heart, I can hear it chanting as it is pulsing: *Allah Hu, Allah Hu, Allah Hu, Allah Hu.* I had forgotten the simple language of the heart, Allah Hu. Everything settled down. Everything is in Allah's hands. Allah takes care of everything.

I got that, at this time in my life, I have little left to do and a lot to give. I especially gave up to Allah all my concerns about MaryRose and me being together, how that will work out. I can't figure it out. I can only open to the Divine Light and the Spirit of Guidance. Allah has brought us together and will see us through.

In the middle of sesshin, we went on total silence. MaryRose was seeing angels descend, hearing angel wings. "I've cried more than I have since I was born." She pulled her Russian hat down over her eyes to keep the world away. The next day, Taj Inayat took her on as a student and answered her heart's desire.

We went on a long walk through the hills in the moonlight. She said, "I'm taking you with me wherever I go." We professed deepest love for each other. I promised her that I will stay together with her wherever she goes. That night Shabda sang ragas, and MaryRose saw the lights in the room modulate with the sound, saw Shabda's body dissolve into space.

The rest of the retreat was very peaceful. We were deeply in love with each other, very comfortable as roommates, very loving and intimate, while we went through all these transformations. We just loved snuggling up with each other each night.

## September 2006

MaryRose and I enrolled in Suluk Academy to study the teachings and practices of Hazrat Inayat Khan with his grandson Pir Zia Inayat-Khan. Suluk was a four-year program, three eight- or nine-day sessions a year, held at the Abode of the Message in New Lebanon, New York. The Abode is located in the historic buildings of an old Shaker community in a beautiful pastoral region.

Hazrat Inayat Khan brought Sufism from India to the West in 1910, carrying the transmission of the Chishti silsila (lineage). He was a musician who chose to lay his veena aside and teach through speech. The teachings we have are transcriptions of the talks he gave until his death at age forty-four in 1927. He was a Muslim who chose not to teach Islam to Westerners at that time, concentrating on what he called The Message of Spiritual Liberty. He initiated many people, some as teachers, and gave his mureeds a wealth of Sufi practices.

Both the Sufi Order International (now the Inayati Order) and the

Sufi Ruhaniat International are in the lineage of Hazrat Inayat Khan. The Sufi Order was founded by Pir Vilayat Khan, the son of Hazrat Inayat Khan, and now is guided by his son Pir Zia. The Sufi Ruhaniat was founded by the mureeds of Murshid Sam, who was a mureed in turn of Hazrat Inayat Khan, and now is guided by Pir Shabda Kahn. The Sufi Order is primarily an esoteric school for the teachings and practices of Hazrat Inayat Khan. The Sufi Ruhaniat is best known for the Dances of Universal Peace but is an equally esoteric school.

At one time all of these Sufis were one big happy family. Many of Murshid Sam's mureeds were also initiated into the Sufi Order. Then, in 1977, Pir Vilayat announced that he wanted none of his mureeds to use marijuana, nor any other mind-altering substance, and asked those who could not stop using marijuana to resign from the Sufi Order. The senior teachers in the Ruhaniat did not want to betray the *bayat* (initiatic link) Murshid Sam had given his mureeds by demanding that their brother and sister mureeds give up smoking dope or leave. Marijuana use had not been an issue for Murshid Sam. In essence, Sam had said, "What's all the fuss about a vegetable?" Murshid Sam's mureeds stood by each other as a group with their own lineage to honor, and rejected the hierarchical authority of Pir Vilayat. It is characteristic of the Ruhaniat that it functions as a group of brothers and sisters rather than a hierarchical order. It could be said that Pir Vilayat disowned the Ruhaniat or that the Ruhaniat deserted Pir Vilayat. Either way it was very painful for all involved. Only thirty years later did all involved begin to engage in an ongoing healing process.

When we returned from Sufi sesshin earlier that year, MaryRose and I wanted to go to a retreat with Taj Inayat of the Sufi Order, a retreat for initiates only. I didn't know if I qualified. Although I had been initiated by Pir Vilayat in 1971, I had resigned at Pir Vilayat's request in 1977. Although I had been engaged in Sufi practices and leading dances for thirty years, I was an outsider in the initiatic hierarchy. I wrote Pir Zia, whom I had never met, about my quandary. His generous reply was, "Once the door has been opened, it can never be closed."

Before I went to Suluk I wanted to be initiated into the Sufi Ruhaniat, which has always been my spiritual family. I asked my oldest friend, Asha, to initiate me. She was the one who first welcomed me to Lama Foundation in 1970. Now she was a Murshida, welcoming me into the Ruhaniat in 2006.

Standing in a beautiful meadow high above Santa Fe, with MaryRose as witness, Asha looked me in the eye and said, "I'm standing here in space and you're standing there in space and between us is an open door which is also in space. If you choose to, you can step through that door."

I stepped toward her, we joined hands, and she said the words of initiation, drawing the Sufi heart and wings on my forehead. We all sat for a while in silence.

After a while Asha said, "Do you feel anything different, now that you're initiated?"

"Not really," I said. "Here we are together in the present moment."

"That's right," she said.

Thus, I was an initiate of both Sufi Order and Sufi Ruhaniat when I went to Suluk Academy.

We slept in the old Shaker buildings and ate together in the community dining room. We were part of the Abode community while we were there and took turns helping with the cooking and cleaning. Every morning there would be a session with Pir Zia and a session with the guest teacher of the week: Azizza, Gayan, Wali Ali, or Zumurrud. Every afternoon there would be mentor group meetings followed by pod gatherings.

Pir Zia was a very refined and beautiful man, with a presence of deep peace. Always dressed in brown Sufi robes, he would enter the meditation hall silently, walking very, very slowly with great dignity and humility. His voice was soft, quiet, distinct, and precise. He was twenty years younger than me but spoke with the authority of embodied traditional wisdom.

Pir Zia had organized a huge body of material around the themes of concentration, contemplation, meditation, and realization, one for each year of Suluk, for us to study.

If Pir Vilayat had taken us soaring to the highest heavens, Pir Zia was deep and grounded. And yet exactly the same thing happened to me with Pir Zia as had with Pir Vilayat—listening to him, I would be absorbed into a white space beyond words and beyond thought. It was like falling asleep. I kept nodding off into the white space.

I knew I wasn't prone to falling asleep in class. I could listen all day and night to Hart DeFouw teaching. Listening to Pir Zia, I was absorbed into a wordless white space. I was aware of talking going on but I couldn't comprehend any of it. It was like having cotton in my ears. I kept nodding off into samadhi. Was this the spiritual transmission Pir Zia was carrying?

I asked my mentors about this. Their replies were always evasive— "Does it make you uncomfortable?" "Are you comfortable with it?" At least they seemed to acknowledge that "it" was something. I even asked Pir Zia directly about this and he was equally oblique. "Shahabuddin complained about the same thing to my father, who said, 'If you only heard my words, you wouldn't get what I am saying. . . .'"

Okay. . . .

Eventually I got to a place where I could be absorbed into the white space and fully comprehend the words at the same time. Maybe that was what I needed to come to. All the same, I remained wary of a state of consciousness that was dependent on sitting with Pir Zia. It seemed like a contact high.

Many of the students were enraptured by the spiritual phenomena they witnessed around Pir Zia—waves of light flooding the room, stardust streaming from his slippers, that sort of thing. Our group mentor, Ishi-Nili, told us, "The very cells of your bodies are being transformed by being with Pir Zia."

Be that as it may, I was not given much ability to see that kind of thing: lights, colors, auras, angels, devas. . . . Any sort of visual spiritual phenomena eludes me. I admire and respect those I know who have such abilities. I trust that it is real, but it is not mine to see. I do have vivid dreams and sometimes fantasies, but the direct perception of etheric light (auras) and spiritual light is rare and elusive for me. I seem to have some clairaudience but not clairvoyance.

The voice of Hazrat Inayat Khan has always resonated deeply in my soul. It is as if my soul already knows what he is talking about, but he has the ability to let the soul knowledge speak. Nothing Inayat Khan says surprises me, but much of what he says delights me. His words are like an ocean of honey, a cosmos of love, harmony, and beauty. My only problem is remembering where to find this or that wonderful thought. Suluk refreshed my immersion in Pir-o-Murshid's voice. Pir Zia gave me more practical application of the teachings and a wealth of practice to embody them. Spiritual practices are dead letters until the teacher gives them life. Sitting with Pir Zia was the core of Suluk. The rest is pretty much a blur.

Pir Zia gave MaryRose a new Sufi name, Widad, meaning "all-pervading love."

Together Ahad and Widad are One Love.

One silent day Widad and I went for a long walk up through the woods, and then down the road into town, where we had excellent hamburgers for dinner. We walked back under the starry sky and saw shooting stars. We sat and chanted zikr with the Sufis.

Widad kept on saying to me, "I have no libido. I have nothing for you. It's all for God! Aren't you jealous of God? He has all my attention!"

I said to her, "There is no separation."

Our class recorded, transcribed, and made a book of all of Pir Zia's teachings over those four years. It was a massive online project involving at least a dozen transcribers and editors. I contributed photography to the book, actually two volumes of over a thousand pages. But I can never show the book to anyone and am sworn to return it to Suluk on my death. This knowledge is not intellectual property but a heart-to-heart transmission. I'd like to think I got the transmission even though I missed some of the teachings.

Toward the end of Suluk, some of us were invited to take a Coordinator training, which would enable us to support the local Sufi Order representatives in holding group classes. In order to take this training, one had to have a guide. Widad had talked with me so much about working with a guide that I wanted to have this experience. I asked Asha if I could work with a Sufi Order guide and she gave me her blessing. I asked our group mentor, Ishi-Nili, if she would be my guide for this purpose. She heartily agreed. I did caution her that I was also a Ruhaniat initiate, that Ruhaniat was my spiritual family, and that at some point, if I was asked to be a teacher, I would have to choose between Sufi Order and Sufi Ruhaniat.

Pir Zia was quite clear that no Sufi Order teacher could teach in Sufi Ruhaniat. The Ruhaniat had no such restrictions. But Pir Zia was definite—if you teach in Sufi Ruhaniat, you're out of Sufi Order.

We were granted only one meeting with Pir Zia per year. In my last meeting with Pir Zia he asked me how I saw myself serving the Message. I said, "Pir Zia, I am not a spiritual teacher like you are, not in the sense of standing or sitting before an audience and discoursing on spiritual subjects. I serve the Message by leading the Dances of Universal Peace." He gave me his blessing.

## May 29, 2010

On the morning of our Suluk graduation, we held a solemn procession, led by Pir Zia, to the top of the mountain where there was a bestowal of blessings, Sufi shawls, and roses on all of us. We each were given a diploma that certified one as having reached the degree of "Traveler on the Endless Path." In the afternoon we had a public ceremony in which our class embodied a living labyrinth of whispered prayer for people to walk through. Widad and I led the assembly in dances.

Ishi-Nili took me out behind the meditation hall and initiated me to the eighth level of the Sufi Order. I began to have monthly phone meetings with Ishi-Nili as my spiritual guide, giving me practices.

Meanwhile my old friend Pir Shabda, head of the Sufi Ruhaniat, had been coming through Albuquerque each summer en route to Lama Sufi sesshin. We had been hosting Shabda and his wife Tamam at Manitoba.

"Ahad," Shabda once said to me, "you really should be teaching. You've been doing sadhana for many years. You're ready to teach."

"If someone comes to me and asks to learn," I told him, "I will teach them."

I asked Asha about this. She said, "Until you have a student, you don't need to put yourself forth as a teacher."

Then the student appeared, Dennis, a very bright man, born on my birthday, two years my senior, who loved our dance meetings. He said to me that he would like to know more about "the Sufism behind the dances." That was the sign.

The Sufi Order has twelve levels of initiation, like grades in a school, as set up by Hazrat Inayat Khan. The mureed is given progressive levels of initiation over time. The Sufi Ruhaniat employs only two initiations: the first level, welcoming one into the tent, and the ninth level, recognizing that one is mature enough to initiate and guide. Traditionally, in India, only these two initiations, called *bay'at* and *khilafat,* are used.

I asked Asha if she would initiate me to the ninth level in the Ruhaniat so that I would be able to initiate and guide Dennis. She gave me this initiation in the fall, in the dark of night, in my backyard.

When I told Ishi-Nili of my decision she was dismayed. She said, "You can't be a teacher in both orders. It does not make sense for me to guide you anymore. I feel so sad. I knew this might happen, but I wish you had chosen *us* rather than *them.*"

It was like a divorce. She made me swear that I would never ever ask anything from her again and basically never talk to her again. Although spiritual friendship and spiritual liberty were ideals promoted by the Sufi Order, when I broke rank with this strict hierarchical order, I was shunned by my one-time spiritual guide and friend. She never spoke to me again.

On a bright spring day, I initiated Dennis into the Sufi Ruhaniat and gave him the name Anwar, a name of light. It was a three-level ceremony, ascending from the sun room to the sun porch to the high tower of our house. Anwar, my first and only mureed, is a lay Christian monk of the Third Order of St. Francis. Anwar joins Christian congregations in prayer almost every day, but he is very devoted to his Sufi practices as well.

One area of life in which Widad and I were in complete alignment was our spiritual path. Although we had different functions according to our natures, her as a teacher, me as a musician, we were both dedicated to the Sufi path and the Dances of Universal Peace. Time with God in meditation and prayer is part of our daily life.

The Dances of Universal Peace had never been firmly established in Albuquerque. There had been various leaders who held meetings in various places over the years, but the dances had never really taken root as they had in Santa Fe. Our desire was to establish a regular dance meeting in Albuquerque.

Before offering a public meeting, we held private gatherings in our homes for those interested and then in a church to begin building community. This generated a lot of interest and enthusiasm in a party-like atmosphere. Then, in 2006, we began having public meetings in the Church of Religious Science on San Pedro in Albuquerque, drawing in good-sized circles of between fifteen and thirty people. We also encountered our first challenges there.

Some people were using the dance meetings for networking and self-promotion, putting out flyers and posters, making announcements about events in the circle, and even bringing goods to sell. Although there is nothing really wrong with this at what is seen as a community gathering, we were seeking to create a sacred container for prayer in which the mundane did not intrude. We put a stop to that behavior. We may have lost a few people who were primarily there to promote their own self-interest, but that was all right. We wanted lovers of the dances, lovers of God.

We also had to disinvite certain people who were being disruptive or disrespectful of the space we were creating in other ways. As an example, I was leading a very sacred dance, Allah Hu Ahad, at the end of a large conference in Santa Fe, when a woman came into the center of the circle and began doing a dance of veils, slowly and seductively shedding her clothes. I was so absorbed that I just ignored this intrusion. I noticed it, but must have thought it was part of everything anyway. Tara Andrea had to escort the woman out of the circle. I learned that I could not be so oblivious of an intrusion on our sacred space.

At some point, the Church of Religious Science on San Pedro changed location and identity to become the Albuquerque Center for Spiritual Living on Louisiana, and we moved with them. Still later we moved the dances to the Albuquerque Friends Meetinghouse.

Tara Andrea, Maboud, and I had become very comfortable with each other over the years in Santa Fe and in some respects had grown very sloppy. We never rehearsed and came to dance meetings prepared to wing it. Maboud and Tara were continually evolving new dances and their creative ferment spilled over into the meetings. Maboud could be working out new steps in the group in the moment, changing and rearranging things. The two of them would sometimes argue with each other across the circle. Our Santa Fe meetings were spontaneous but not always consistent. Mostly it was love and light—but there was a shadow side. It was in this atmosphere that Tara had certified Widad as a dance leader.

Widad and I took a different approach to our dance meeting in Albuquerque. We rehearsed extensively before each meeting. We sought to carefully construct programs of dance that would lead from harmonization to exaltation, often evoking certain themes. I brought thirty years as a musician and dance leader. To some extent I served as Widad's mentor, even as our rehearsals showed me that I still had a lot to learn. Widad brought a spiritual attunement, a very high sense of the sacred that is rare and that I have learned to trust, as well as an ecstatic, embodied femininity. Our rehearsals were often as high as the public meetings.

One of our agreements is not to criticize or correct each other when we are leading dances in public. We support each other as dance leaders, even if we think the other is making a mistake. We save our opinions for later.

The Dances of Universal Peace are participatory body prayer, not performance art. The basis of the Dances of Universal Peace, Murshid Sam says, is the repetition of the sacred phrase. Chanting the divine name embodies the divine presence. We begin our dance meetings by holding hands in a circle and reciting the Sufi Invocation:

*Toward the One,*
*the Perfection of Love, Harmony, and Beauty,*
*the Only Being,*
*United with All the Illuminated Souls*
*who form the Embodiment of the Master,*
*the Spirit of Guidance.*

Then we string the prayer beads of our own sacred names. I say "Ahad" and the circle responds "Ahad," my beloved standing next to me says "Widad" and the circle responds "Widad," and so on around through each person in the circle. The first dances are usually simple group dances to attune the group, to get us holding hands, stepping together, and chanting together. Even just the fact of holding hands in a circle with other people is a minor blessing most of us rarely experience in everyday life.

The whole dance meeting is a process of attunement and harmonization, drawing us ever closer to unity in heart and breath. Hazrat Inayat Khan says,

> The work of a mystical teacher is not to teach but to tune, to tune the pupil so that he may become an instrument of God. For the mystical teacher is not the player of the instrument; he is the tuner. When he has tuned it, he gives it into the hands of the Player whose instrument it is to play.

As each dance progresses the leader may or may not say "women's voices only" or "men's voices only," alternating the voices of the sisters and the brothers. The leader may say, "On the breath!" and we continue to dance in silence, keeping the prayer on the breath. Or when the group is really attuned, the leader may say "voices only, no instruments," which is often the most glorious moment, hearing our open hearts singing in praise. Murshid Sam says,

> The essence of prayer should be praise. . . . The words, the attitude, and the motions, when these are made, are directed upward, away from self, toward God. Offering praise to God and blessing for God—these are the ultimate duties of the devotee.

In the partner dances we hold hands with one another, look into the eyes of one another, greet one another with peace, and bless one another with love . . . and then move on to the next partner. It is one thing to open our hearts to the all-pervading divine presence. It is the same thing in a different form to open our hearts to the divine light in each other, which may be challenging and often is delightful. The partner dances often evoke joy and laughter as one finds partners, loses partners, makes mistakes, and we play with each other. The point of the dances is not to avoid making mistakes. Joy is sacred. Mistakes are just like grace notes, accidentals, in the light playing among us. There is no right way to pray.

The dancers are not always perfect. Some people just can't seem to get the step or the melody perfectly. Some people sing loudly and out of tune. I just stand next to them and sing louder. I have a duty to teach the dance clearly, which may involve some repetition, but I do not have to perfect each dancer. Harmonization of voices and hearts does happen in its own way over the course of the evening.

Sometimes God throws in a wild card, like the large drunk man who wandered in and joined the dancing circle, whooping and hollering, "Amen! Alleluia! Praise Jesus!" in the silence after each dance. He reeked of booze and melted hearts and prejudices that night.

Toward the end of a dance meeting, we typically do deeper, sometimes longer, dances now that the hearts and voices are harmonized. This is when the Holy Spirit can come in. Sometimes, the longer we dance, the deeper the surrender happens. Although many dances have exquisite complexity, over the years we have come to value the simpler, deeper dances as a more effective "means of transportation" to ecstasy.

We close with the dedication: "May all beings be well . . . May all beings be happy . . . Peace . . . peace . . . peace."

Widad and I have hosted several guest dance teachers over the years, including Pir Shabda, Murshid Allaudin, Murshida Asha, Murshid Abraham, Murshida Halima, and Murshida Darvesha. Pir Shabda has been particularly supportive with his warm relaxed atmosphere, large heart, and clear, incisive mind.

I discussed with Pir Shabda the difference between the teaching model in the Sufi Order where the students always sit in front of the teacher, the star and crescent formation, and the Ruhaniat model where we all stand together holding hands in a circle.

My experience at Suluk was that Pir Zia, the star, was protected and unapproachable, maintaining a rarefied atmosphere around him. The students would sit passively in front of the teacher, soaking up the divine light. Many of these students just can't wait to get home and be the shining star for their own crescent of students. There was a certain amount of unaddressed rivalry, jealousy, judgment, and other shadows that murked the atmosphere at Suluk.

In Ruhaniat gatherings, the atmosphere is much more egalitarian and down-to-earth. We hold hands together and dance in a circle. We dance together and sit alone. The teachers are approachable, hang out with us, and even eat meals with us. As many of us are dance leaders, the teachers are always asking members of the circle to lead dances.

Pir Shabda told me: "In Ruhaniat we do something for a while, and then we let someone else do that something for a while."

I had not traveled at all for a good thirty years. Now, later in life, I traveled extensively with Widad. We visited the temples of the Goddess in Crete and Naxos and Delphi. We visited medieval castles and the grotto shrine of Saint Sarah the Black in Provence. We toured through Tuscany

Ahad and MaryRose, Camp de Aigles, above Chamonix, France, summer 2010.

and sailed on Lake Como. We cruised down the Rhine, through the land of the Holocaust, and into the Danube. We hiked the Swiss Alps and the Colorado Rockies, the Canyonlands of Utah, the cloud forests of Costa Rica, and the jungles of Belize. We snorkeled the vanishing coral reefs in the Caribbean. We walked the beaches by the oceans every year. We were blessed to see what we were able to see of the glory of creation.

## February 2012

Widad and I flew to India to join the celebration of Hazrat Inayat Khan's *Urs* (death day/wedding night) at his *dargah* (shrine) in New Delhi on a pilgrimage led by Pir Shabda and Taj Inayat. The dargah compound is a two-story walled garden compound in the Nizamuddin *basti* (neighborhood) of New Delhi. Inayat Khan chose to be interred near the dargah of Hazrat Nizamuddin Auliya, his most illustrious predecessor.

The central event of the Urs celebration every year is the blessing of a chador or grave covering at the dargah of Nizamuddin Auliya, which is then carried by the pirs and the mureeds to the dargah of Inayat Khan and draped over the grave.

The dargah itself is a large free-standing structure on the second story of the compound. A tree grows inside it and up through the roof of the large gathering room. The canopied burial is covered with a golden jeweled cloth and red rose petals. When I first prostrated and put my forehead on the cool marble footing of Inayat Khan's casket, invoking Toward the One, I fell into vastness, emptiness, and absolute silence. Everything stopped.

Pir Shabda later commented, "How wonderful! You had an experience of the not-self."

Other prostrations were like plunging into webs of light rippling on the surface and in the depths of a pool of water, both here and at other dargahs. I experienced absorption into the samadhi, the baraka, the presence held in this place by the illuminated soul buried here and the devotion of the people to the memory of the saint.

The Urs celebration was a three-day gathering of Sufis from all the Inayati orders. Pir Zia was there, as were many of our fellow students from Suluk. There were talks and concerts, singing and dancing, meditation and Universal Worship—and tragedy. When Pir Shabda arrived, he learned that his son, Solomon, had been killed in a car accident in Thailand. Shabda was open with us about his grief while being fully present as our magnanimous host, a heart-wrenching demonstration of equanimity. He wanted to be with his family in California, but he said, "You are my family, too." After three days he left early to go home.

Pilgrimage to dargahs and holy places is integral to Chishtiyya Sufism. Some may see this as saint veneration or close to idolatry. At certain times and places, it has aroused the destructive wrath of fundamentalist Muslims. But India is an extraordinary spiritual environment, in which one is free to be whomever one imagines oneself to be, spiritually.

We visited the dargah of Nizamuddin Auliya and the dargah of Bibi Fatima in New Delhi, the dargah of Moineddin Chishti in Ajmer Sharif, and the dargah of Salim Chishti in Fatehpur Sikri. All these shrines are very much alive with fervent prayer, impassioned singing, palpable baraka, and deep serenity.

Shabda tells the story of Murshid Sam arriving in town and asking to meet the sheikh, only to be informed that, sadly, the sheikh had just passed away, to which Murshid replied, "That's okay. I'll meet him at his tomb."

As in the Catholic faith, Sufi saints, when prayed to or through, are seen as capable of answering prayers and granting wishes. The custom is to make a prayer and tie a string, strands of thread dyed red and yellow, to the lattice windows of the dargah. People meditate, contemplate, pray, converse, discuss, release, whatever the soul needs, at such sacred sites. Often, it is simply to breathe in the sublime presence and peaceful atmosphere found in such a location.

It is like this at Murshid Sam's maqbara, where he was buried high on the hillside above Lama Foundation. People have always made pilgrimage to his gravesite, which is a simple mound of white quartzite from the mountain, with an open-air dance ground made on the earth nearby. The maqbara used to be sheltered in the piñon forest, but since the fire, it lies open to the elements. Some people report having all sorts of conversations with Murshid Sam up there. When I visit the maqbara the only voice I hear is "Allah Allah Allah," so I simply walk around the grave, chanting *"Allah Allah Allah."* Now there is a beautiful formal dargah there, which Pir Shabda caused to be built.

Hazrat Khwaja Nizamuddin Auliya was a medieval Sufi mystic who welcomed people of all faiths and classes into his assembly and his discourses on divine love. His many mureeds spread Sufism throughout India. He is greatly loved by all the people to this day.

The Nizamuddin basti has changed very little since medieval times, goats on the rooftops, homes over little one-room shops on narrow streets, a very close community. As one approaches the Nizamuddin dargah, one is asked to take off one's shoes. There are vendors selling rose water, garlands of roses, chadors, tasbihs, and religious artifacts. One goes through marble-floored corridors with lattice windows to a large marble plaza surrounding the dargah that is filled with people sitting and praying and *qawwali* singing (a form of Sufi devotional singing). The dargah itself is a square building surrounded by a covered porch and surmounted by a white dome. Men enter the central chamber and stand in prayer or walk around the chador-covered grave, strewing roses on it. Women cannot enter the dargah itself but have to sit outside on the verandah and peer through the lattice work. The atmosphere is highly charged with baraka and continual prayer.

After a week in Delhi we took the train to Ajmer to visit the dargah of Moinuddin Chishti, which is built on a much vaster scale, third only to Mecca and Medina as the most visited shrine in the world of Islam. Ajmer is located in the relatively pure air of the Rajasthan desert. A long, crowded bazaar street leads to a towering green gate, which allows entry to a huge marble complex of porticoes and mosques and vendors, all strung with brightly colored lights.

We visited Moinuddin Chishti's dargah just after sunset. Long lines of men and long lines of women of all faiths were patiently waiting to go into the central-domed dargah while qawwali groups were singing. Our group sat under a tiled portico, awaiting our turn. Birds flocked and sang in the trees, creating serenity amid intensity.

When we were led inside the dargah, we were immersed in a mass of people crowding around the silver-fenced grave, praying loudly, praying silently, young men shouting fervently, everyone strewing roses on the tomb, crowding in to touch the chadors on the grave, to prostrate themselves at the feet of the saint.

Hazrat Moinuddin Chishti is known as Gharib Nawaz, the protector of the poor. Twice a day there are *langars,* public meals, where thousands of people are fed from two *degs,* enormous iron cauldrons, ten feet in diameter, on either side of the entry. The atmosphere at the dargah is one of continually intense fervent humanity and deep serenity at the same time.

We visited the dargah of Salim Chishti in Fatehpur Sikri. Salim Chishti is known as the wish-fulfilling saint. Emperor Akbar petitioned him to pray for the birth of a son. When this wish was fulfilled, Akbar built a new capital city around the dwelling and now the dargah of Salim Chishti. The dargah is a gleaming white marble shrine set in a huge red sandstone palace complex. Pilgrims come to Salim Chishti to pray for what their heart desires—marriage, children, prosperity, success, health. They leave their prayers as strings tied on the marble lattice—and when their children are grown, their children come on pilgrimage out of gratitude.

In Fatehpur Sikri, we went inside the Diwan-i-Khas, a very unusual building with a central pillar that supports a platform high above the floor and four walkways reaching it from the second-story balconies. Emperor Akbar would summon representatives of various religious communities to come and hold discussions about God while he listened out of sight from above. Murshid Sam received some initial inspirations for the Dances of Universal Peace here in Fatehpur Sikri.

After Ajmer, Widad and I parted from the group of Sufis we had been traveling with and went on our own way. We drove over the hill to nearby Puskhar, a Hindu town on a sacred lake, to visit one of the very few Brahma temples in India. I had to take the rare opportunity to visit my jyotisha *devata* (personal deity), Brahma.

Under the *shikara* (red spire) of the open-air Brahma *Mandir* (temple), I had the darshan of a small thirteen-hundred-year-old, four-headed black-marble murti (idol) with intense white eyes, wrapped in red cloth and marigold garlands. I was pierced by the gaze of what seemed like an ancient hunk of black stone meteorite with white bugged-out eyes. I still don't know what to make of it. We went to the lake and had a Brahman priest bless us and welcome us to Hindu India. We scattered our prayers as rose petals on the lake.

If Sufi India was power and peace, baraka and salaama, then Hindu India was *ananda marga,* the path of bliss, for me.

We visited the main Krishna Temple in Jaipur at noontime, when the priests open the doors on the murtis, who are sheltered most of the day. In India the murtis are considered living beings and are clothed, garlanded, washed, and fed every day—and given lots of down time to rest between viewings. Hundreds of people come and line up for darshan, the gaze of Radha and Krishna. Widad joined a group of women dancing ecstatically, chanting to Krishna, holding up the thumbs-down mudra of the teats of the divine udder full of love.

We visited the sprawling Galta temple complex, where monkeys are worshipped and fed. We visited Neem Karoli Baba's ashram in Vrindavan, where we were astounded by a life-size murti of the blissful baba and charmed by the sweet temple cows. We chanted Ramnam (the name Ram) in a shady room with his tucket and ate kedgeree with the residents in a metal cage with monkeys crawling all over it. We visited the golden-domed Sikh Temple in New Delhi, where holy books are chanted and thousands of people are fed every day.

## April 2014

Widad and I went on a tour of Andalusia and Morocco. Muslims, Christians, and Jews shared a common culture for eight hundred years in Andalusia until the Reconquista and the Inquisition purged the Iberian Peninsula of Muslims and Jews for the next five hundred years. We visited Toledo, Granada, Cordoba, and Seville. We came to appreciate the beauty and the richness of the Andalusian culture that was a shining jewel while much of the rest of Europe was in the Dark Ages. We learned that Greek and Roman literature had been completely lost to Europeans in the literally Dark Ages until the Andalusians undertook the great task of translating the Greek and Roman classics from Arabic into European tongues.

In Morocco, we experienced the deep sweetness of a country where Islam had been the cultural norm for twelve hundred years. Islam in Morocco was neither compulsory nor intolerant. Islam permeated the entire culture with a peaceful atmosphere. We were told that if you are respectful of religion in public, you can do what you like in private. If you want to eat lunch during Ramadan, just do it at home. Morocco did not seem to be threatened by modern culture and was not infected by fundamentalist Islam. Moroccan women had made great advances toward independence in the last fifty years.

In the mountain town of Chefchaouen, we were privileged to hear a group of Sufi women, dressed in green and white robes, singing devotional songs that had been nurtured in the privacy of home for hundreds of years. In Rabat we listened to a group of men playing and singing Andalusian Sufi music. We visited the white domed tombs of *marabouts* (saints) next to the ruined mosque where storks nested, in Chellah. We had numerous encounters in the street with strangers who would say enigmatic things such as, "There is nothing under this cloak but God. . . ."

## Sunday, October 2, 2016

MaryRose and I got married—after eleven years of loving each other and being together. We invited all our family and friends to come to our wedding celebration. It took us a full year of working with vendors and planning every last detail to create a beauty so sublime, an event so seamless, that everyone was transported.

We were already married in every sense but legally. We both lived and worked at home. We had been together all the time, sleeping and waking, walking and talking, cooking and cleaning, celebrating and recreating, living and loving, fussing and fighting, singing and dancing, and everything in between, for the past eleven years. Now we had decided to take our reality to the next level—because having a wedding and actually getting married changes everything.

On Friday, MaryRose had high tea with the women at the St. James Teahouse while I took the men on a hike in the wilderness to visit Ganapati. On Saturday we held Universal Worship at our house, lighting candles for all the spiritual traditions of the world, reading sacred verses, chanting, and dancing together, followed by dinner on the patio at El Pinto.

Sunday was a glorious crisp fall day, bright blue sky, high wispy clouds, Sun with Jupiter and Moon with Venus. We were married under a canopy on the patio of the Tanoan Country Club, with green lawns and the Sandia Mountains behind us. MaryRose, exuding glamour, overflowing with joy, looked like a fairy-tale princess in her vintage wedding gown and huge bouquet. We were all singing, "Allah Hu, El Allah Hu, Pour upon Us Thy Love and Thy Light," as she came glowing down the aisle. We exchanged vows and lit the unity candle. Widad and Ahad were getting married to God and to each other. We exchanged rings and had all sorts of blessings bestowed on us. We were pronounced husband and wife. We kissed. All present released scores of painted lady butterflies into the air and then

October 2, 2016, Albuquerque, New Mexico, image courtesy of Dolores McDuffie.

formed an archway chanting *"Ya Fattah, Ya Fattah"* (May the Way Be Open!) as we left the patio—followed by dinner and toasts and cake and dancing and bouquet toss and garter toss and more dancing.

We are married in the higher love, married to God and to each other. On her finger, Widad has three gold bands with diamonds from my mother. I have a broad gold band with three diamonds as shooting stars. The rings on our hands signify Ahad, Widad, and God. This marriage is my spiritual path in life now, may God preserve our secrets—between the sheets of our marriage bed.

# 11    THE INNER LIFE

We had a sublime honeymoon in Bar Harbor, at the peak of the fall colors in the forest by the ocean in Acadia National Park. Marriage brought about some profound changes in our life together, even though we had been together for eleven years.

When the honeymoon was over, in the depth of winter, my reactions to stress intensified and I found myself occasionally overwhelmed, out of my mind, acting out in ways that were damaging to our marriage. The two psychologists I had been working with had diagnosed this as the result of trauma and told me that this trauma could not be cured, it could only be managed, which was not very helpful.

Then I turned seventy. My father had died in his seventieth year and my seventieth year represented some kind of longevity buffer to pass through. I felt my father had died early, bored and weary of life—that was my inkling. Wracked with cancer, he just stopped eating, stopped talking, turned his face to the wall, and died on the third day. But I was not there, as I had not been there for most of my father's life, so I really don't know.

My seventieth birthday was lived with my wife at Lama Foundation's fiftieth anniversary reunion with hundreds of my brothers and sisters dancing in the dome and praying at Murshid Sam's glorious new dargah. Then I had two heart attacks.

One warm night in July, Widad and I went downtown to the zoo to hear a concert by the Wailers. Thousands of people flooded the park, camping out on the lawn in front of the bandstand among huge old cottonwoods. Once we found our place and set up our chairs, I went to get drinks and snacks for us. It took time. After the band began to play, I was carrying a glass of wine and a can of beer back through the crowd when I felt pressure in the center of my chest, pain in my heart. I wondered if this was the pain of my heart opening up to embrace all of the humanity here. When I got back to Widad, the pain subsided. We danced to the music ("One love, one heart . . .") and connected again as joyful lovers dancing in the stars ("Let's get together and feel all right . . ."). As we walked back to the car the pressure in the center of my chest returned, along with some shooting pain in my arms and wrists. I hoped it would go away again, but by the time we had driven home and lay down in bed, the pain was still there. We went to the emergency room, where they tested my blood and informed me that I had had a heart attack and needed to be hospitalized.

*I am looking at Widad across the crowded room. A lot of light fills the room. Looking at her, loving her, my soul says to me that I am ready to go, I clearly realize that I am ready to go, to leave this life, that every-thing is complete. Even my memoirs, which I wrote from my soul, are com-plete. And yet, looking into her eyes in this moment, I know that our time together is not complete and I want to stay with her. She sleeps with me on the narrow bed. Angel wings brush her hair.*

When I was hospitalized all the tests were run and they found nothing, no plaque, no blockage. They concluded it must have been an arterial spasm. But then I had a second heart attack two weeks later and a second hospitalization. This time, by comparing x-rays, they concluded that a tiny artery in the wall of the heart had blocked up and sealed itself off, no problem. They gave me some meds and sent me on my way.

I felt like I had lost something . . . but there was a new opening as well.

After the heart attacks, my doctor recommended I work on the emotional component with Gautama Katzman, a trauma therapist in Albuquerque. Gautama's approach to healing trauma was not analytical. His approach was neurological—becoming aware of how the nervous system had been imprinted, programmed if you will, by traumatic experiences, and working with a wide array of methods to loosen, lessen, and release these frozen patterns in the neural pathways. These methods include rhythmic breathing, EMDR (Eye Movement Desensitization and Reprocessing), TAT (Tapas Acupressure Technique), and many others.

In my layman's understanding, trauma occurs when the nervous system is overwhelmed by intense reactions, such as fear or terror, to severely distressing events, and the stress is more than the nervous system can cope with. One is unable to integrate the emotions generated by the stress. One has to dissociate (disidentify, often literally leave the body) in order for a sense of self to survive. The extreme (traumatic) emotions imprinted on the nervous system then remain unconscious until similar emotions are stimulated by stress in present time and a traumatic response bursts forth with a vengeance, with an intensity far out of proportion to present events. So, there is the original traumatic event, recurring traumatic events throughout life repeating and amplifying the original trauma, and traumatic stress reactions in present time.

When my trauma is stimulated in present time, I am overwhelmed with fear, terror, rage, and despair, all jumbled together. I can't think things through. I am out of my mind. I don't know what I am saying. My nervous system is flooded with chemicals that demand flight (there must be somewhere out of here!), fight (pacing around the house, shouting and yelling), and ultimately freeze (mute, defeated, senseless paralysis). This trauma is debilitating, humiliating, and, worst of all, harmful to the one I love.

Forty years ago, when my mother told me I was a horrible baby, howling and screaming for the first three months of my life, I was surprised. I had always thought I was the golden child—everyone was so happy to see me and my mother loved me my whole life. She had been a horrible mother at first, but neither of us knew it.

As an infant I had been left alone much of the time, hungry, crying, starving, howling and screaming, angry, terrified, and ultimately numb and dissociated. Decisions were made in my soul, not conscious rational decisions, but intentional resolves in my newly embodied soul.

*I am all alone.*
*No one is holding me.*
*I am hungry.*
*There is no one feeding me.*
*There is no way to get fed.*
*There is no help.*
*I ask for help but no one comes.*
*I can't ask for help.*
*Nobody is here for me.*
*I'm not going to need anybody.*
*I can't ask for what I want.*
*I can't get what I want.*
*Asking for what I want seems to push away what I want.*
*It's better not to want anything at all.*
*Exhausted, I suffer in silence.*

I feel myself as a little boy, age three or four, locked in his room, yelling and screaming, enraged at not being seen, not being known for who he is—playful, creative, fun—enraged at being shut up, locked up, dignity wounded, vowing, "I'll never do this to anyone."

I remember arriving at a decision to suppress my energy, rage, and enthusiasm in order to be fed and survive. I remember the decision to go into hiding, to pretend, to be well behaved, not to let them know who I am. I remember the decision to suppress my throat and not give voice to the feelings in my body, to let my mouth express only the thoughts in my mind.

I pretended that I forgot, and then I forgot that I pretended. I chose to become invisible to my world, my parents and my teachers, and then became invisible to myself. I developed a personality as a bright empty intellect, composed of ceaseless chatter, knowing it all and feeling as little as possible.

So here it is—the traumatic imprint of the first three months, then the first three years, of my life, which has structured and defined my entire life journey, which structured and limited the choices I was able to make, which lay behind everything, unseen and unknown, until MaryRose dared to love this reclusive, stoic astrologer, who dared to love her in return, and over time everything that was hidden came into the light.

The healing continues. The journey goes on. Right now, all I can say is that I have a lot more space to allow her to be who she is without reacting so strongly—and that this has made space for more peace and more love in our lives.

This was the beginning of my inner life—not infant bliss but infant dissociation.

We live in two worlds: the inner world and the outer world. These worlds overlap and interpenetrate each other. These two worlds project on and reflect each other. Yet each world has its own logic, its own dynamics, and its own laws, so to speak. We see with two eyes: the inner eye and the outer eye. In order to live fully we need to develop, as Pir Vilayat said, stereoscopic vision, or, as Murshid Sam bluntly put it, controlled schizophrenia. The inner life is always present, always alive, coexistent with, distinct from, yet interpenetrating, the outer life. Yet for the most part, attention is on the outer life in the world.

After the grandiose dreams and fantasy play of childhood, my attention was focused on the outer world of school, sports, homework, and family dynamics. Only in adolescence did I become aware that part of my consciousness was discontinuous with consensual outer reality, that there was a self-arising, independent, authoritative mentation within me.

While sitting and sipping cocktails with my family in the backyard on a balmy summer evening, I had become aware of blood calling out from the earth, the blood of Native Americans slaughtered, the lives of black slaves sacrificed, so that we could sit in the shade and get a buzz on. Who could I tell this to?

No one was going to validate my inner world. In fact, I soon found out that the expression of my knowingness was considered subversive and unacceptable. My father would call me into his den for long serious talks after dinner. He would try to educate me in history, politics, and economics, to the point where I would become bored. When he asked me what I was thinking and I told him, his standard response was, "Frank, I think you're crazy." I learned to keep my thoughts to myself.

I wrote down my thoughts and feelings extensively in diaries and journals. My journal writing—vital, vernacular, vulgar, enthused, stream of consciousness—came to an abrupt end one day when my father violated the privacy of my room, read what he needed to read of my journals, confiscated and destroyed them all—along with my love and trust in him.

Despite the atmosphere of paternal repression and censorship, there developed a very rich if submerged and inarticulate inner life, along with my sisters who tried so hard but at times could not contain their giggling and laughter from bursting forth during the solemnity of dinner time.

> *Darkness gathers in family dinners*
> *in shells of laughter*
> *in lions of prayer*
> *Silent children run away*
> *through galleries sunk in the silverware*
> *through floodlit cellars and golf courses*
> *tunneling through secret love*
> *in the summer houses of the moon*

Poetry and prose fiction turned out to be a more socially acceptable form of giving some expression to my inner voice, and even got some marginal recognition. I began to develop a craft and some identity around being a poet. By the time I was in college, what I came to call "the singing voice" of my inner world was far more essential and life-giving than the outer world of classwork and homework assignments.

By the time I heard Robert Bly say, "If you want to be a poet, you need to go be alone for a while," I was ready to take the plunge. I spent one whole summer totally alone on retreat in the White Mountains. I didn't write a single poem, so immersed was I for the first time in the silent world of essence.

☙❧

Absorption into unity, expansion into diversity—this is the inhalation and exhalation of spirit, the ebb and flow of consciousness. All life rides on the swing of the breath—in and out, in and out. Absorption into unity returns one to essential simplicity. Expansion into diversity brings one forth into the glorious, creative complexity of the manifest world.

My experiential reality is largely a matter of where and how I focus my attention. When focused solely on the external world, I find myself trapped in what seem to be endless cycles of suffering and self-replicating economies of conflict, futility, and despair: *samsara* . . . *dunya* . . . let alone the inevitable old age, sickness, and death, which we do our best to ignore.

Suzuki Roshi said, "Life is like stepping onto a boat that is about to sail out to sea and sink."

We don't want to look at that. In every age and in every condition, the single most valuable thing one can do is to take time to be alone with oneself outside of social influences, whether through meditation, retreat, solitude, or wandering, to let oneself know the silence of the inner life.

☙❧

I wasn't born to be a hippie, spiritual or otherwise. I was born to be an investment banker, seduced by the muse in my youth, but eventually coming to my senses and perpetuating my genes in the good life in suburban Baltimore. But a massive wave of spiritual awakening swept through the post-war world in the sixties and seventies, and I was a sparkle in that wave. Ancient streams of blessing were flooding into the post-industrial West.

In my beginning God was dead—or hidden, or inaccessible. God was not alive in my family, nor in my school, nor, as far as I could tell, in my church. Life was obedience, discipline, and achievement in a very privileged prison, but the rewards were mostly empty. Something was missing, but I didn't know what it was. The family and culture I had grown up in was achievement oriented, cold, competitive, and mental. My soul had a song to sing, a life to live, but could not see its reflection in the world I grew up in. So, I developed brilliant, sarcastic, cutting, cynical, hyper-linguistic mental abilities, even as my heart lay dormant, with no companion other than the sweet soul music on the radio.

The promise of Holy Communion in the Presbyterian Church turned out to be a dud. There was no Christ in the thimble of grape juice or the cube of Wonder Bread. The presence of Jesus in his words has been with me throughout life, but the belief systems that grew up around the figure of Jesus made no sense to me. Although millions of people for thousands of years have been united in Christian belief systems, it still made no sense to me.

The Buddhist concept of enlightenment and the high of smoking marijuana came into my life at the same time, and for a while they seemed to be the same. I had no teacher or guide other than my friends. I learned that nirvana was "a place or state characterized by freedom from or oblivion to pain, worry, and the external world," which seemed to be precisely the result of getting high. Time stopped, mind stopped, vision and hearing were acute, everything appeared as it really was, infinite . . . for a moment. Nirvana is "a blowing out," and getting high blows the mind . . . for a moment, a split second in eternity . . . until the music starts singing, the muse starts chanting, and ultimately . . . until the munchies come on with a vengeance. Although getting high was initially liberating, it turned out to be an addictive trap that it took me way too long to get out of.

Enlightenment may have been an appealing ideal, but it was the teachings of Mr. Gurdjieff that first awoke me to the reality of the human situation—that ordinary man is a machine, an automaton, with no free will, no real "I." I recognized that I had no real identity.

I had nothing but a mind that was ceaselessly churning information, words, and ideas, a mind on automatic, a mind that would not stop. I tried the stop exercise. I tried self-remembering. I tried and I tried. But I had no awareness of my emotional suffering. My mind would not permit it. I was not ready for this way of conscious labor and intentional suffering.

Ram Dass and the Maharaj-ji satsang welcomed me into a love I had been yearning for my whole life. What attracted me was not the philosophy or the mythology. The whole gestalt of guru yoga, Sanskrit chants, and blue-skinned, dewy-eyed multi-armed deities was strange to me—but the love I could feel was for real, the love, the joy, and the peace. Despite my skeptical mind, I experienced God as a living reality, living within and among us just as Jesus promised, and my heart blossomed.

The way given was to love, serve, and remember God always and everywhere. The methods given were to quiet the mind and open the heart through meditation, devotional chanting, and selfless service (seva). This path and these methods remained constant throughout all my years at Lama Foundation, with my further initiation into the Chishti Sufi path through Pir Vilayat Khan and Murshid Samuel Lewis, into the practices of divine remembrance (zikr), invocation of the divine names (*wazifahs*), and the ecstatic Dances of Universal Peace.

The goal of all these Hindu and Sufi practices seemed to be mystical union, union with God, union with the Beloved. As articulated by Hazrat Inayat Khan, "There is one Path, the annihilation of the false ego in the Real. . . ." I vigorously pursued practices that brought me experiences of unity, not-self, no mind, white space, emptiness, and so on—but these were all temporary states. I rapturously fantasized in poetry that I had touched home plate.

But what no one told me and what I could not see for myself was that, in order to function in life on the Earth plane, one must have an ego to begin with. In order to annihilate ("soften" is the preferred word these days) the false ego in the Real, one must have an ego to begin with. And my ego was vague and fuzzy at best, shattered and disintegrated at worst. I could barely function outside of spiritual community. I was on a major spiritual bypass, using spiritual beliefs and practices to avoid dealing with my debilitating emotional pain.

My inner work with Joanna Walsh involved embracing an alternative and idiosyncratic belief system, which was a derivative of Scientology and Kahuna wisdom. The model was that the cause of dysfunction and suffering lies in the subconscious, in past-life traumatic recordings that automatically react out in present time, and that the dissolution of these past-life recordings removes obstacles to healthy functioning as super-conscious in present time. I took all this at face value because the love between us was real and it gave me a way to begin to work on my emotional wounding that I had been in denial about for so long.

The study of jyotish connected me back with the sanatana dharma, the perennial philosophy of Hinduism, specifically Sankhya and Vedanta, a window initially opened by Ram Dass, now exquisitely articulated by Hart DeFouw. Jyotish was a method by which pure awareness (*chit*) of the soul (*atman*) could witness the delicate intricacies of karma manifesting in time and space—and see the unseen (*adrishta*). Jyotish offered practical and spiritual means (*upayas*) of engaging with karma in intentional ways.

I studied Sanskrit for two years. I studied both the Bhagavad Gita and Yoga Sutras with Nicolai Bachman. Vedantic philosophy and vocabulary deeply imprinted me. Sanskrit mantras joined my Sufi practices.

And for a while I sat on the back porch smoking and reading non-dual advaita teachings, which assert that the soul is the same as the ultimate reality—until I realized that, although my soul recognizes the truth of these teachings, without a living teacher they result in little more than the spiritualization of the ego.

But when love came to town, and for the first time in my life someone loved me deeply, passionately, and truly, and that someone, MaryRose, was a practicing depth psychologist, I found that I finally had to engage in long-neglected personal work on my emotional complexes. For starters, I had to get out of my head, get in touch with my feelings, and learn how to communicate my feelings to my beloved. This may sound simple, but for me it was not.

More recently I have been working with the Jungian belief system, which posits two distinct psychological centers: the ego and the Self. The ego is the conscious personality—who I think I am. The Self is what we might call the higher self, the totality of conscious and unconscious, the inner presence that many of us know simply as God. What is crucial is the connection between—the dialogue between ego and Self—a dynamic process that never resolves but keeps moving toward greater wholeness, constantly cycling through ego inflation (identification with the Self) and ego alienation (disconnection with the Self). There is no get-out-of-jail-free card.

The Jungian belief system gives me a model with which to engage and unveil my actual psychological experience and to deal with long-suppressed emotional wounds and trauma in a much more grounded way than chasing past-life fantasies. There is ample space for all the previous belief systems I have embraced to function without being invalidated or supplanted.

Reflecting on the Sufi symbol of the heart with wings, Widad and I agree that personal psychological work *and* spiritual practice are the two wings on which the soul soars.

I had been seeking love, lover, and beloved my whole life, and coming up against what I took to be my own inability to love, time and time again, until finally I just gave up. I couldn't get what I wanted, so I resolved not to want what I wanted and that left me very unhappy, or very stoically "content." I learned to live with unfulfilled desire. Dissociation, defiance, deception, and repression may have been necessary strategies for getting through childhood with some authenticity intact (and well-hidden), but these habit patterns were disastrous obstructions to loving another person. My ingrained sarcastic responses undermined me at every turn.

Marriage is the belief system I subscribe to now, monogamy with my wife, who loves me and opens the way for me to love her. Ours is not a young marriage for creating a family. Ours is a mature marriage for bringing soul into the world, for polishing the mirror of the heart, and trusting each other when one says, "Hey! It looks like you missed something there!" I cannot see my own blind spots without the reflection of someone I know loves me and sometimes sees what I cannot. We definitely have a subscription to each other's issues, along with devotion to similar spiritual practices.

We all have belief systems, everything from cargo cults to ascended masters. Most of us have multiple belief systems, although we may not be aware of it. Our minds are like the blind men with the elephant, touching a part of the elephant and taking it for the whole, touching multiple parts and holding multiple "truths"—without apprehending the greater reality, which in truth is beyond the mind.

> *When one looks at the ocean,*
> *one can only see that part of it which*
> *comes within one's range of vision;*
> *so it is with the truth.*

HAZRAT INAYAT KHAN

Hart used to say that the jyotishi should have lots of tools in his bag, lots of methods and approaches. The master golfer never approaches the same tee in the same way. The master investor does not make the same play the same way every day. Learn a new technique, try it for a while, use it all the time, then put it into your tool bag and move on, he would say.

A Quaker woman once said to me, "No religion has all the answers. That's why we study all the religions."

The overall dynamic of this inner life narrative has been the urge of the unconscious to move into consciousness, to bring forth richness and beauty, to liberate the conscious self from limiting conditions and identifications, and to bring that self into awareness of and alignment with the superconscious presence, divine life energy that lives in all beings, in all things.

We are all related. We are all one. There is no separation among all my relations.

Hazrat Inayat Khan speaks of the intoxication of life. I imagine that we are all packed into a crowded bar, drinking, smoking, talking, laughing, dancing, and carrying on. All the drinks are passed around and I taste everything. I'll have what you're having and more! Everyone is having a good time with good friends, except for a few inevitable loners. A good time is had by all—until it starts to feel too loud and noisy. I feel overheated and dizzy from too many drinks. I go outside into the cool night air and climb up a hill. I sit under a tree and gaze at the moon in the starry sky. Warm light and laughter spill out of the tavern far below. Sitting quietly in the still of the night, I slowly sober up and become alert and aware. In sobriety I touch my essential presence, the truth of my being. I sit there a little longer and then go back down the hill, back into the barroom, and greet my friends, and choose my booze. . . .

I try to do my spiritual practices first thing in the morning upon awakening and after writing down my dreams. I sit in formless meditation, riding on awareness of the breath. I put Sanskrit mantras on the breath, followed by Sufi purifications, wazifahs, and zikr on the breath, vocal practice, singing zikr, and writing down what is given to me. Any and all, or none of the above.

And when my wife needs to talk with me, that takes precedence over my personal practice, although generally, she has her own morning devotions. And sometimes we sit together.

It used to be that spiritual practice was rigidly maintained and set apart from the rest of my life. Now spiritual practice is a good part of my life and permeates all that I do.

I return to sitting in silence, breathing. At first, I was disciplined, even rigid, about spiritual practice, enthusiastic, excessive, and then I grew lax and forgetful, then devoted and daily, now natural and flexible, almost casual. There is no longer a dividing line between meditation and everyday life, although I always love to, in the words of Pir Vilayat, take time for the timeless.

*Just before the dawn*
*I awake and I am gone . . .*
*and the road goes on and on and on*
*in the breath of Er-Rahman*

*When I feel the morning breeze,*
*see the light come through the trees,*
*then I fall down on my knees and breathe . . .*
*Allah Hu Allah Hu Allah Hu*

When I stay overnight in Santa Fe and take my morning walk along the river, each portion of the walk is the container for a particular prayer. The landscape remembers my prayers along with me.

I gaze directly into the light of the morning sun, filtered through the branches and leaves of a tree, and greet the path of light: *Om Bhur Buvaha Swaha*. . . . Then I walk on down the block: *Om Gam Ganapataye Namaha* . . . I walk down the street, until I reach the park and turn left, breathing a Brahma mantra. I reach the river and walk along the green path, breathing presence of the Goddess: *Hrim Shrim Klim Parameshwari Swaha*. . . . I walk on until the path stops curving and lies straight ahead. I say the invocation, "Toward the One," and begin my Sufi practices: purification breaths all the way out until I turn around, then wazifahs and zikr all the way home, breathing "Allah," essence presence, into the very cells of my body.

Meditation engenders a state of bliss in the whole body, essential bliss, ananda. For me, this sensation of bliss concentrates in the forehead, just above the eyebrows. In meditation, my brow becomes open and expansive like vast blue sky with occasional wispy thought clouds drifting through. Behind the bliss is an abiding calmness, spaciousness, emptiness.

*My body is like a mountain.*
*My eyes are like the ocean.*
*My mind is like the sky.*

Essence is simple like sunlight is simple . . . pure white light that contains all the rays of color in its wholeness.

Spiritual practice can be very boring, boring to the ego, although the ego can seek to attach its values to spiritual practice in all sorts of subtle and not-so-subtle ways. Spiritual practice can be beautiful, uplifting, inspiring, and all that, and still be empty and boring to the ego. As Reb Zalman says, "When zikr gets boring, that's when it gets really exciting."

I am aware of being the space surrounding the Earth, the space within and around the Earth. I am the atmosphere and all lives and breathes within me, all my thoughts and feelings, all my relations and creations, all my lifetimes and wife-times, all my ancestors and lovers and children, all live and breathe and move and love in the space I am.

It is all so intimately familiar and poignant. I have seen myself take birth and play and work and love and suffer and die time and time again, over and over and over again, and here I am, the seemingly eternal, unchanging, luminous space in which it all happens and to which it all returns.

The soul comes into life in order to have experiences. In order to have experiences, the soul needs to see its reflection in the world.

> *I was a hidden treasure and I desired to be known so I*
> *created a creation to which I made Myself known. Then*
> *they knew Me.*
>
> HADITH QUDSI

Pure awareness is conscious—but not self-conscious. In order to be conscious of self, soul seeks reflection in experience by identifying with whatever is experienced. Soul itself is free from any identity.

*The soul has no birth, no death, no beginning, and no end. Sin cannot touch it, nor can virtue exalt it. Wisdom cannot open it up, nor can ignorance darken it.*

HAZRAT INAYAT KHAN

In order to have experience, the soul can and does identify with whatever is presented to it and whatever form it finds itself in.

What I experience as reality at any one moment is largely a result of where and how I focus my attention.

Over time, a series of self-identifications coheres in memory to form a self-image with a personal history. Writing these memoirs re-creates a personal history. The process of writing these memoirs is a letting go of all of these experiences.

Hart says that *moksha*, which is usually translated as liberation, means the ability to let go of experiences. Without letting go of experiences we cannot have new experiences. We just keep on recycling the same old same-old. When we can let go of experiences, we can have new experiences.

*Hold on tightly and let go lightly.*

RAM DASS

Each morning I sit in a column of breath,
inscribing names on this tower of breath,
writing light on luminous space,
windows of presence,
power and glory,
tap-tap-tapping the telegraph of my heart,
imprinting every organ and cell,
divine life presence awareness
silent and utterly still,

and feeling the blood pulsing and flowing
at the base of my skull,
*Ya Hayy Ya Hayy. . .*

*O Life O Life. . .*
deeply embedded in heart throbbing,
*libb lubb, libb lubb, libb lubb, libb lubb . . .*
*live love, live love, live love, live love . . .*

Deeper the secret
the heart mouth utters
*Hu Allah Hu Allah Hu Allah Hu*

As I live and breathe,
(as my grandmother used to say)
there is something someone living and breathing,
something someone so much greater,
so awesomely powerful and infinitely loving,
living and breathing in every creature,
listening to the heart in the center of my chest
*Hu Allah Hu Allah Hu Allah Hu*

*Friends, we are all on the journey; life itself is a journey. No one is settled here; we are all passing onward, and therefore it is not true to say that if we are taking a spiritual journey we have to break our settled life; there is no one living a settled life here; all are unsettled, all are on their way.*

HAZRAT INAYAT KHAN